Reflections

Evangelical Messages for the Modern World

ALEKSANDAR BIRVIŠ

WESTBOW
PRESS®
A DIVISION OF THOMAS NELSON
& ZONDERVAN

Copyright © 2017 Aleksandar Birviš.

Translated from the Serbian by Christopher Daniels. Proofread by Mark Daniels.

All rights reserved. No part of this book may be used or reproduced by any means, graphic, electronic, or mechanical, including photocopying, recording, taping or by any information storage retrieval system without the written permission of the author except in the case of brief quotations embodied in critical articles and reviews.

WestBow Press books may be ordered through booksellers or by contacting:

WestBow Press
A Division of Thomas Nelson & Zondervan
1663 Liberty Drive
Bloomington, IN 47403
www.westbowpress.com
1 (866) 928-1240

Because of the dynamic nature of the Internet, any web addresses or links contained in this book may have changed since publication and may no longer be valid. The views expressed in this work are solely those of the author and do not necessarily reflect the views of the publisher, and the publisher hereby disclaims any responsibility for them.

Any people depicted in stock imagery provided by Thinkstock are models, and such images are being used for illustrative purposes only. Certain stock imagery © Thinkstock.

Scripture taken from the King James Version of the Bible.

ISBN: 978-1-4908-3177-0 (sc)
ISBN: 978-1-5127-8574-6 (e)

Library of Congress Control Number: 2014905750

Print information available on the last page.

WestBow Press rev. date: 11/12/2019

Contents

HOW TO READ THIS BOOK xi

AKNOWLEDGMENTS xiii

THE LORD'S PRAYER DURING

THE CIVIL WAR (1991) 1

Foreword.. 1

Introduction 3

The Heavenly Father 3

His holy name 5

The Kingdom of God... 6

The Will of God 11

Give us this day 16

Forgiveness for forgiveness' sake 18

As Christ has forgiven you..25

Trials — an everyday challenge 30

Deliverance from the evil one..38

For Yours is the ... forever...43

REGULAR SERIES OF SERMONS................................49

I THE LORD SANCTIFY 50

A MAN WHOSE NAME WAS JOHN 59

CHRIST — GOD INCARNATE.......................................68

THE GLORY IS NEAR...72

A TEMPLE NOT MADE WITH HANDS.......................79

The dwelling place of a holy God...................................79

The temple of a new people...81

A Spiritual House 81

The temple and its court...83

The Holiest of Holies 85

THE RICH FOOL...87

Indifference towards the time that we live in.........................87

"This night" but not unexpectedly 89

Think "today"..90

Belonging to Christ — now 94

IN THE SCHOOL OF BLESSING......................................95

Teaching and missionary aspects of blessing..........................95

ABOUT FOREGIVENESS 99

The art of small steps..99

CHRIST THE HEALER 106

WITNESSING 110

Our part in God's work..110

Witnessing about God and man..110

The enemy wants to shake man 113

PARDON AND WITNESSING ABOUT PARDON...........117

ABOUT OUR TESTIMONY 123

Some aspects of our testimony..123

TRIALS — THE TEST OF THE KINGDOM OF GOD 131

Righteousness in the Holy Spirit —what are the
temptations of righteousness? 132

Peace in the Holy Spirit — what are the temptations
of this peace? 135

Joy in the Holy Spirit — what are its temptations?............138

FROM CONFLICT TO CONFLICT – CHRIST 142

I LOVE MISSION...151

Mission is a question of love 152

Mission is the work of the Holy Spirit 154

We are not alone.. 155

BEFORE THE THRONE AND BEFORE THE LAMB....... 157

ETERNAL KING — ETERNAL KINGDOM...................... 164

HOW TO DEEPEN YOUR FAITH 170

WHO BELONGS TO CHRIST? 176

Measures of closeness.. 177

Fulfilling God's will... 179

Authentic belonging 182

CHRIST HAS RISEN FROM THE DEAD!.......................... 183

BREAD FROM HEAVEN... 188

CHRIST — THE GOOD SHEPHERD 193

What do I expect from the Good Shepherd? 194

Christ has fulfilled all our expectations............................ 195

The Shepherd — our confidence 199

WRITTEN IN THE BOOK OF LIFE 201

BROTHERS AND DISCIPLES 205

THE BIBLE HAS COME TO US FROM THE JEWS.......... 209

The Word communicated.. 210

The Word received... 210

The Word passed on 211

Our debt to the Jews.. 212

Somewhere, far away 213

THE SAVIOR GOES AWAY — WE REMAIN 216

THE ASCENSION 226

Meditation for the Lord's Supper 226

WHAT SHALL WE SAY ABOUT THE HOLY SPIRIT?...... 232

I BELIEVE IN THE HOLY TRINITY 238

THE SPIRIT AND THE BRIDE SAY:............................. 243

THE WILL OF THE FATHER....................................... 252

Fear not, little flock 254

Little Flock 257

The Will of the Father...259

The Kingdom is given 260

GOOD NEWS FOR EVERY CREATURE 265

GOD CREATES A NEW MAN 274

I BELIEVE IN LOVE...281

LIFE IN THE LIGHT OF THE SPIRIT 289

STRENGTH, PROTECTION AND VICTORY..................300

THE TRANSFIGURATION....................................307

HOW CHRIST WOULD THINK............................311

FIVE PRAYER MINIATURES 319

1. More of the Gospel.......................................319

2. Deeper faith...320

3. Greater calmness...322

4. Richer love 324

5. Strengthened hope.......................................326

ADDRESSES ON SPECIAL OCCASSIONS 329

THE AUTHORITY OF THE SCRIPTURES IN

RELATION TO THE CHURCH 330

Authority...331

The Scripture 332

Experience...333

A Book about God 335

Certainty...338

Enlightenment..341

The Church...342

Nevertheless..344

ADDRESS AT THE OPENING OF HOLY TRINITY

CHURCH..345

THE DESIRED TIME 349

FOR THE WOMEN'S CONFERENCE..............................354

A word about ministry 356

A word about mirrors....................................357

A word about the laver 358

EDUCATION: CONDITIONS, DEVELOPMENT

AND PURPOSE (I)..360

Beginning of the academic year............................360

Watchmen throughout the country 361

An ordered life 366

EDUCATION: CONDITIONS, DEVELOPMENT

AND PURPOSE (II) 370

The academic year..370

Primary education 373

Secondary education....................................374

Higher education....................................376

Consequences 377

Appendix..383

WHY I WRITE OUT MY SERMONS..............................383

Notes..385

HOW TO READ THIS BOOK

Sermons, like other forms of public speaking, should be read slowly and at a rate of not more than one a day. It is better to read one several times over a period of two days, rather than two or three a day.

We recommend the reader keeps a Bible by him. Lovers of good reading material will read a sermon and then take the trouble to find the passages quoted in the sermon and spend a few minutes meditating on them. As they then read the same sermon again, they will understand the things they have enjoyed as well as enjoying what they have understood.

Reading like this is not entertainment. It is hard work. It requires the use of the mind and the imagination. None of these sermons was written for strangers but for a specific audience. Each one was preached in a church service, mainly at the First Baptist Church in Belgrade (Slobodanke Danke Savić 33), but also in other places. Largely the same group of widely-differing people listened to these sermons, Sunday by Sunday and Wednesday by Wednesday, as they sought to hear the Word and to experience God.

The aim of this book is just that.

Aleksandar Birviš

AKNOWLEDGMENTS

On 17th August 1994, Dr. Čedomir Drašković, a retired professor from the Belgrade Orthodox Theological Faculty, was buried at the New Cemetery in Belgrade. The writer of this book is thankful to God for the many pleasant hours he spent from 1951 to 1953 as a student of the late professor, listening to his lectures in preaching, pastoral theology and other areas of practical theology. If there is anything of any value in these sermons, that is due to Dr. Drašković. The weaknesses are the writer's, because the late professor undoubtedly deserves better and more commendable students.

THE LORD'S PRAYER DURING THE CIVIL WAR (1991)

Our Father which art in heaven,
Hallowed be Thy name.
Thy kingdom come,
Thy will be done
In earth, as it is in heaven.
Give us this day our daily bread.
And forgive us our debts,
As we forgive our debtors.
And lead us not into temptation,
But deliver us from evil:
For Thine is the kingdom, and the power, and the glory, for ever.
Amen.
(Matthew 6:9-13)

Foreword

Many young men's lives have been snuffed out. Their names will no longer be called out at roll call. Their officers will no longer deploy them on the front line. No one will send for them anymore. Some of them will have a proper burial. Some will have no burial at

Aleksandar Birviš

all. Strangers will bury them, who knows where. Their friends and family will be informed with just a few short words, if at all.

Were they on the right side or the wrong? They didn't know. In a year or two that won't matter.

So-called resourceful people are already taking advantage of their death and their shed blood. The careers of well-known people and the recognition they receive will prosper on their marked graves. The right side will accuse the wrong side. The wrong side will continue to devise means of revenge and await their moment.

The glorious heroes will soar on the wings of achievement, where there are no traffic tailbacks. Taxes will go up, purchasing power will decrease, and the economy will go into decline, as many get rich quick. There will be new upheavals.

Those who have grown wings will soar above all this. As everything else deteriorates, they will prosper.

Nobody will take any notice of the young men, women and children, just as they did on the Srem Front in 1944-45. Today, those responsible for what happened then are joining forces again to polish their medals and talk about the victories they won. They have no remorse for those they callously sent to their deaths.

What is there to say in these tough times? Is there any point in preaching when no one will listen? I am not so pessimistic. No one wants to listen to those who have spoken only untruths and continue to do so. But there will always be ears open to hear the truth. There are those whose hearts have not been hardened – not everyone is evil. Not all evil people are without hope. The Lord's power has not disappeared.

Reflections

Introduction

The weapon of the Christian is prayer. We pray in exaltation before God. That is worship. We pray when God gives us something, or when He takes something away, when something happens or when it doesn't happen. That is thanksgiving. We pray when God stirs our consciences and our understanding, as we realize how much sin there still is in us and how many sins we have left behind us. That is confession. After we have confessed, we pray that we may continue to live without sin and without the devil spoiling things. We strive afresh for holiness and sanctification. That is the promise.

But the largest part of our prayer is supplication. There are so many things we need (at least we think we need them). I used to think that our prayer meetings and Bibles studies encouraged supplication. ("Lord, give peace to this country! O Lord, save those who are on the front lines! Set the captives free! Bring the leaders to their senses! etc."). But when I began to pray I realized that we shouldn't ask for the things unbelievers ask for. Our Savior taught us how to pray. The Lord's Prayer or "Our Father" is a well-known prayer. Let us apply the lessons of this prayer to the times and events we are living through.

The Heavenly Father

We all have a Heavenly Father. That's true both for believers and non-believers. God is the Father of those in uniforms and those in civilian clothes. Both those who shoot and those who die belong to Him. He is our Father. He is not my Father, nor the Father of my

Aleksandar Birviš

church, nor the Father of any particular people or country. Every man is dear to Him.

So we find divisions strange, especially when they involve suffering.

> *Like as a father pitieth His children,*
> *So the LORD pitieth them that fear Him.*
> *For He knoweth our frame;*
> *He remembereth that we are dust* (Ps.103:13–14).

People are not aware that they are made of dust. The Heavenly Father wanted us to be made not just of clay and dirt. That is why we are not what we used to be.

The Father is in heaven. How insignificant borders seem. In the regions within those borders, companies go into liquidation, workers are made redundant, employees are not paid (and what they are paid is not worth much), pensions are paid out erratically and many other misfortunes happen before the eyes of the Heavenly Father. He sees it, while those who are responsible do not. He is far off, but He is the Father. Those responsible are on the earth, but they do not behave like fathers even to their own children - instead they force them to commit mindless acts.

This is why we pray to the Heavenly Father. He has not betrayed our trust nor will He. When we are abandoned by all, and when our loved ones become like animals, God remains our Heavenly Father. He never stops loving. *God is love*, writes the apostle John, *and he that dwelleth in love dwelleth in God, and God in him* (1 John 4:16b).

Reflections

His holy name

The main trouble with those around us is their lack of respect for God's name. People have a name that they shout out, that they use as a swear word, that they sing songs and write fairy tales about. Quickly, far too quickly, the people of the Balkans are beginning to reject that same name, to spit on it, to curse it, to ascribe stupid things to it, to say revolting things about it. As time goes by, yesterday's god becomes the devil, yesterday's flower an object of shame.

And so we say, "Sic passit gloria mundi." But the Word of God says something different (Ps. 135:15-18):

> *The idols of the heathen are silver and gold,*
> *The work of men's hands.*
> *They have mouths, but they speak not;*
> *Eyes have they, but they see not;*
> *They have ears, but they hear not;*
> *Neither is there any breath in their mouths.*
> *They that make them are like unto them:*
> *So is every one that trusteth in them.*

Idols are a reflection of those who worship them. Those who created the myths about mighty leaders are no better than those leaders. Those who denigrate them today without repenting as God commands, are still idol worshippers - they have just changed their idols in line with changing fashion. They will worship these new ones, because idol worshippers are accustomed to changing the object of their worship. If a particular god is not suitable or if some other power conquers those who trust in one group of idols, they will turn to the gods who win.

Forced conversion was not invented by Islam. There have always been turncoats and there always will be as long as man is on this earth. There are many haters of freedom who have become defenders of democracy overnight.

Christians preach the Holiness of God's name. That is their duty. That name sets men free from idols. If anyone wants to discover where victory lies and what is really going on among men and nations, let him observe how the Holiness of God's name is honored. It is the only name that brings salvation (Acts 4:12).

The Kingdom of God

A discussion of the Kingdom of God will take a little more time. The conflicts and worry that are part of our life are the results of a power struggle. Tanks, rockets, grenade launchers, mines, Kalashnikovs and everything else that is coming out onto the streets and heading into the fields and forests, are indications that a struggle for power is being waged, that the kingdoms of this world are doing their worst, because they can do nothing else.

Not until people accept the rule of the living God, will they have true life. They will exist, go about and multiply, consume food and dump dangerous waste, but they will not live. In particular, their common life will be tense, artificial and full of obstacles. There is no life for the oppressed, but there is no life for the oppressors either. There is no life for those who are governed, but those who govern do not live happily either.

Reflections

The Lord offers us His rule. That is the Kingdom which we pray for in the Lord's Prayer. Other forms of power may be similar to or different from the Kingdom of God. But they are not true Kingdoms. They cannot be until they completely return to God, in other words until they come to sincere repentance.

The man who repents has realized that sin is a reality. Our understanding of the world may differ, but our attitude to sin, that is our own sin, must be profound and in complete agreement with Scripture. In it we read, *The LORD looked down from heaven upon the children of men, to see if there were any that did understand, and seek God. They are all gone aside, they are all together become filthy: there is none that doeth good, no, not one* (Psalm 14:2-3). If this is what God's Word says, then man has no choice but to confess: a) his sinful nature and sin, that is, his tendency to sin and his attachment to sin, and b) his individual sin. Neither individuals nor whole nations have any right to believe in their own sinlessness and innocence. To believe in sinlessness is to disregard the conclusions of God's Word.

Awareness of sin leads to confession of sin. Blessed are the people and the nations who receive from God the strength to confess their own sin and who take advantage of that mercy before it is too late. That willingness is what distinguishes a repentant man. He knows that the perfect rule of God cannot compromise with sin. I have met people who have grasped this in a very simple way. They come to me immediately after their conversion to talk about their own personal sins and ask me: "Do I need to say this before the whole church? Can I do it straightaway on Sunday?" Such an attitude should not be anything unusual. I would like every new convert to cultivate in himself or herself a readiness to confess sin. It is, of course, important to see this in the context of the Kingdom of God, as there are those who are not aware of their sin and are so insensitive that they say, "I

Aleksandar Birviš

would confess my sin if I had any." The Kingdom of God is not for those who are steeped in self-deceit.

In order to experience the Lord's rule it is necessary to feel sorrow for sin. Sin is an insult to God. I cannot expunge that sin by my own means. By falling I mock God: Satan uses the sin that I commit to mock God's perfection. Because of my mocking attitude I am powerless to redeem myself before His righteousness and goodness. And so I mourn. Without profound sorrow I cannot enter into joy. Without sorrow for the sins of those around me, the state of the nation in which I live will not improve.

Sorrow is a good thing. But it is not enough. We must cry out for forgiveness. The Lord is willing to forgive those who turn to Him. The Almighty promises: *I, even I, am He that blotteth out thy transgressions for Mine own sake, and will not remember thy sins* (Is. 43:25). *I have blotted out, as a thick cloud, thy transgressions, and, as a cloud, thy sins: return unto Me; for I have redeemed thee* (Is.44:22). *And they shall teach no more every man his neighbour, and every man his brother, saying, Know the* LORD: *for they shall all know Me, from the least of them unto the greatest of them, saith the* LORD: *for I will forgive their iniquity, and I will remember their sin no more* (Jer.31:34) etc.

How can God not forgive? He has given these and other promises, and on top of the promises He has given His only-begotten Son. God expects His people to begin to forgive others and not to do, or even think of doing, evil. Not to talk about what has happened – that can't be changed – but to bring restitution and restoration and to ask for forgiveness. *For if ye forgive men their trespasses, your heavenly Father will also forgive you: But if ye forgive not men their trespasses, neither will your Father forgive your trespasses* (Matt.6:14–15). The incorruptible and eternal Judge forgives those who reject their sin and try not to sin any more (John 5:14; 8:11).

Reflections

People usually expect the Kingdom of God to be a list of rules and institutions. That is the nature of this world's kingdoms. If the truth be known, man has grown accustomed to such forms of power and finds it strange that there can be forms with different incentives and different structures. The Kingdom of Heaven is different. It does not place the emphasis on the coercive methods of this world but on righteousness, peace and joy in the Holy Spirit, as the apostle Paul puts it (Rom.14:17).

May righteousness in the Holy Spirit come. The righteousness offered by countries and societies has nothing to offer, nothing for us to hope for as Christians. Worldly righteousness will always be imperfect, and nobody can guarantee that it will not be opposed to Christ. We are not saying that it will not be helpful to some churches and religious fellowships, societies and associations. By its very support for such groups, the righteousness of this world will diverge from the Savior and the redemptive news of Christ.

We await peace in the Holy Spirit. Today there are many who hope for peace. This is understandable. War has broken out. A shaky ceasefire has been agreed. Foreign politicians come to bring local leaders to their senses. Young men are losing their lives, their parents protest, and reports flow in from all sides. Everyone would like peace, but a peace without God or at least a peace that will be indifferent towards the Lord. That is why God says back in the Old Testament, *There is no peace unto the wicked* (Is.48:22). In order for peace to be established evil acts must cease. Unregenerate men will never give up evil, especially if that evil brings them profit without effort and encourages them in their desire to assume power and to continue in their disobedience towards God. Peace must be in the Holy Spirit, and not in the spirit of existing decisions and regulations, especially if the proposed rules aim to maintain injustices that have already been achieved.

Aleksandar Birviš

I would like us all to be clear about this. God does not forbid us to pray for peace. On the contrary, in the Epistle to the Hebrews He encourages us (12:14): *Follow peace with all men, and holiness, without which no man shall see the Lord.* This should be the aspiration of every Christian. *If it be possible,* writes the Apostle Paul, *as much as lieth in you, live peaceably with all men* (Rom.12:18). But there are situations when God does not want peace. He tells us through the prophet Jeremiah (6:13-14): *For from the least of them even unto the greatest of them every one is given to covetousness; and from the prophet even unto the priest every one dealeth falsely. They have healed also the hurt of the daughter of My people slightly, saying, Peace, peace; when there is no peace.* Where greed has taken hold of the servants of God, (and we don't need to look at other fellowships to find that), there is no peace. So, instead of praying for peace, let us first drive out the unclean spirits of greed and lies, let us pour out the riches we have amassed and help those in need. Let us right injustices, let us bring order to disorder, let us settle accounts as honesty demands, and then we can ask for peace at least amongst ourselves. As far as the men of evil are concerned, let us pray for their conversion. Let us not be concerned which side they are on, for they are on the side of sin wherever they are, until they receive the Gospel.

Likewise, the Kingdom of God is joy in the Holy Spirit. Where does this joy come from, when all is so miserable? Joy in the Spirit does not depend on unspiritual influences. When we seek the Kingdom of God, we have accepted in advance the conclusion that Christ has to destroy the works of the devil (1 John 3:8). Where the devil stops working, sin loses its power and joy commences.

Joy in Christ makes us stand out against the general mood of the nation. How can a father rejoice at the knowledge that his child has been killed in an attack from the rear or killed by the officer who until yesterday was sitting beside him? No, that father cannot rejoice. But if we Christians help him in his grief and worry, his sorrow will reduce, and that is a step closer to joy.

God reigns. Let us accept His rule. Let us set our hearts on it and we will transcend the boundaries of men and time and space. We are truly at home only in the Kingdom of God. Outside of that we are strangers and pilgrims on the earth (Heb.11:13b).

It needs to be said that in longing for the Kingdom of God Christians do not bring down the kingdoms of this world. They crumble by themselves. The involvement of the Christian in this is not necessary.

Belgrade, 10th July 1991

The Will of God

Christians honor God's will in good times and in bad. In heaven, that is in the world of spiritual existence, the will of God is carried out without hesitation or objection. The Lord does not enforce it Himself but the angels and all the hosts of heaven joyfully carry out every command of the Lord.

All our knowledge, including our knowledge of God's will is limited by human imperfection. But that knowledge is by no means small. In fact, everything that our God reveals about Himself gives us the answers to two questions: What does God want? and, Who is God? According to some rules of thinking this second question should come first. But, in terms of importance the Will of God comes before thinking about the nature of God.

The question of who God is is one for philosophers. For believers that question is resolved through experience. Man has experienced God and no further thinking can add anything to that. But experience, of course, does not like to be alone. The believer is joined to the body of Christ, which is the Church. It is within the Church that he now lives, in the sense that it is the Church that holds out to him the Savior who is life.

The question of what God wants belongs to the realm of philosophy and theology. For Christians this has always been a question of everyday life. In today's world we hear of wars and rumors of wars (Matt.24:6). We know that this must be so, in other words, God wants it that way or at least has allowed it to happen. So then, how can we lose our fear or at least our anxiety?

Ferment, unrest, and even wars are not something that is meant to be, nor are they something that was not meant to be. They are not against God's will. But those evils are not part of the will of God in heaven for which we pray to the Almighty. God has not given up on His intention that His Will be done on earth as it is in heaven, in perfect harmony. Driven by human weaknesses and the storms of the flesh, we give up on God's plan, not of course every time, but frequently enough.

Experiential knowledge of God's will is still linked to events on earth. We are focused on heaven and strive to enter it. This we do through our prayers, study of the Scriptures, by fasting, and especially by worshipping God. But no matter whose we are and where we belong we still live on the earth. And so no one should be surprised at the presence of fear and apprehension. Even very spiritual people sometimes lose their calmness and boldness.

We can begin to see why Christ declares, *Let not your heart be troubled: ye believe in God, believe also in Me* (John14:1). The will of God has been revealed and we know it by faith. We don't close our eyes to the unrest and war around us. We just open one more pair of eyes, our spiritual eyes, and see what the Lord has prepared. We don't close our ears to wars and rumors of wars. We simply open our spiritual ears to hear what the Holy Spirit is saying.

12

Reflections

God is completely independent. No one is like Him. No one can be His master. He is not responsible to anyone. We know that God's will is totally free. In times when freedom is obviously being curtailed it is good to know that oppression is not a part of God's will. God does not like slavery either. If there is oppression and slavery, then they are the consequence of some earlier sinful acts. Subversion and armed conflicts can bring nothing without sincere repentance. When he repents man is ready to accept the will of heaven on earth.

Can anyone oppose the will of God? No. Why? Because God is omnipotent. Whenever you pray for His will to be done, you are praying for the fulfillment of the only will that cannot be thwarted. Once the will of the Almighty is carried out, all other wills vanish. Spiritual growth appears stunted in many cases because of a refusal to accept this fact. Man, insignificant and small as he is, would like to hold on to his own little whims and to be spiritual at the same time.

Autocratic men do not like the will of God. They may love the Church as an organization that gives them political support. And for that reason they are prepared to pay the clergy (they don't, of course, pay them out of their own money). The moment Christians stop thinking in line with the demands of the world, the authorities will not hesitate to use cruel methods. Christians respect the authorities, but cannot accept perversity and distortion. It can cost them their lives. In the same way that Christians were persecuted by the autocratic Roman Emperor Diocletian around 303 AD, so in Serbia some nine hundred years later Stevan Nemanja[1] exterminated the Bogumils,[2] and Quirin Kuhlman[3] was burnt at the stake in Russia in 1689. We could quote many more examples too. Men paid with their lives for being obedient to the will of God. They were not disobedient to the authorities; they were just more obedient to God's voice.

Aleksandar Birviš

We must tell everyone that God's will is sacrosanct. We dare not take it lightly. God does not approve of men who trifle with His will. God's will is that men should not perish, that peace should come, while the leaders argue about where they are going to meet. Some of them now refuse to go to the place they used to consider it an honor to be invited to, others won't go to the capital even though nothing will happen to them there, while others suggest some venue right at the other end of the country and all the time the bloodshed continues[4]. How foolish!

God's demands are a reality. Whoever ignores them, ignores reality, and is liable for the repercussions. This applies to individuals, as well as to whole nations. No one can say that God didn't give him the opportunity to change for the better and to be blessed. Instead of accepting God's gift, men are carried away by victories, celebrations, and stories. They have forgotten the will of God. They have neglected it and rejected it.

God is not forgetful. He remembers the tears of the righteous, and also the sneers of the unrighteous. Some people are now complaining that they have been forced out of their homes but they conveniently forget how today's occupants of villas in Dedinje and Topčider[5] entered them in 1944 and 1945. It won't make it any easier for those who have been driven out of their homes to know this, but we must all remind ourselves that our Holy God is carrying out His holy will. He is doing it in the best way possible and just at the right time.

There is no need to sigh. Let us accept God's will and everything will turn out for the best. The Lord Jesus promises, *If any man serve Me, let him follow Me; and where I am, there shall also My servant be: if any man serve Me, him will My Father honour* (John12:26).

Belgrade, 17th July 1991

(credit Matija Žaknić)

Aleksandar Birviš

Give us this day

Economic problems would largely be solved if people grasped the meaning of the words *Give us this day our daily bread*. I am not going to spend any time talking about the meaning of 'our daily bread'. Some say that it means basic food. Some say that it means food for tomorrow. While others say it is talking about bread of a different quality from ordinary bread that we eat every day, supernatural bread, that is Jesus Christ.

These are interesting questions. They are important too, since it is quite possible that the Lord Jesus is talking about himself: Christ our everyday need. Nevertheless, our current circumstances require that I pay more attention to the words *Give us this day.*

God is the eternal giver. He always gives. According to His standards everyone has the right to His gifts. This day is an infinitesimal part of God's eternity. But even so a day is the unit of time by which we live. We are not living in some other time, but in the present. Now is the time that we expect God's gifts.

In business or in other everyday tasks, we do not put off tasks until tomorrow. We expect God to give us everything at the right time. God expects us, too, to fulfill our obligations on time. Today He surely gives what He has always intended to give. Have you done what God requires you to do in the course of this day? How happy will the people be who grasp this. Their finances will not go into the red, because they don't follow a human model, but depend on the generosity of the heavenly giver of gifts.

With such a Giver we do not need a bright future. He who has Christ is not in darkness even in these times. His spiritual eyes are open as they reflect the light of God. He is not prepared to destroy the people of today at any price in the name of some future bread.

Reflections

Revolutions and counter-revolutions have alarmed many people, and have destroyed or ruined many more and what have they brought us? Some people of course have taken advantage of them; just as in the current situation some people's greed will be satisfied. But hatred has replaced common sense in men; the worldly has taken over the spiritual, and with it have come murder, destruction, alienation and disappointment.

By honestly restricting their demands just to the needs of today Christians limit those very needs. Man would like to have more and more. In fact, what we today call re-privatization and enterprise are just more acceptable names for greed and selfishness. It sounds crude, and maybe not very attractive, but the committed follower of Christ consistently limits his needs. There is no need to be a miser or an eccentric. You just need to check each day what you really need, and what you can do without. This is the fruit of love. Instead of hoarding treasure, that is, the love of wealth, Christians focus entirely upon God and their fellow men. They praise the Lord, and help their neighbors.

We ask the Lord to provide what we need for today. Have we resolved to live as if there is no tomorrow? No. For some people the future is a life based on plans, preliminary draft plans and projections. No one is saying that Christians should reject that approach. They just try to carry out their Savior's demand. He says, *Take therefore no thought for the morrow: for the morrow shall take thought for the things of itself. Sufficient unto the day is the evil thereof* (Matt.6:34). Worry distorts the soul, and is of no help. The more a Christian commits himself to his Lord, the brighter will be his outlook on the future. Christian mothers know that their sons will not be exempt from the troubles to come. But they know something more than that: the Lord has need of their children and He knows with absolute certainty what

Aleksandar Birviš

He will do with them. What is there left for us to do? What are we to do? We are left with today. Today our sons and daughters must belong to the Lord. This is the day of great needs, their needs. The answer is in our hands.

Do those who need that answer know what it is?

Belgrade, 24th July 1991

Forgiveness for forgiveness' sake

At first sight forgiveness seems to be the opposite of justice. For example, you receive your salary and take it home. Then a pickpocket snatches it from your pocket. You grab hold of him. You hold him firmly by the arm. He is holding your wallet in his hand. You take the money out of the wallet and put it in the pickpocket's pocket. Then you let him go.

You say to Him, "Go in peace. In a month's time I'll have my salary in my wallet. In the meantime my family goes hungry. My wife will leave me, because she is not obliged to live with an irresponsible man. But never mind. You just enjoy yourself and I will be happy you are enjoying yourself."

People have gathered round. The pickpocket is trying to run away. Some of them grab him. And they have him in a tight grip. They shout:

"Where are the police? Off to prison with him!"

"Please don't," you beg them, "I have forgiven him. He hasn't stolen anything from you. Your families will not go hungry. Neither you nor your wives will have to go begging to borrow money. You saw that I gave it to him freely. I could have taken it from him, but I didn't. I am not going to bring charges against him."

Reflections

"Police! Police!" The people shout and won't let the thief go.

Two policemen arrive and one of them asks, "Who's that shouting? What's happened?"

People are shouting. Their voices are all confused. "This man is a pickpocket. We saw him steal this other man's wallet."

The policemen take hold of the man. They hold him in a strong grip. Then they bring him over to you.

"Sir," they ask "has this man stolen anything from you?"

"I don't want to talk about him," you say.

The people around begin to protest.

"We saw him. He pinched your wallet."

"Where is the wallet?" asks one of the policemen.

"I have it here," you say.

"And where is the money?" the policeman says again.

"He has it," you reply.

"Aha!" the people exclaim.

"Aha!" the policemen breathe a sigh of relief.

But you continue, "I gave him the money. You all saw me. The money is his now."

"This man's mad," say the people around pointing at you.

The policemen release the pickpocket. The bystanders try to grab him again. The police shout, "That's enough! Leave the man alone. Whoever chases him and shouts out will be taken before the magistrate for causing a public disturbance."

The people disperse. The performance didn't turn out as they had imagined.

But would you act like that? I don't think so. It would be the Christian thing to do and in keeping with the spirit of the Lord's Prayer, but it is a type of Christianity that you are not used to. Neither are your preachers used to it.

Aleksandar Birviš

Let me give you an example. On 1ˢᵗ May (1991) shooting broke out in Borovo Selo, some little way from Osijek[6]. Up until the end of May and even later than that there was no shooting in Osijek. On the 23ʳᵈ May I was at a meeting of ministers. Most of our ministers didn't come to the meeting. They gave all sorts of reasons, even though they preach that not a hair of our head will fall out apart from the will of God. Just imagine that, God forbid, the six men who came to the meeting had been attacked by someone. There would have been protests and bitter reactions but no forgiveness.

Many people, very many people say in their prayers, *...forgive us our debts as we forgive our debtors.* Many of us know that the Lord Jesus explained it like this: *For if ye forgive men their trespasses, your heavenly Father will also forgive you: But if ye forgive not men their trespasses, neither will your Father forgive your trespasses* (Matt.6:14–15).

Surely people condemn themselves with their own words? If they have not forgiven others they will not be forgiven.

Forgiveness is a great art. Just like every great art it demands much study and practice. It begins with simple realizations and actions, and then gradually becomes more complex and difficult. It's like that with forgiveness too. I want to suggest some steps for you to take. They aren't meant to be a recommendation for everyone to follow, but I hope that they will be helpful to everyone who tries to apply them.

Step One: the stimulus. The Lord Jesus said, *Therefore all things whatsoever ye would that men should do to you, do ye even so to them* (Matt.7:12). You be the first one to forgive. You get on a bus and nobody wants to give up his seat. Don't hold it against them. Forgive them in your heart and pray for them. The check-out assistant in the supermarket tries to shortchange you. Tell her nicely she is obliged to give you the money. Don't make a scene because you are out of pocket. Forgive her, whatever happens, no matter how much you are short. You won't go short, and if she has done it deliberately, she won't be absolved from her sin like that. Rather, offer her a tract and pray for her.

Step Two: absence of pride. We are no better than the world; it is just that the Lord has chosen us to realize that we are even worse, and that we need to repent. Forgive because you know that you are capable of performing even worse deeds and misdeeds (it is God's grace that you don't do them). Don't boast of your being born again, just be aware of what God wants from you. One of the tasks He has given you is to forgive. It is not your job to decide what God has ordained. Do what Christ requires of you. Don't be proud of forgiving others, nor of any other virtue. If you want to ruin the good works that you have done, just blow your own trumpet. If you want to spoil the forgiveness that you have shown, boast about it.

Step Three: grief. In spite of the joy which is planted in your heart, every sin – be it yours or someone else's — should make you sad. You can dispel that grief through forgiveness. As soon as sin rears its ugly head, you must put a stop to it and seek forgiveness. Grief over sin leads to repentance. You must not forget that sin grieves the Almighty. Sin is a betrayal of God's expectations. No one is happy when his children get into bad ways. The Heavenly Father is also grieved at such behavior. If we are true children, we will be hurt by what grieves our Father. In our everyday business let us not be happy in situations when sin appears. Misplaced joy is not joy but sin, and it should make us sad. Joy comes through a careful assessment of sin and sober immersion in the truths about forgiveness.

Step Four: meekness. The apostle James writes, *But the wisdom that is from above is first pure, then peaceable, gentle, and easy to be intreated, full of mercy and good fruits, without partiality, and without hypocrisy*

Aleksandar Birviš

(James 3:17). Meekness (gentleness) or a refusal to use force is good preparation for confession of ones own sins and forgiveness of others. This step is not easy. True meekness is impossible without the true life from God (conversion, new birth etc.). And even then we don't see much meekness. A quick look at the curricula of theological colleges and the behavior of Protestant theologians show that there isn't much wisdom from above, and very little meekness. But if you are not meek, your prayers for forgiveness of sin will not be answered.

Step Five: righteousness. God is holy and righteous. There is no power — not even the power of forgiveness — that can overrule holiness and justice. I can forgive someone for swearing at me, but that doesn't mean that he should be left to continue to swear. On the contrary, he needs to be taught not to do it, even if we have to be strict with him. It is much more important to be concerned for holiness and justice when human lives, property and honor are at stake. I can forgive a pickpocket for taking my money, but he must be held to account for stealing it, and make restitution and learn not to live a life of crime. If only those who have brought the economy to its knees would be forgiven the personal insults they have spoken, while at the same time being punished for their incompetence. At the moment it works the other way round: people are being charged for personal insults, while they are calmly forgiven, almost unnoticed, for ruining companies large and small. Righteousness demands that we carefully distinguish between what should be forgiven and what needs to be made good.

Step Six: mercy. Christians don't forgive because God has commanded it. They forgive because the Lord has shown mercy in their lives. They don't expect forgiveness as if their opponent is obliged to forgive them. Christian men and women hope that the Lord will place forgiveness into the other person's heart too. Mercy

Reflections

doesn't stop at forgiveness. A merciful man carries on doing good deeds. When he has forgiven he gives the other person something to eat, something to wear, or some other form of help that he has available, and above all he will pray for the man to whom he has shown forgiveness.

Step Seven: a pure heart. Forgiveness is only of value if it is done sincerely without any intention of distorting the truth. Care must also be taken that the one who forgives has as little evil as possible in his heart, as little offensiveness and fear as possible. Everything that casts any kind of shadow over a man's life, any kind of animosity, will destroy sincerity and give the lie to forgiveness. There is a story about a man who kept on taking his neighbor to court — for no real reason, except that he enjoyed upsetting his neighbor. Then the man got ill. After a while it seemed that the illness was incurable. So the man sent his friends to the neighbor to say to him, "Sorry I kept taking you to court." The neighbor came round to see him and they made their peace. All the judges heaved a sigh of relief. The neighbor carried on visiting the man, finding doctors for him and getting his medicines. The illness started to subside and the man got better. He got out of bed and was restored to health. Then one day his neighbor came to visit him and he kicked him out and shouted at him, "What are you doing messing around in my house? Get out!" And he started all over again thinking up reasons to take him to court. The judges couldn't believe it, "We thought he said that he wasn't going to court again!" He answered, "I didn't say I wouldn't if I got better." God doesn't recognize that sort of forgiveness. And most forgiveness is like that. Maybe it is not so blatant, but it's still the same when there are hidden motives. An impure heart cannot forgive. So we need to clean it out from the bottom up, throw out all insincerity, corruption, pollution, ambiguity and the rest of it.

Aleksandar Birviš

Step Eight: peace-making. What do men achieve by forgiveness? They achieve peace with God, peace with each other and peace with themselves. Forgiveness certainly leads to peace, but peace also leads to forgiveness. Where peace is more comprehensive, more complete, forgiveness is deeper. Enmity makes a man shortsighted. In the upheavals people are going through, a whole generation of young people is growing up that will need many years to learn forgiveness — if God allows them to survive the extermination which is aimed at them. If a young girl of just twenty years old has to defend her scorched village with just a dozen others, to take on a hugely superior force of bloodthirsty men for ten hours, to shoot and watch as young men fall dead from her bullets — one of whom she was yesterday maybe expecting would ask her to marry him — what possibility is there that she will even begin to forgive? Can even the best evangelism make any difference in such a situation? No, not until the Lord Himself brings peace and commonsense to the hearts of those who have suffered and to their neighbors. We know there will be no peace until God's justice is satisfied, but we also know that inner peace can be nurtured even in the most unfavorable circumstances. Then it will be easier to begin to forgive.

There are other virtues which create the ability to forgive. I will finish by mentioning just one, and that is perseverance.

Step Nine: It is written, *Who shall separate us from the love of Christ? shall tribulation, or distress, or persecution, or famine, or nakedness, or peril, or sword? As it is written, For Thy sake we are killed all the day long; we are accounted as sheep for the slaughter. Nay, in all these things we are more than conquerors through Him that loved us* (Rom.8:35-37). Let us try and think about these words like this: God's love undoubtedly includes forgiveness as well. No one can separate us from forgiveness. If I want to forgive the most wicked enemy I have, there is no power

Reflections

that can stop me forgiving him. Someone may try to persecute me. I won't stop forgiving. Someone may deprive me of food and drink. I won't stop forgiving. Someone may take all my possessions so that I have nothing to wear and nowhere to lie down. I won't stop forgiving. One of my nearest and dearest may turn against me. I won't stop forgiving. Someone may strike fear into my heart through their savage behavior or just their incompetence. I won't stop forgiving. Someone may kill me and my loved ones. I won't stop forgiving. My forgiveness will be Christ's victory, and it will bring me blessing as long as I hold on to the Lord Jesus.

Belgrade, 31ˢᵗ July 1992

As Christ has forgiven you

With regard to the theme of forgiveness in the Lord's Prayer, I need to spend a little time addressing some words from the Epistle to the Colossians — because of the confused thinking of the society in which we live. *Put on therefore, as the elect of God, holy and beloved, bowels of mercies, kindness, humbleness of mind, meekness, longsuffering; Forbearing one another, and forgiving one another, if any man have a quarrel against any: even as Christ forgave you, so also do ye (Col. 3:12-13).*

Forgiveness develops as other virtues are nurtured. That is why the apostle doesn't write only about forgiveness. He mentions mutual tolerance before forgiveness. The same preconditions are required for forgiveness as for tolerance. It would be helpful to look at each one in turn.

1. **Being elect.** We have a duty to instruct all our fellow men. We must teach all men to forgive. But not everyone will

25

Aleksandar Birviš

accept that teaching. Few will understand. Even fewer will agree to forgive.

2. **Belonging.** In a democratic society everyone chooses where they belong and who or what they belong to. It is plain that both individuals and nations are making the wrong choice today. This is happening even in fellowships of God's people. Men decide to opt for what is temporary and worldly, under the assumption that eternity will come whatever they do. But it's wrong to say it doesn't matter; if you have to spend eternity without God because you belong to the wrong side, then you need to take a clear decision straightaway. If you belong to God now, you will belong to Him after the resurrection from the dead and in eternity too.

3. **Holiness.** How can we maintain holiness? Society is in upheaval. All sorts of filth and scum are floating to the surface. Twisted and distorted minds are trying to take over power — and some of them have succeeded. How are we to heal others while still remaining sane? How can we clean up the filth and still stay pure? We have only one option: we must pray, we must never give up the study of the Scriptures and we must continue in fellowship with God's people.

4. **Amiability.** Christians are loved (at least they should be). They are loved by their Savior. And others will love them. Not just those whom Christians have done good to. You remember when those young people from Holland[7] in early summer (1991) were singing and praising God near the monument in town. Then the "White Eagles"[8] turned up and began to beat them up. There was no sign of the police. The fight lasted twenty minutes. It only ended when some bystanders got involved and restrained the White Eagles.

Reflections

Somebody showed love, no matter how small, towards those young people.

5. **Bowels of mercies.** A Christian who forgives becomes a channel of gentleness. His whole being is sweet and it exudes sweetness. One can hardly expect the art of forgiveness from men who have never penetrated the hidden storerooms of their own souls. How are they to penetrate? How can they break through? By confessing their sins, by a constant attitude of prayer and by being spiritually immersed in the revealed truths of God. Then true mercy will radiate from them.

6. **Kindness.** It is the sort of kindness that willingly makes itself available to others. In our efforts to be kind we must avoid the tendency to separate ourselves from other people. Christians don't become worldly by serving men. Who ever heard of a cook who feeds himself? Christian kindness is not selfish kindness, it is not kindness in isolation nor is it intrusive. Witnessing about the gospel is often fruitless because we are too intrusive in our witnessing. People look on intrusiveness as an infringement of their privacy, not as healing. Only through the kindness which helps the other person to be set free can we achieve forgiveness.

7. **Humility.** The proud forgive in order to make a show of their magnanimity. Is this really forgiveness? The humble forgive because of Christ, without making a show and not asking for any reward or recognition.

8. **Meekness.** No one can be forced to forgive. The meek reject force even in places where it is normal. For example: no one should be forced to belong to any particular state or to not belong to it. The state has limited my right to forgive as soon as it becomes convinced of the existence of an enemy of the

Aleksandar Birviš

state whom I cannot verify for myself. It's the same with belonging to a particular people. I want to choose a nation, consciously and unhindered, that will not prevent me from being meek and that will not tell me whom I can forgive and whom I can't. Even less should anyone tell me that I should belong to a particular church. Maybe that church has done great things in the past. But the past should not be allowed to compel me to tie my present and my salvation in Christ to anything else. The meek are sickened by violence, especially violence against children, when they enter into the most intimate connection with God without their knowledge or assent. How much forgiveness is required in such situations — from the times of the Bogumils right up to today's victims, slaughtered just for belonging to a different ethnic group or a different faith! How many layers of oppression, violence, force and compulsion need to be exposed and completely rejected!

9. **Longsuffering.** The meaning of the word longsuffering covers two main areas: behavior and stability. As far as behavior is concerned, the man who suffers voluntarily accepts what God intends. No matter how great the difficulties are, the follower of Christ carries out the will of God as fully as he can, both in everyday life, and in exceptional circumstances. Stability in suffering is seen in a readiness not to turn ones back on the Savior, as well as in a lack of concern about how long the suffering will last. Suffering always seems to go on too long, and often the person suffering thinks they can't endure any more. But suffering prepares people to forgive according to Christ's example.

Reflections

Christ's example of tolerance, and especially His example of suffering, can be put into practice. But first it is necessary to achieve and continually maintain at least the nine factors we have listed. They are the spiritual garments of the person who forgives.

How did Christ forgive?

First, Christ forgave in the same way as He loved. His forgiveness isn't a down payment in return for some favor or demand. The Savior doesn't make accusations, He doesn't keep accounts. He simply forgave because He loves and in the same measure as He loves (that is without measure).

Secondly, the Savior knew whom He was forgiving and what He was forgiving. His forgiveness is all-embracing, but it wasn't universal. Whoever encountered Christ encountered forgiveness. But only those who sought forgiveness actually received it. It doesn't all have to be worked out in detail and reduced to an itemized list. For Christ it is important that a man express his need as explicitly as possible. The Lord will expand our knowledge if we forgive one another.

Thirdly, Christ forgave in all situations and circumstances. He forgave while talking to people, while keeping quiet, while eating and drinking, while at religious services, when He was with the healthy and the sick, and even on the cross. Nothing could stop Him forgiving: not people, nor places, nor time, nor events, nor location, nor any other circumstances.

Need I say more?

Belgrade, 14th August 1992

Aleksandar Birviš

Trials — an everyday challenge

Trials[9] are a form of test. God tests people. That was what was happening when God tested Abraham. The Lord asked him to sacrifice his only son Isaac (Gen.22:1-19). We know that the Judean king Hezekiah (died 691 BC) was also tested (2 Chr. 32:31). This test came after Hezekiah was healed, that is after God confirmed it by the miracle of the moving of the sun, or rather the shadow from the sundial. Hezekiah was imprudent and failed the test (2 Ki. 20:1-19).

Not only were individuals tested, so were the people of God. We see Moses telling his fellow countrymen, *And thou shalt remember all the way which the* Lord *thy God led thee these forty years in the wilderness, to humble thee, and to prove thee, to know what was in thine heart, whether thou wouldest keep his commandments, or no... Thou shalt also consider in thine heart, that, as a man chasteneth his son, so the* Lord *thy God chasteneth thee* (Deut. 8:2, 5).

There is no doubt that we can view trials as part of God's discipline. Consequently the children of God have no need to shun trials. Trials may be tough, but that is nothing to be surprised at. The Apostle Peter writes, *Beloved, think it not strange concerning the fiery trial which is to try you, as though some strange thing happened unto you: But rejoice, inasmuch as ye are partakers of Christ's sufferings; that, when His glory shall be revealed, ye may be glad also with exceeding joy* (1 Pet. 4:12-13).

The request, *Lead us not into temptation* seems rather puzzling to the reader of Scripture. Why pray that we may escape trials, if they are essential for us as part of our education? But let's think for a moment about the fire that the apostle Peter mentions. Trials can be so tough that the one who is going through them begins to think that he would be justified in giving up. You don't have to go as far

Reflections

as denying your faith. You can give in to other smaller or greater forms of dishonesty, and that will be seen as apostasy before the Lord.

I often quote this example (I hope I won't bore you with it). In Romania, during the so-called golden era, that is the time of militant atheism and severe poverty brought on by a command economy, somewhere around spring 1989, a committed Christian (we'll call him Dmitru), his wife and six children were on the verge of starvation. The children were aged from three to ten years old. He worked in a large joinery company, his wife worked in a shoe factory. They both received a salary as well as a children's allowance and food coupons (for example, two eggs each every three weeks). What use was that when there was no food? The coupons were invalid after a certain time, and there was nothing to buy in the shops. Those bits of paper just became worthless.

Middlemen and people from the villages began to appear selling food secretly. But they weren't interested in money because what they wanted couldn't be bought in the shops.

"Dmitru," said one of the peasants, "I can bring you some cheese and milk. They have taken my wheat but I still have a few potatoes and some maize flour. When I have any fruit I will put some aside for you."

"How much will it cost?" asked Dmitru.

"Nothing much," said the peasant.

"What do you mean nothing much? How much is that?"

"Well for a start: two and a half kilos of nails, you know those strong ones."

"But man..." Dmitru tried to interrupt him.

The man carried on without looking at Dmitru.

"I am building an extension to my house, and I need some large nails. We'll get the other ones I need later."

Aleksandar Birviš

Dmitru tried to explain:

"You know, my friend, that I..."

But his friend wasn't listening. He carried on:

"I need a pair of shoes, but not now. My daughter is getting married in October, the first Sunday after Saint Paraskeva's day."

"Congratulations," said Dmitru.

"I'll sort out something for my daughter with your wife."

"With my wife? Leave her out of this."

"Sorry, Dmitru, I didn't mean anything bad or dishonest. I'm an honest man."

"What do you mean honest when you want me to steal, and you expect my wife to steal as well?"

"That's not stealing. Everybody does it. How would they live if they didn't do it? You can't eat coupons. You haven't taught your children to chew paper have you?"

"Listen to me," said Dmitru, "if you want me to do something to help you, I'm ready. But there is no way I will steal."

"What is a man to do? You need to sand your floor boards and fix up the roof beams. I haven't got any floorboards or beams, nor any nails. It's all propped up with pipes at the moment. I gave them some wool and some mutton, and the men who repair the water system gave me some pipes. So we had a deal."

"Listen, I don't work like that."

The peasant stood up and walked off.

"Drop dead then," he said, "People like you don't deserve to live. At least not in this country."

Dmitru and his family put up with hunger and shortages for a few more days. As soon as he and his wife got their salaries they bought what there was available, gave some to the church, and bought tickets and set off for Resica. The next night at about half past one they made it across the Romanian-Yugoslav border. The Romanian guards tried to shine their spotlights on them. But the power supply was poor, and the floodlights just flickered on and off so that the guards had to shoot at random. The woman and the youngest child were just grazed by bullets.

Thank God, the family arrived in Vrsac. They were transferred to Padinska Skela, then to Koviljaca. The children spent the summer at the sea. In the middle of autumn (1989) they left for Canada.

I'm sorry to say that some of the Christians in this country said to them: "Why did you run away? You want America; you want the riches of this world. Your place is in Romania. That's where you should be witnessing about the Lord."

Dmitru replied wisely:

"If I steal, I am not a witness for God. Nor am I if I die of hunger. The dead do not praise God."

There are many trials like this. Millions of Christians are confronted with hardships and suffering every day. They don't always have the Yugoslav border nearby to escape over, nor can the High Commissioner for Refugees solve all their problems. But they all have to be solved somehow.

So it is important to bear in mind the words of the apostle James (1:12-15), *Blessed is the man that endureth temptation: for when he is tried, he shall receive the crown of life, which the Lord hath promised to them that love Him. Let no man say when he is tempted, I am tempted of God: for God cannot be tempted with evil, neither tempteth He any man: But every man is tempted, when he is drawn away of his own lust, and enticed. Then when lust hath conceived, it bringeth forth sin: and sin, when it is finished, bringeth forth death.*

We need, then, to avoid sin, to stand firm trusting in God's goodness. The outcome is blessing. This prospect gives hope. But

Aleksandar Birviš

there is a whole range of trials which are not caused by our own desires, but which are the result of a combination of circumstances. The individual cannot influence what has already happened to him but he has to take a stand against it, and more often than not to oppose it. That is why it is good to pray that our Heavenly Father would protect us from such trials or show us the way out so that we can act in accordance with God's will.

Today the main trial is politics. Man has been a political being ever since Cain murdered Abel. By murdering his brother Cain demonstrated four political principles:

1. the individual man resolves issues of social relationships by specific behavior;
2. man is the cause of conflict and man bears the consequence of conflict;
3. politics are conducted within the boundaries of community (even if it is made up of only two men), but they are also conducted outside that community;
4. men love power.

Our current political experiences and trials revolve around a similar circle of challenges which we must respond to.

Firstly, politics is a form of regulated social behavior. Not to be involved in politics is also politics — the worst kind of politics. Men of violence and the riff-raff come to power through non-involvement, in the absence of genuine, audible political voices, or standpoints. Some people have failed to express their will out of fear for their own lives. They have saved their own lives but because of them many others have met their fate in prison camps, prisons and as refugees.

Reflections

Of course we should pray against becoming politically insensitive. The Church must open people's eyes, but how can it open their eyes if its own are closed? Christians see what the world does not see. The world sees institutions, political parties and their actions. Christians see God's will. They weigh up what is God's will and what is not. God's people think and act on the basis of such assessments.

Secondly, the Church does not get involved in political conflicts. Disagreements and conflicts belong to this world. In the world there is no right or wrong side, just convincing and unconvincing parties. When you look at the work of Parliament you can easily see: a) that there is no one born of God there, and b) that more often than not it is not truth that is being offered but a lesser lie. The members try to promote themselves and their efforts as being the best solution, in as convincing a way as possible. Disagreements arise out of the struggle for power, and not from a desire for the truth. The truth is helpful if it suits one's intentions and aspirations but not vice versa: truth is an objective, an aspiration and an intention which has to be attained regardless of whether it is helpful.

Christian witness in the field of political conflicts takes on four dimensions:

1. Truth is the only power which liberates. Christ said, *And ye shall know the truth, and the truth shall make you free* (John 8:32). There is no good politics without an unshakeable striving for the truth. Rejection of truth cannot be justified by any higher goals (national sovereignty, freedom, success, financial gain etc.).

2. Where there is no repentance, there are no regenerated people, and where there are no regenerated people there is no progress. There is a need for change in the laws, property rights, the

judicial system, electoral and parliamentary procedures, the economic system, the health service, education and many other areas. But this is of little use if it is in the hands of men who have not been transformed by God. What is important for progress are not political parties, nor systems or programs, but repentance. John the Baptist's message is: *Bring forth fruits meet for repentance* (Matt. 3:8). In simple language this means, show by your deeds that you have really repented.

3. We expect nothing from the world. The world has nothing to offer which is not worldly. There is a saying that you can't make a silk purse out of a sow's ear. In the words of our Savior: *For of thorns men do not gather figs, nor of a bramble bush gather they grapes.* (Luke 6:44b). The Word of God points us in a different direction: *And we know that we are of God, and the whole world lieth in wickedness* (1 John 5:19). We ask the Lord to change us, to change politicians and at the same time protect those men who have been changed from giving in to the illusions and deceits of this world.

4. Let us give priority to apostleship. The world is the Christian's field (Matt. 13:38). The world is not there for us to rule over, but to bring the gospel to it. Wise Solomon instructs us: *Prepare thy work without, and make it fit for thyself in the field; and afterwards build thine house* (Prov. 24:27). We are too busy sorting out the Church, when it should be the Church sorting out the world. That is what Byzantium and Rome did, and that is the reason for all the horrors which have occurred from the time of the Huns up till today and which non-Christians use to mock us. The Church must make the Gospel known, in spite of the shortage of people, resources and virtues. If we are not great scholars, no one will force us to speak about

Reflections

what we don't know. If we lack something let's get out there with what we do have. Everything that the Lord has given us is great and good. To those who work He will give more. Of course, the Almighty gives us what we really need and not what tickles our vanity.

Thirdly, we must not lose sight of the fact that there is internal as well as external politics. The Savior requires His fellowship of believers to live and work both in this town and beyond it, both in this country and abroad, amongst this people and amongst others, in places where there is shooting as well as in places where there is no shooting, in Korea, in Africa, at the Equator and at the poles. Christians bring to politics the ability to tear down borders. Borders exist, they are a reality, but we are the only ones who can see what purpose they serve. Their function is to prevent Christians from winning souls, *For though we walk in the flesh, we do not war after the flesh: (For the weapons of our warfare are not carnal, but mighty through God to the pulling down of strong holds;) Casting down imaginations, and every high thing that exalteth itself against the knowledge of God, and bringing into captivity every thought to the obedience of Christ; (2 Cor. 10:3-5).* This task obliges us to think about external politics. It is not our job to be concerned with borders, but we must know about them. It is good to know what is on the other side of the border and much further afield, for the same God is at work there too.

Fourthly, power is not privilege. It is service (Rom. 13:3-4). Christians are the only people who are clear about this and they need to make it known to others. The world will not receive this message easily. But nevertheless, the most successful parts of the world are those where the leaders serve the people. Then the temptation to abuse power disappears and no one can easily resort to force and

Aleksandar Birviš

coercion. Where the government puts its own objectives before the need to serve the people, there poverty is rife. The more the government uses coercion the greater are the temptations of power. The desire for repression gives rise to new means of repression, and new means of repression strengthen the desire for repression, and it all develops to a frightening degree, and all sense of proportion and taste is lost. To make things worse, such a type of government — under the pretence of the protection of higher goals — consumes lives and resources and money in unprecedented amounts. Someone has to pay for it all by going hungry and becoming poor. This gives rise to the temptation that Cain faced: to kill the one who is better than you.

Of course there are many other trials. We can't list them all, and it is almost impossible to foresee what ones there still are to come. Every time has its trials and every trial has its time. And so we still need to pray: Lead us not into temptation.

Belgrade, 21st August 1992

Deliverance from the evil one

Evangelical Christianity seems to have forgotten about the struggle against evil spirits. Most of our ministers do not know what to do if demons show up. Should we do what witch-doctors and fortune tellers do? They leap about, blow on the evil spirit, spit on him, use garlic against him, trick him with false names etc. Should we light fires, write out mysterious messages and use incense to drive out the devil and his helpers?

The struggle against spirits is a fact of the Bible and of life. How come men are so ignorant? Is it just a lack of knowledge?

Reflections

No, there is something worse at work here. Satan has succeeded in convincing the majority of Christians that he is harmless, and even that he does not exist. As a result evil spirits are of little significance. Everyone behaves as if they don't exist. Men believe in God — it's fashionable today — but belief in Lucifer seems childish and old-fashioned. As if it is beneath an educated man to believe in the existence of the devil.

Is it possible to believe in demons in the 20th century?

It is true that Christians repeat the Lord's Prayer, where it says *but deliver us from evil.* But the devil has been up to his tricks with that as well. Because of certain doubts about the translation, men pray for deliverance from some kind of impersonal evil, whereas they should be praying to the Heavenly Father to deliver them from the evil one, the devil.

Satan is a person. Every evil spirit is a person: he is personally aware; he knows who he is and who he is not. The devil often knows his place better than Christians, but he is also very good at knowing how to be where he does not belong.

There is no place for the devil in the presence of God or men. He has fallen and has perished. He belongs in the place of eternal torment. The place of the ruler of darkness and all his followers is in the pit.

The fact is, evil spirits are at work where they don't belong. That is their temporary field of activity. That state of affairs will continue until our Savior comes again. *And then shall that Wicked be revealed, whom the Lord shall consume with the spirit of His mouth, and shall destroy with the brightness of His coming* (2 Thess. 2:8). The work of unclean spirits is only temporary. It is not easy for us, since it is difficult to fight against them. But the forces of evil have been defeated by the

Aleksandar Birviš

cross of Christ. We just need to rebuke them in the name of the Conqueror from Calvary.

What are we to do against the manifestation of evil spirits? How can we drive Satan away? How can we keep the evil one at bay?

Let me offer one course of action. (This is a suggestion based on the Scriptures and experience given by the Holy Spirit. I would be most pleased if someone were to suggest a better idea).

We should begin with prayer, something along these lines:

> Holy Father, Righteous Lord, Son of God, Lord Jesus, Holy Spirit, Lord of life, Glorious God, the only Lord — there is no power but God alone. No one can help us but You, Lord, our God. You are glorious, almighty over all, and so we come to You. Do not look at our weakness, forgive us our sins, protect us in these struggles and defeat the unclean spirits, cast the evil spirits into the abyss, break all the powers of the devils, and completely overpower Satan, destroy all evil by the power of Your breath so that they are mentioned no more. This we pray in the Name of Christ, in the Name of our Savior and Lord and Son of God. May all glory be to Him and to the eternal Father and the Holy life-giving Spirit, both now and for ever and for all eternity. Amen.

After an introductory prayer a suitable portion of Scripture should be read such as for example Eph. 6:11-20 or Rom. 8:33-39 followed by another prayer of thanksgiving to God for His Word and for the victory in Christ. Then it is a good idea for all those present to speak out together the first three verses of Psalm 68: *Let God arise, let His enemies be scattered: let them also that hate Him flee before Him. As smoke is driven away, so drive them away: as wax melteth before the fire, so let the wicked perish at the presence of God. But let the righteous be glad; let them rejoice before God: yea, let them exceedingly rejoice.*

After this reading comes the rebuke. It should be spoken out loud. According to ancient texts I suggest the following rebuke be given:

> Listen you devil, the Lord rebukes you; God Almighty, the living God who came to this wicked world and dwelled amongst men rebukes you. The Lord Jesus comes now, and easily destroys all your power. He delivers men from bondage. He is Lord, He has conquered, He overcame His enemies and all their forces on the cross. He triumphs over you, you evil spirit. When the sun hid its face, when darkness fell in the midst of the day, the earth was suddenly shaken, and the graves opened up in Judea, holy men rose up from the dead, and the Lord cast down the devil. Christ has destroyed death through death, and has overcome you, Satan. The Lord has stripped you of your strength. I rebuke you in the power of the living God, who protects all the approaches to paradise, who protects the tree of life and all places where God's glory dwells. I rebuke you, evil power. I rebuke you in the power of the mighty cherubim that wave the flaming sword, and prevent sinners from entering eternity, and do not allow access to the tree of life. The Holy Name of the Lord Jesus comes against you to repel you. May the Lord cast you into the abyss! May the Son of God crush you, may the sovereign Savior who walks on water as if on dry land trample you under His feet. With one look from the Savior, the ocean depths dry up, the hills tremble, and the mountains melt. He puts you to flight now. Tremble before Him, you devil. Satan,

Aleksandar Birviš

get lost, leave this place, give way, and take your hands off this child of God, whose name is (say the name of the person for whose deliverance we are praying) and leave this place of God, this building and everything that is in it. The Lord Jesus forbids you ever to enter this man (or woman or girl) again, either openly, or secretly, or to hide in him (or her), or to meet him (or her) or do any evil to him (or her) either by day or by darkest night, at midday or at midnight. You have no right to dwell anywhere except in the depths of the pit, where you will remain until the day of God's judgment which surely awaits you. Fear God, you evil spirit, for God sits above the cherubim and clearly sees the depths of darkness. All the holy angels shine before Him, all the archangels tremble before Him, and all thrones, principalities, powers, authorities, the bright cherubim and seraphim — the chief servants of God — tremble before Him. The heavens and all that is in them shake and tremble before the Lord. The whole earth and all that is in the earth and all that is under it shakes before the Lord. The sea and all that is in it fears the Lord. You too, Satan, you devil, tremble, let all the evil spirits shake, all the devils shriek for fear — for our Lord is coming to reign. You evil powers, leave this faithful warrior of Christ alone. God has prepared him (or her) for war, has chosen him (her) to defeat all of you, and has set His seal upon him (her). He protects him (her) and will let no one have him (her), and so get out of him (her) at once! Satan, you wicked antichrist, I rebuke you in the name of Christ, I rebuke you by the heavenly Horseman, who rides on the wings of the wind, who makes the fiery flame become God's angel servant. You devil, shameless tempter, I rebuke you by the cross of

Reflections

Calvary, I rebuke you by the empty tomb and the risen Son of the living God: you and your rebel hordes leave this child of God whose name is… Leave all these rooms, and don't come near ever again, keep right away from this area, do not come back again, do not show your face again. And we will praise the Lord who made the heavens and the earth, who was and is and who will be for all eternity: He is the mighty Lord of hosts, glory to Him now and for ever! Amen".

That is the end of the rebuke. After that we praise God – we praise the name of the one God: Father, Son, Holy Spirit — Three in one, God indivisible. We praise Him now; we praise Him for all eternity. Glory to the Lord for ever and ever. Amen, Hosanna and Hallelujah! Amen.

If circumstances allow, more prayers, psalms, singing and readings can be included.

I must add this: Satan is especially active in our country at this time. Christians are capable of thwarting all the activities of the devil. Their duty is to drive out evil spirits in Christ's name wherever they have the opportunity and wherever it is necessary. *Submit yourselves therefore to God. Resist the devil, and he will flee from you* (James 4:7).

That is God's promise. Blessed are those who believe those promises. God will deliver them from the evil one.

Belgrade, 28th August 1992

For Yours is the ... forever

The Lord's prayer finishes with words of exultant praise: *For Thine is the kingdom, and the power, and the glory, for ever. Amen.* Different

Aleksandar Birviš

manuscripts and translations have different versions of these words. They are generally missing from the most reliable copies of the original text. Experts believe that they were added later and they assume that they were not spoken by the Lord Jesus.

Be that as it may, these words belong to our Lord because He is the true owner and representative of the Kingdom of God, the power of God and the glory of God. For this reason it would not be right to leave out the interpretation of this song of praise. It would be incomplete before God and irresponsible before men.

The Heavenly Father is the undisputed Master of the Kingdom of Heaven. In that Kingdom righteousness reigns. It is not a civil society — something that we hear a lot about today. In contrast to a state with a legal system (laws), a civil society is a country where the rule of law prevails and laws are passed consistently and implemented successfully. But the rule of law doesn't ensure that the state is just, because its laws may make lawlessness the norm. Men regulate some of their relationships through laws. The more evil there is among people, the more evil those relationships are. The Heavenly Father is infinitely removed from evil. He is the perfection of goodness, and in His Kingdom there is no injustice just as there are no other evils.

That is why we need constantly to turn to the Heavenly Father. Only in fellowship with Him can justice be achieved. God's justice is sometimes unpleasant. We must not forget that God never promised that His justice would be pleasant and that His Kingdom would be a party. For men who love God all God's actions are fascinating, and His words bring enjoyment whenever they appear.

You cannot love God if God does not give you love. It is a gift from the Almighty. A man may want to love, but in order for him to love properly, the Lord must plant it in his heart. Since no one can force the Lord to do anything, we cannot demand of Him that He

Reflections

plants love in our hearts. We don't need to. He is willing to make us a people and individuals that love Him. He doesn't hold back this gift, in fact He rewards us. We must not stop asking, and He will certainly give us His love.

God's Kingdom is a land of peace and calm, but it is not dead or forcefully suppressed. In the difficult times we are going through we long for the good times, or rather for some unspecified time when we were supposedly living in peace and no one was being killed. It's true, no one was being killed on the battlefield, and old scores were not being settled by destructive action, but our church in Belgrade was demolished in 1973[10] without war being declared, and it was condemned by a simple court ruling and an exemplary town plan. Men have been swallowed up by the darkness with no possibility of finding out anything about their fate. There was no peace, for there can be no peace where wickedness, lawlessness and godlessness prevail.

Men desire peace. That is good but it is in vain. Peace cannot be built on injustices. Not even a simple ceasefire can hold until injustices are rooted out. The blessed task of peacemaking can be performed by those who have already grasped and achieved poverty of spirit, sorrow before God, meekness, hunger and thirst for justice, mercy and purity of heart. Peace must not just be a temporary breathing space before another period of hostilities. Even less may it be a means of confirming and establishing privileges, injustices, oppression and everything else that is against God's will. In times of turbulence and hostilities we must lift up our heads (Luke 21:28). That is the prime task of Christians in times of crisis. Caution and political factors are of secondary importance.

The Scriptures teach us that worshipping the Lord in difficult times brings joy. Are we to rejoice when we see so many disfigured corpses, villages burnt down, people's homes taken away and the

Aleksandar Birviš

power of darkness triumphing? No. Nobody can or should rejoice at such things. But love for God opens up much wider horizons. If we have decided on this love, then we will view all the horrors of life in a different light: they point to worldliness, and worldliness cannot exist without destruction, deceit and horrors.

So let us talk freely about joy. It will still exist within us even after all around us falls apart and unimaginable atrocities are perpetrated. The evil one is constantly trying to take away our joy. There are many traps that he places within us and around us, activities that he tempts us with which are against our convictions and the beliefs on which our church stands. But that in no way reduces God's authority and the care of the Heavenly Father, and so it cannot reduce our joy.

God's power keeps us when we adopt such a frame of mind. We believe that God has a power above all powers. The Heavenly Father does all things by His power. He does whatever He desires. Holiness is pleasing to Him and He makes it possible. He is pleased when everything happens in accordance with His superior wisdom and understanding. He defines His purpose and does all things as He has ordained. Men and angels see that what He determines is the wisest solution. All other decisions lead to extremely harmful consequences, and only God's decision brings blessing.

The power of God does not prescribe anything that would be opposed to God Himself. In fact nothing can oppose Him. Our Heavenly Father remains faithful to His most noble purpose because that is His will and because no one can oppose Him or dissuade Him from His intention, and not because it cannot be otherwise.

For us who believe in the fatherhood of the Almighty, it is a comfort and an encouragement to know that there will never be a time when He does not want to be our Father. By His almighty power the Lord makes His fatherhood unchangeable and permanent.

Reflections

Men can behave like children of God, or they can rise up as His enemies. The fatherhood of God has such power that it does not cease because of unseemly human behavior.

The Father showed His almighty power in the very first pages of Scripture. He creates the world by speaking forth the Word. By the power of His Word He brings order to the world and upholds it. When He thinks it is necessary, God creates; when He finds it necessary, He destroys. This doesn't look like fatherly behavior when we see Him doing such things. We forget that the Father isn't only He who feeds us but also He who disciplines us. He knows best what action to take in disciplining His child. It is a Christian conviction that nothing happens by accident, but that everything occurs in accordance with God's perfect and almighty will. Whatever happens, God's solutions are the best and the most profound. It is difficult to penetrate their depths. But in such circumstances we still believe that the most wise God will not let men fall into all sorts of tricks and misconceptions. He removes them.

God's glory is also mentioned. There is in the human spirit a yearning for that which dominates the human personality both in individuals and in the human race as a whole. There is a desire for the infinite even though no one has any experience of it. In fact man yearns to know the glory of the living God. It is sought by people who have nothing else to seek, but it is hoped for — often completely unconsciously — by the man who has become so independent that he does not need God. Where does this come from? It comes from the fact that the glory of God has existed since time immemorial and remains the desire of man's heart. Man has lost the glory of God but he has not forgotten it.

The Heavenly Father rejoices over every person who seeks His glory. The glory of God is the one thing that can satisfy all the various

Aleksandar Birviš

human desires. Man desires something more, and then something more than that, and then more, and so on without end. The glory of God is the answer to such a desire.

While man is occupied with all these efforts life just rushes past. What is even more difficult is that man brings misfortune on himself in all this. He stops doing that when he realizes that God in His glory is willing to reveal Himself to him and he just has to turn towards Him. Then man begins sincerely and enthusiastically to praise the Lord. In spite of what men call success or failure, man emerges from the vicious circle and does not fall into despair. It is true that Satan will rush to offer him disappointments, and even despair. But God's glory gives the power so that anyone can resist Satan's enticing offers.

The material that carnal man is made of would never seek for God's glory of itself. In the first place all physical possibilities are limited. Also, there is a lack of awareness of something that is beyond man's horizons: man is too concerned with himself, and less with what is outside of him. When a man begins to delve into spiritual factors, he finds it very difficult to accept them in any way apart from what the limits of his own habits permit. How often do we notice that even believers talk about God and think about Him as if He is a man?

Is there anything more important than complete commitment to the glory of the Father? Maybe that glory will not be revealed as it was to the prophets. The follower of Christ must not lose sight of the fact that the Father does not have to show His glory to every child of His in the same way. He will surely reveal it.

Our Father has given us physical existence, salvation and holiness. From Him come the Kingdom, the power and the glory. As we approach Him as Father, we Christians open ourselves up to all His blessed gifts and expectations. The Lord will not withhold them.

Belgrade, 1st September 1992

Reflections

REGULAR SERIES OF SERMONS

I THE LORD SANCTIFY

First Sunday in Advent
Subject: Expectation of the Savior

The word of the LORD *came again unto me, saying,*

Moreover, thou son of man, take thee one stick, and write upon it, For Judah, and for the children of Israel his companions: then take another stick, and write upon it, For Joseph, the stick of Ephraim and for all the house of Israel his companions:

And join them one to another into one stick; and they shall become one in thine hand.

And when the children of thy people shall speak unto thee, saying, Wilt thou not shew us what thou meanest by these?

Say unto them, Thus saith the Lord GOD; *Behold, I will take the stick of Joseph, which is in the hand of Ephraim, and the tribes of Israel his fellows, and will put them with him, even with the stick of Judah, and make them one stick, and they shall be one in Mine hand.*

And the sticks whereon thou writest shall be in thine hand before their eyes.

And say unto them, Thus saith the Lord GOD; *Behold, I will take the children of Israel from among the heathen, whither they be gone, and will gather them on every side, and bring them into their own land:*

And I will make them one nation in the land upon the mountains of Israel; and one king shall be king to them all: and they shall be no more two nations, neither shall they be divided into two kingdoms any more at all.

Neither shall they defile themselves any more with their idols, nor with their detestable things, nor with any of their transgressions: but I will save them out of all their dwellingplaces, wherein they have sinned, and will cleanse them: so shall they be My people, and I will be their God.

And David My servant shall be king over them; and they all shall have one shepherd: they shall also walk in My judgments, and observe My statutes, and do them.

And they shall dwell in the land that I have given unto Jacob My servant, wherein your fathers have dwelt; and they shall dwell therein, even they, and their children, and their children's children for ever: and My servant David shall be their prince for ever.

Moreover I will make a covenant of peace with them; it shall be an everlasting covenant with them: and I will place them, and multiply them, and will set My sanctuary in the midst of them for evermore.

My tabernacle also shall be with them: yea, I will be their God, and they shall be My people.

And the heathen shall know that I the LORD *do sanctify Israel, when My sanctuary shall be in the midst of them for evermore* (Ez. 37:15-28).

Let us look first at a Jewish interpretation of the passage.

Ezekiel, the son of a priest, was one of those taken into exile in Babylon. He became one of the spiritual leaders who helped the people of Israel maintain their spirits during the years of despair. He was both a priest and a prophet, a preacher and a writer, the inspirer of a nation and pastor of individual souls. The key note of his teaching is *personal responsibility*. He is a great preacher of repentance and God's forgiveness extended to those who truly seek it. *Again, when the wicked man turneth away from his wickedness that he hath committed, and doeth that*

Aleksandar Birviš

which is lawful and right, he shall save his soul alive (Ez. 18:27). If those who dwell in the house of Israel would be purified in this way, Israel will once again be restored and will become a holy people in whose midst God will be seen to dwell.

Ezekiel uses live allegories, symbols and parables more than any other prophet. The first half of the chapter (verses. 1-14) is his vision of the Valley of Dry Bones. The Prophet sees the nation as if dead (which it was), where the fires had gone out in the solemn cold of exile. Then he sees Israel brought back to life by the Spirit of prophecy and rising up to a renewed life in glory.

In the second half of the chapter (verses. 15-28), which makes up our haphtarah (reading from the prophets), the prophet depicts the continuing national resurrection. Finally he announces the unification of the two kingdoms of Judah and Joseph (The Northern Kingdom of Israel). This is symbolized by the coming together of two sticks, which reminds us of the picture we have in the main reading about Joseph and his brothers who meet after being separated for many years.

v.16: The symbolic act of the prophet is intended to draw attention to his message. One piece of wood represents the Kingdom of Judah (two tribes); the other the Kingdom of Israel (ten tribes). This second one is often called Ephraim (one of Joseph's two sons) as is the case here.

v.18-22: The people ask what Ezekiel's action means and he explains it like this: the two kingdoms will join together, as they once were under Saul, David and Solomon.

v.23: The result is not just political union but also spiritual renaissance. Israel is united — but united in returning to God and faithfully fulfilling God's Law. Then they will deserve the name of People of God.

Reflections

v.24: David, that is, the perfect ruler in the future Kingdom; in the messianic era he will be a leader like David was.

v.27: The Shekinah. God's majestic presence will be clearly seen amongst them when they are faithful to their calling as a Holy People. Also Israel will in this way be the means for God to be revealed to other nations (verse 28).

For us Christians there are other points to be made. I don't say that the Jews don't have more to say or know more. Maybe I have selected a Rabbi who assumes that his readers know a lot more, and he tells them only what he thinks his readers don't already know. But I will pass on to what I think I need to say.

v.15: The coming of the Lord's word. Man has been found worthy to hear and to listen to the living God. We live with the conviction that the Lord cooperates with man. Man should be thankful and carefully participate in that cooperation with God. God never says anything to harm anybody or anything. Dire consequences may result if His voice is not heeded or we ignore the good thing that He Himself has prepared.

v.16: Two sticks. God joins together. He is able to join that which to men appears irreconcilable. This is the right place to remind ourselves of politics and wars. The huge injustices today taking place over a small area and in a short space of time seem to be encouraging people to become fiercely alienated one from another. We wonder whether some of these people will ever be able to live together again. The answer is: if God wishes it they will live in closer unity than before.

v.17: Little and disunited. A remnant is a sad thing to see. From the human point of view it is a painful experience when only a small number survive out of a great people. It is even more embarrassing when the remnant is not united. It is disunited and alienated from

Aleksandar Birviš

the Lord, but the Lord has not separated Himself from them. He sees the trouble that the people are going through and He is closer to them than they think.

v.18: The people question. The people have the right to know. There is no need to fear people who ask. Prophets are there to give answers. He who believes, seeks. God's answers are not far off; God's explanations come at just the right time.

v.19: The hand of God. The hand of man does not know how to unite. All human communities are temporary, even the ones that last the longest and are not broken up by the will of man. The hand of God unites permanently and for eternity. It is true of course that the Lord does not unite by force. He seeks and finds and brings together. He finds the best way to achieve unity. A prophet may hold a stick in his hand, or he may hold a man's hand, but the Lord holds the heart and the soul, life and eternity, individuals and tribes, families and nations, villages and states. We must not be deceived by made-up stories about brotherhood and unity. Let us leave it to the Lord – He forms the assemblies of men, He appoints rulers and deposes them. I know a man, a Jew, who was tortured and mutilated in German concentration camps. When the Second World War was over, he underwent a whole series of operations to enable him to lead some semblance of a life. The first two things he did when he came out of hospital and convalescence was a) to become a Christian and b) marry a German girl. I had the opportunity to see him and hear him preach – he has an unshakeable faith in God's mighty hand.

v.20: Plainly and in writing. Writing is an art. For Christians writing is essential. As the people of God we are assured of the holiness and authority of God's Word. The Lord has granted that His will be written down by His Spirit. He has confirmed it in practice, and confirms it today that His Will is all-powerful, holy and revealed

Reflections

for the good of those who believe. It is no good running from the written word. That is to obscure the truth, to deny the evidence. And it is foreign to the Gospel.

v.21: Existence in accordance with God's will. Israel does not exist on the basis of its merits. The real reason for its existence is the Lord's choice. The Almighty wished a nation to exist and for that nation to be God's revelation to the world. There are no other nations that can boast of such an ancient tradition of literacy and such a youthful willingness to accept all that is progressive. The future of this scattered people lies not in further migrations and dispersal but in the nearness of the living God. How much more do Christians need to see their present, future and eternity in close fellowship with Christ? For Christians have no true home on this earth. This turns them more to the Savior.

v.22: One nation — one king. Divisions exist. A united Europe is for the time being more of a story for the future than a future for a story. Divisions can only be overcome by the One who is Himself indivisible — the Lord. Politicians and armies have no answer. Even if they could resolve these issues, they still wouldn't solve them. Because of course, if there were no divisions, opposition and enmity, these people would no longer be necessary. What would they do? They do not know how to till the land, they are ashamed to beg. And that is why they need wars, just as doctors and vets need illnesses. But the Almighty thinks and acts differently. He will overcome divisions in those same centers of idol worship where they began (the mountains of Israel). God's chosen Anointed One (Christ) rules over a united people through the foresight of God.

v.23: Cleansing. God wants a people for Himself. His people must be pure. And so the Lord will purify them. The Omniscient One knows all idols, both hidden and unhidden, the ones men

Aleksandar Birviš

are aware of and the ones men are not aware of. God removes the detestable things (sin) and takes away the existing hindrances. He also suppresses future hindrances. That is why He shed His blood and keeps us as His people.

v.24: The long-awaited David. God foresees that a new Anointed One (Christ) will come to rule. His rule will consist of serving God. The Messiah will not impose Himself upon His people; instead His service and His Holiness will raise Him up to the throne. As well as being ruler Christ will be a shepherd. He will take care of every individual. It makes absolutely no difference how many there are in the earth - the Savior is able to save everyone who believes and, of course, wants to be saved. The Shepherd is not intrusive; Christ's rule is established through fulfilling the will of God. God has made known what He wants. He has appointed whom He wants. Man is not left to the confusion and upheavals of life. Everything is in God's hands.

v.25: A true dwelling place. The Savior creates and maintains fellowship with the saved. Christ's fellowship is the true dwelling place for the present, the future and for eternity. In the present that fellowship is the Kingdom of God: righteousness and peace and joy in the Holy Spirit (Rom. 14:17). In the future this fellowship will be the place where relations between people, primarily families, will be built and fostered. In the world it will be more difficult because these vices will take over: self-interest, the love of money, self-promotion or boasting, pride, blasphemy, disobedience, thanklessness, gossiping, lasciviousness or licentiousness, anger, malice, treachery, intemperance, conceit, hedonism, empty piety (the form without the power), lack of sensitivity, savagery, hot temper and so on. (2 Tim. 3:1-5). That is the future of the world. The future of the Christian is in the confines of the Savior's eternal rule in an extended family. Eternity is ineffable, unutterable and indescribable. It is meaningful

Reflections

that eternity is in the uninterruptible and permanent presence of Christ. I am not interested in heaven or hell because I have been promised the presence of God.

v.26: The eternal covenant. Our God is the covenant Lord: He enters into covenants with men. All the covenants He has ever entered into are condensed into one covenant. The characteristics of that covenant are eternity and peace. Peace in Christ is the absence of all war, the reality of covenant with God, peace with our neighbors and peace with ourselves. That peace and all that goes with it will be everlasting - it will not be violated, it will not be interrupted. Eternity brings much more. It is not, to be specific, just uninterrupted and indestructible existence — it is an extra quality and dimension of life. The Savior describes it in His promise that His followers will be like angels (Mark 12:25). Additional promises are focused on blessings such as steadfastness and multiplication, and on the Holy of Holies. With the coming of the Lord Jesus the Holy Place, that is the temple, is among men. In praying to Christ the people of God bow down to the living God. The Savior will never be separated from His followers. That is our indestructible temple. All the expectations of both Jews and Christians and of all who seek the Lord are centered on and fulfilled in Him.

v.27: God and His people. A dwelling place in the Holy Spirit, that is the living God in the midst of His people, is the result of the covenant of God with men. Men are not alone; God is amongst them and is willing for His glory to be present in the human race. In that light the covenant is mutual - the Almighty loves His people and does everything in order that this people may become and remain holy; whereas the people of God love their Lord and endeavor to glorify Him as worthily as possible. While the covenant with the Jews was limited, the eternal covenant is independent of time and

Aleksandar Birviš

space. Wherever there is just one Christian, there Christ is, for the covenant is entered into with the ever-present God. We do not look at the size and number of God's people. There are no big and small churches — there are just those that are close to Christ and those that are closer, that is, those who have grown into the covenant with God to a lesser degree and those who have grown into it more than others.

v.28: New members: waiting for Christ is also a period of waiting for new Christians. When the Savior's birth in Bethlehem was expected it was known that He would bring a new Kingdom and a new people. Wherever and whenever Christ is sought, new Christians are expected to appear. Christians of today live, or at least should live, with the same zeal for winning souls that the apostles and other followers of our Savior had. Nations can see Christ, but we need to do all we can to let them see their need of Him. Witnessing originates within the Holy Place. The presence of God increases the awareness of the Lord and the awareness of a personal need for salvation. We should remember that in times of general confusion neither Christians nor non-Christians have anything or anyone to wait for except Christ, and this is proclaimed to all both near and far.

★ ★ ★

We await Christmas. Our Savior is born. We await the celebration of His birth. If we cut out the dreamy mood and cute little songs that make Christmas pleasant and attractive to us, we are left with inescapable impressions of a year which has already shown that the civilized are not civilized, and that the cultured in general lack culture, but that believers have in many ways betrayed Christ. All of them will welcome Christmas. Will they welcome the Lord Jesus?

Belgrade, 15th December 1991

A MAN WHOSE NAME WAS JOHN

Third Sunday in Advent
Subject: The Forerunner

There was a man sent from God, whose name was John. The same came for a witness, to bear witness of the Light, that all men through him might believe. He was not that Light, but was sent to bear witness of that Light (John 1:6-8)

1

John the Baptist was sent by God. John was a man with a task entrusted him by God. It was not men who sent this forerunner of Christ and prophet to the Jordan. Nor did John dwell in the desert before that at the command of men. This holy man was ordained before his birth to glorify the Almighty.

Worshipping God is a natural act that can be carried out anywhere. Nature praises God in its own way. Men do it in their way. Every Christian glorifies God in the way God instructs him and enables him.

Everyone is required to glorify God according to His will. And so all ways of glorifying Him are not equal. John praises God by speaking out what God wants and what He is like. He was a prophet and his task was prophetic. Others have a teaching task or an apostolic task. The Lord sets the task. Does anyone want to be a blessing to

Aleksandar Birviš

others? He can't choose his own task. We cannot seriously struggle for our neighbors where the mission is not fostered in complete submission to God's will.

The Baptizer of Christ was a hermit. Men without a true understanding of God's gift look down on hermits. They look on them as cowards, men who are afraid to confront social realities. They say that men who live in the wilderness cannot have any influence. What a delusion! Hermits are often aware of evils which many conceal. The man from the wilderness sometimes has such influence that even men of violence fear him.

John the Baptist came into his ministry from the wilderness. He was a blessing for all who love the truth. Today, as in the past, the people of God enjoy reading about the gospel truths of his life. Because of his truthfulness and boldness John the Baptist was cast into prison and executed.

His task did not end with his death. When the Savior began to perform miracles, Herod and others whose consciences were not clear, thought that John had risen from the dead. Such was John's standing and influence. He was a blessing to many, not by baptizing, nor by preaching, but by his personal influence.

2

The primary task of John the Baptist was not to baptize in the River Jordan. The Scripture sees John as a witness. He bore witness to Christ. That is a task intended for all of us. Apostles, prophets, evangelists, emperors and other rulers, miracle-workers, those who brought gifts, shepherds and teachers, the bringers of good news, the martyrs and all other Christians, of both sexes, from all nations, from all walks of life and all age groups have witnessed about the promised Messiah.

Reflections

Witnessing is not the main task, nor is it a secondary one. It is a feature and a most valuable part of every task. John the Baptist witnessed by baptizing and preaching and answering questions, by suffering, believing, doubting, and even when they cut his head off.

Christians live as witnesses. They would much prefer to behave as advocates: it's a more prominent occupation and it seems more important at first glance. But Christ has no need of lawyers. Why defend Him when He Himself is the evidence? And who do we defend Him against? What is there to prove? If Christ needed men to defend Him, He would not be God.

A witness is concerned with facts. He doesn't present evidence. He just tells what he saw, heard, experienced, what happened, who was involved etc. No accusation, no defense, no politics, no argument — just reality.

Each individual witness experiences the facts in a way peculiar to himself. If he is honest, he will not change his statement according to what others have experienced. That is what dishonest, weak-willed witnesses do. Truthful and truth-loving witnesses don't do that - their statement is more often than not unpolished, sometimes crude, but it is faithful to the truth.

This is the case with preaching too. John the Baptist did not include in his sermons things that people do not know. His comparisons were known by all, his recommendations direct, his speeches clear. His aim was to tell the truth. He didn't praise and flatter. He didn't insult or blame. He spoke what he had to and in the way that he had to.

For many John the Baptist was an embarrassing witness. But he was the complete witness - without ingratiating himself and without compromise. They tried to silence him and reject him but those who understood him received a blessing.

Aleksandar Birviš

3

Every testimony brings light. The courts wouldn't call witnesses if everything was clear. Both the prosecutor and the defense try to cloud the issue. They keep explaining things, but most often their intention is not to get at the truth. They want to serve the interests of their clients. The judge is the one who is interested in the truth – he has to listen to all sides and all the witnesses.

Christian witnessing brings light where it is most needed. The general awareness of God is vague. In human nature that is the darkest part of the consciousness. Science is trying to illuminate the secrets of the mind. Art struggles to disperse darkness. Sport is a search for what is purest and best. Only in religion and politics do men try to make things indistinct.

Why do priests and theologians behave like this? They act as if they were drawing the curtains, preventing the light from entering, building up walls of darkness against the light. In the world there have never been more books about religion, more services and prayer, while people are more empty, violent and godless than ever.

It is obvious: something is wrong.

I don't propose to go into an examination of the reason at the moment. It is better for us to look at the content of our testimony, the one and only possible content — Christ. In other words, John the Baptist did not bear witness to anyone else except the Lord Jesus. The forerunner of the Savior was only one of a long line of people who witnessed about the promised Messiah. Talking of Christ is a means of not only bringing light but also of witnessing to the light.

The task is clear: to tell the facts about Christ. Whoever has any experience of the Lord Jesus is obliged to share his joy with others. That is how joy will increase. The blessing of God is multiplied

Reflections

by division. The selfish have very little joy. The generous and big-hearted have blessing upon blessing.

Facts must be separated from everything else. If Christians want to be effective witnesses they must carefully avoid what is not fact, what they have not personally experienced. The word about Christ must not be mixed with our many human conventions.

One of these conventions that we have is the large number of human traditions. The Savior and salvation did not appear yesterday. The Gospel has been preached for a long while: for twenty centuries after Christ, but also thousand of years before He came among men. The truth is hidden under many layers of history. Some of these layers have been accepted as additional revelation. The inclusion of human traditions weakens the testimony and undermines the blessing.

The same applies to folk customs. They have been formed down the ages, and have often been assimilated into religion. Men lose sight of the Savior, while holding on to customs that will not save them. Customs can be damaging in more ways than one. They are passed on to future generations. These generations accept them without questioning. They are willing to impose them on others, especially on their children. If someone turns their back on their customs they call him a traitor and a degenerate.

Customs cannot give new life and blessing. The fewer customs and human learning there is, the closer Christ is.

4

There are some pitfalls to be avoided in witnessing.

There are those who believe you can witness better if you are better educated. That is fine, but a witness is not expected to be educated but truthful. Learning has its advantages. If we speak good Turkish then it will be easier for us to win over a Turk. If I am

Aleksandar Birviš

familiar with the Talmud, then Jews will accept me more readily. But what use is all knowledge if I lack love and integrity? I won't be a blessing to anybody if I know the Kalevala[11] by heart, whereas two or three words about the blood of Christ will mean eternal life for someone.

One pitfall is to forget who we are. It was said of John the Baptist that he was not the Light, but he bore witness to the Light. Many are convinced that they are the light, and not just lamps. This is just where Satan has caught them out. Children don't give birth to parents, parents have children. A lamp is there for the light. A witness is there because of Christ, and not Christ because of the witness.

Christ did not need to have a special representative. Many people fall into this trap: they don't witness about the Savior, instead they depict themselves as the Savior's substitute, representative, agent or similar. The Lord is the Lord, and a witness is a witness.

Witnessing about the light must not be reduced to cursing the darkness. Thousands of words spoken against the darkness will not illuminate one inch of ground. One little lamp makes every step safer. Christianity must not neglect to point to sin, the struggle against evil and the driving out of unclean spirits. But that isn't Christianity. Christianity is Christ. Witnesses speak out about Him. He is the content of their testimony. Such a testimony brings blessing and such witnesses serve their neighbors.

The pitfalls of witnessing include self-praise. It can happen that the witness unwittingly stops talking about what he has heard, seen, and felt and so on, and begins to talk about himself. In worldly courts that can lead the listeners astray and can be of interest to the judge. Christian witnessing begins, continues and ends with the Lord Jesus. If a witness replaces that with himself then he does the Gospel a disservice. The Devil encourages human arrogance and

Reflections

often tricks Christ's followers into this pitfall. There is no blessing in that. Witnessing has its full power only when those who witness exclude themselves, their arrogance and conceit. Humility, meekness and calmness are the essential marks of a faithful witness.

5

The aim of witnessing is faith. John the Baptist testified with the intention that all should believe. Communicating Christ is not a desire to give a better picture of the Savior or to give a literary description. Christ must be believed, believed correctly and believed for salvation.

In his encounter with Christ, John the Baptist demonstrated that he believed in the prophetic word concerning the promised Messiah. Even when he doubted, the forerunner showed that he believed in the expectation of God's people. People today expect and believe the same things. The promised Messiah came among men, but many deny and reject that fact. The Kingdom of God doesn't suit some people. Others don't find the fact of Jesus as Lord to their taste - they would like to put themselves in the place of God.

True faith is a sign of the maturity of each individual witness. Men believe all sorts of things. The media are not always inclined to tell the truth. Lies are represented as truth, and men believe them. People sometimes don't have a choice; they know of nothing else and just believe in what they are given.

Maturity in faith gives the ability to choose the content. John the Baptist could have kept quiet about some things. He had the opportunity to be inconsistent in carrying out God's will. He chose consistency. Inconsistent witnesses do not point to Christ. Blessing cannot be expected from them.

Aleksandar Birviš

When I talk about faith I mean saving faith. That is the only faith which is worth preaching. If faith is not saving faith, Christians need not take it seriously, how ever useful it may be.

Saving faith relies on Christ the Savior. There is no other support. Many changes take place in the man who relies upon Christ. They are inevitable. Many people today profess to be believers. Some openly state that they have suddenly realized that they have been wandering and they are coming back to their roots. But they are just coming back to further wanderings: they believe that they have become something different just because they have begun again to observe some customs or, even worse, they now observe those customs openly, whereas up to 1989 they did it in secret.

Somewhere around 1960 I heard of a man who had no contact with the army except from doing his military service. He used to come to his office every year on the 19th December smartly dressed. He would tell his colleagues that when he finished work he was going to a celebration lunch at his father's house and in the afternoon some sort of small reception. When the asked him: "What are you celebrating?" he would reply, "My father is celebrating Army Day in advance because he is busy on the 22nd of December." His superiors would let him go early and the political leaders were kindly disposed towards him. But in actual fact he was celebrating St Nicholas' day.

The man made every effort to hang on to that custom. In doing that he was prepared to lie and deceive, thinking that he was preserving his faith. Today (1992) he thinks he has earned faith. That is why he rejects the Word of salvation. He cannot grasp the need for personal repentance, because he sees himself as a defender of truth, justice and spirituality. Others look up to him and he doesn't see he has any need to change. The testimony of such a man does not lead to Christ because his actions have nothing to do with the Lord Jesus.

Reflections

Our testimony will bring saving faith to others only when that faith is focused on the Savior. That is why we need witnesses who are totally committed to Christ. Christian witnessing is a struggle, and in a struggle there is no place for retreat, even less for treachery.

At that time God sent John the Baptist. John came to witness to the Light, so that all might believe through him. John was not Christ, but he witnessed about Christ.

Today God sends you. You are a Christian because God wants you to witness about Christ, so that men may believe through you. You are not Christ, you are His witness. Accept the calling and continue in it and you will be a blessing.

Belgrade, 29th December 1992

CHRIST — GOD INCARNATE

Let us read some verses from the beginning of John's Gospel (1:9-14):

That was the true Light, which lighteth every man that cometh into the world.

He was in the world, and the world was made by Him, and the world knew Him not.

He came unto His own, and His own received Him not.

But as many as received Him, to them gave He power to become the sons of God, even to them that believe on His name:

Which were born, not of blood, nor of the will of the flesh, nor of the will of man, but of God.

And the Word was made flesh, and dwelt among us, (and we beheld His glory, the glory as of the only begotten of the Father,) full of grace and truth.

God decided to become man. He carried through the decision that He had made. No one could prevent Him.

God took on a human body. Christ's body was not a prison into which the Spirit of God entered. In our Savior the family of man attained its true appearance and true value. He was and remained sinless (this experience is still unattainable for men). The Lord fulfills His intention of sinlessness.

How does the Lord accomplish it? Today He does not create some new paradise or return man to the paradise where Adam and

Reflections

Eve dwelt. Instead of doing that God sent His Son, and our Lord and Savior, Jesus Christ.

By coming down among men, the almighty Christ gave up His heavenly throne, that is, His honor and dignity. This was His by rights, being that He is God, but He gave up His equality with God. In place of undisputed authority, the Savior accepted the role of serving men and taking on human form, that is, equality with men. His identification with man brought Him death. He accepted torture and execution without objection. He was born as a baby, He lived as a workman and a teacher and was crucified like a slave, but He is still the Son of God (see Phil. 2:5-8).

Through His birth Christ became God incarnate. The human race was deemed worthy for the God-man to live amongst them.

God incarnate is fully God and fully man at the same time. However much He set aside His honor and dignity, Christ did not cease to be God with all His divine characteristics, and the Lord Jesus did not lack anything of the Godhead. All God's qualities are Christ's too.

Christ was not lacking anything human either. He had all the qualities that other men have. He willingly submitted Himself to all the circumstances in which human life unfolds. Even though He was the most independent person, He was totally obedient and submissive. He fulfilled all righteousness, that is, all that God demands. In the Son of God, nothing of what graces men was lost, nor did anything that men are exposed to cease to apply to Him.

Were these two natures in conflict? When we talk of the Lord Jesus, they were not opposed to each other nor was there any disagreement between them. Christ our Savior is perfectly God and perfectly man. If He had been imperfect in anything He would not

Aleksandar Birviš

have been God — which would make our discussions about Christ irrelevant.

Were these two natures of Christ merged into one? No. That which is of God, is God's— and what is of man is man's. Christ was never confused or in a dilemma. His divine nature did not overstep His human nature, nor did His human nature ever overstep His divine nature.

Are the two natures of Christ interchangeable? No. A God who changes is not God. False gods, idols made by men, change and have to be changed. They are subject to decay, being made of the same material as nature. Nature is sinful, idols are sinful — and those who bow down to them sin and are sinful.

The same applies to the human nature of our Lord: it does not change. Individuals change but everyone remains unique as a personality. With Christ things are different. He is perfect. Perfection is not perfection if there is a possibility of it ceasing or being distorted. If perfection still needs to be perfected then it isn't perfection. If the Savior's human nature were in any way subject to change, He would not be Christ, since He would fall short of perfection.

Are Christ's two natures mixed together? No. The Lord needs no mixture. A mixture requires that first of all both natures should be broken into small pieces or dissolved, and then mixed together. This can be done to creation but not to the Creator. A mixture is not a mixture if each ingredient is not present in approximately equal measure. (To tell you the truth: this is a totally carnal way of thinking, unworthy of spiritual men).

Can Christ's two natures be separated? No. There is no power that could do that, and no reason to do it. It would be difficult to imagine the separation of Christ's two natures. Men may talk and think about the two natures of our Savior, but they can't define them,

Reflections

organize them and control them. The unity of the two natures in Christ is such that the Savior always talks about Himself in the first person: I and My. When others talk about the Lord Jesus, they also use the singular form. Christ's behavior shows that He has in essence a unity of personality, and remains so throughout eternity.

That is the sort of Savior that we need. All ages have yearned for Him, as does our age. God appeared and became a true man of flesh and blood. He remained as such but in a glorified body. We need to open up all our desires to Him, all our feelings and thoughts.

I have never been to Bethlehem. I have seen what you can find in the newspapers and on postcards. At the place where the Lord Jesus was born there is a Latin inscription which says in translation, "This is where the Word became flesh."

I cannot see your heart either. There are no postcards from which I could discover your desires, feelings and thoughts. But I do know one thing: the most beautiful thing that could be written on your heart is, "This is where the Lord Jesus Christ was born and reigns."

Belgrade, 12th January 1992

THE GLORY IS NEAR

Third Sunday after Epiphany
Subject: Revelations — the signs of glory

I believe in God's glory. I do not believe in the glory of man. All that is glorious amongst men decays, because human glory must pass away. If anything remains it does so by God's gift. Only those deeds that man does to please God, consciously or unconsciously, are lasting.

I am glad that He has given me an opportunity for us to consider His glory together. These are not my thoughts, nor are they yours. I will try and present what arises from God's Word, to be more precise, from Isaiah (60:1-7). We will look at each section in turn.

> *Arise, shine;*
> *For thy light is come,*
> *And the glory of the* LORD *is risen upon thee.*

It is time for the world to see Christ. How will they see Him? God has raised up a holy people. He has made this people a light to the other nations of the world. The glory of God must be displayed because the time for the light of the Gospel to break through has come with Christ.

Reflections

We must make an effort. God commands us to arise. Sleepy Christians and a sleeping Church will not experience the glory of God. Men drunk on passing pleasures will not notice significant events passing them by. They will miss the best opportunities. They will be caught by surprise, busy with less important things. Why? Because they have not raised their heads, they have not arisen.

The glory of God is over all men. It is also over the people of God. All men alike have the opportunity to enter the glory of God if they believe and if they are willing. The glory of the Almighty is not far from men but they are far from the glory of God.

> *For, behold, the darkness shall cover the earth,*
> *And gross darkness the people:*

What has come between God and men? Sin. From this same book (Is. 59:1-2) we learn that there is no distance too great that God would not span to save man. He shows understanding for man's troubles. The Lord will answer every prayer if it is sincere. But sins, lawless deeds, murders, malicious actions and other evils separate man from God. I come back to the truth I have already stated: God will not distance Himself from man even if man distances himself from God.

Praise God who is able and mighty to bring light into the deepest darkness. The world would be desperate, life would be horrible and man's existence on earth would be intolerable if it were not for the Lord's supreme enlightenment.

The glory of God pierces the darkness and despair. The Almighty reveals Himself. The light dispels the darkness. Sin is continual destruction and eternal ruin. God's glory ends all that because it comes from the Almighty.

> *But the LORD shall arise upon thee,*
> *And His glory shall be seen upon thee.*
> *And the Gentiles shall come to thy light,*
> *And kings to the brightness of thy rising.*

Christians are God's emissaries, emissaries of His glory. Wherever they appear, God's glory takes over. Glory becomes a force of attraction. Holiness, truth, and especially love, attract from afar.

That is why it is appalling if Christians do not show the glory of God but instead strut around displaying their own glory. It is even worse when the children of God do not belong to God, that is, they belong only in name, but have surrendered to the authority of Satan. No one is so effective in destroying the Kingdom of God as so-called Christians, or as the Bible terms them, false brethren. They spread darkness with terrible and destructive effect.

This prompts Christians to carefully open their spiritual eyes. Is the glory of God over men or are men over the glory of God? I count it a special blessing that the Holy Spirit has always kept me from those who set themselves up over the glory of the Almighty. I am not talking about worldly men. The process of separation has been painful, but there is no freedom without struggle, and no struggle without wounding. After all, I prefer people to wound me than for me to wound the glory of God by dabbling in dishonest things.

> *Lift up thine eyes round about, and see:*
> *All they gather themselves together, they come to thee:*
> *Thy sons shall come from far,*
> *And thy daughters shall be nursed at thy side.*

Reflections

What does a Christian look like as he stands before the Lord? As man looks at the holy and most righteous God, faith gives him the standards by which he can place himself in the correct position: in first place — God, in second place — my neighbor, in third place — myself.

The people of Christ gather in this order and unite. If the glory of God is over me, many will join me. The Lord himself brings them. The Son of God thought the same - He gave thanks to the Father for those whom the Father had given Him. He didn't boast that He had won those whom He had chosen, even though He was the incomparable ruler and soul-winner.

We don't know through whom the Lord will bring us souls. Sometimes inconspicuous and unsung members of the fellowship stand continually before God and pray for one or two souls, and the Almighty gives them whole families. While others, those who are intelligent and specially equipped, don't bring anyone, and their whole Christian life is spent in fear and disputes. Therefore when we give thanks we should include those unknown and unsung soul-winners.

> *Then thou shalt see, and flow together,*
> *And thine heart shall fear, and be enlarged;*

God's glory radiates. If it is over someone, that person will also radiate. That is also true of women and children, of whole families, tribes and nations. Glory is passed on like light: in the places that it reaches new sources of glory appear, and they begin to radiate and reach others who also become sources and so on, as long as there is darkness. And there will always be darkness.

Aleksandar Birviš

The existence of darkness should not discourage us. The children of God should not lose heart. It was to a world of darkness that Christ came. At that time the Roman authorities had succeeded in suspending the small amount of Greek democracy there still was, and the Pharisees and Sadducees had obfuscated authentic Mosaic and prophetic thought, while outside the Greek and Roman world all was steeped in witchcraft and superstition. It seemed there was no place for the light.

Nevertheless the light did come. The Glory of God dispersed the darkness. The presence of Christ and the activity of the Holy Spirit made the first disciples the bearers of the glory. Their joy could be seen clearly: our life is something different, we live for the Lord.

Soon many people began to live with this joy. In contrast to physical light which drives darkness away, spiritual light is not intrusive. The Savior reveals Himself and gives proof of His existence, but He does not force anyone to be saved. He does not use force. He wins over by love and encouraging other virtues.

In encountering Christ man must make up his mind whether to belong to Christ or to reject salvation. Christianity is the faith of free, decisive, serious-minded and enthusiastic men and women. There are no hidden pitfalls, secret teachings and underhand deals in it. Whoever comes to Christ, knows who he is coming to, why he comes, and what to expect. The man who rejects Christ also knows who he has rejected, what he has forfeited and what awaits him today and in eternity.

> *Because the abundance of the sea shall be converted unto thee,*
> *The forces of the Gentiles shall come unto thee.*
> *The multitude of camels shall cover thee,*
> *The dromedaries of Midian and Ephah;*

Reflections

All they from Sheba shall come:
They shall bring gold and incense;
And they shall shew forth the praises of the LORD.
All the flocks of Kedar shall be gathered together unto thee,
The rams of Nebaioth shall minister unto thee:
They shall come up with acceptance on Mine altar,
And I will glorify the house of My glory.

The Church is a fellowship of poor people. But the Church is not poor. All the best things belong to Christ, including the best of the poor, the best outcasts and the best exiles. Wherever they go, Christians come to Christ.

The nations have raised a commotion. The rich of this world are in turmoil. Financial power is changing hands. Intellectual ability is overflowing. If we watch with due spiritual attention, we will see that behind these phenomena is stratification: away from Christ and towards Christ. All Christ's adherents who are close to Him will gather around Him.

The assembly of the saints brings all its treasure to the Lord Jesus. Along with their wealth, Christians offer up their prayers. Gold and incense go together. Both of them joyfully announce God's glory. The presentation of gifts and prayers are linked: those who are generous pray better and those who pray give more.

I make so bold as to point out the presence of those who declare the glory of God. They have not separated themselves from men. In spite of the disintegration we have mentioned, the children of God do not avoid their fellow citizens, nor their false brethren and those who once were their brethren. The saved shun sin, but they don't forget that we must love sinners. That love is planted in them by the Heavenly Father. The Church is in the world, and in serving men it

Aleksandar Birviš

serves God, and serving God it serves men — but nevertheless the Church of Christ is not the world or part of the world.

God's glory appears in His holy ones. Every gathering of believers is a temple not made by human hands. That which is focused around the glory of God is the noblest offering and most pleasant adornment. Maybe some of the offerings and adornments don't seem to suit the holiness of the altar and the splendor of the temple at first sight. The Almighty promises that they will contribute to His glory as is befitting. He changes people. He changed those who joined with Him. He will change others who attach themselves to Him.

The Lord God has shown us His glory. It is available for all who believe. Who will accept it? How are we to accept the glory of the Lord? What does a man gain by accepting it?

These and other questions arise spontaneously. The answers may be long and tortuous. They won't be exact and will not satisfy. How are we to arrive at the correct answers?

Let us turn to the Lord Jesus. All answers can be found in Him. He didn't wait for our questions. Before raising His friend Lazarus from the dead our Savior said, *Said I not unto thee, that, if thou wouldest believe, thou shouldest see the glory of God?* (John 11:40)

Believe in Christ and in His almighty power to save. There is no other way.

Belgrade, 9th February 1992

A TEMPLE NOT MADE WITH HANDS

Is the temple holy because it contains the Holy Place or is the Holy Place holy because it is in the temple? There can be all sorts of things in a temple and it can be made of anything you like. That does not make it holy, nor is everything in the temple holy. The temple is holy because of the Holy Place in it and because of the Holy God who dwells in the temple. The temple does not make the Holy Place, but the Holy Place sanctifies the temple.

Holiness doesn't relate just to the Holy Place. Besides the holy places there are certain times, people and rituals that can be holy.

All that comes from God has the mark of holiness. All that is set apart to God should be holy. The standards of holiness were set by the Lord. He gives holiness. All that falls short of God's standards is not holy. Church services are an important factor in holiness, but they are not the only one, nor the most important one.

The dwelling place of a holy God

The temple is a holy place because the Lord in His goodwill towards the human race has ordained that He should dwell there. That is the place where men appear before God at specific times and those are holy times. Holy times are the times when Christians are in their churches, but they are also times when men think about God

Aleksandar Birviš

outside of the temple, when believers read the Scriptures and when they pray to their Lord.

Men participate in prayer and other activities. Those other activities are communion, baptism, confessions of sins, weddings, various dedications, special services, repentance and conversion, sanctification, justification, entrance into glory and numerous others. As they perform them, the people of God receive holiness from God. All these activities and functions also have God-given holiness.

In this way the role of the temple expands. That which is in accordance with God's will is holy. That which is holy belongs to the Lord; He adapts it to Himself and continually perfects it according to His own standards.

In the epistle to the Romans (15:15-16) we read: *Nevertheless, brethren, I have written the more boldly unto you in some sort, as putting you in mind, because of the grace that is given to me of God, That I should be the minister of Jesus Christ to the Gentiles, ministering the gospel of God, that the offering up of the Gentiles might be acceptable, being sanctified by the Holy Ghost.* It is not difficult to follow the apostle's thinking. The Word of God admonishes freely and quite straightforwardly. A whole set of attitudes must be adopted. A Christian accepts them and consciously engages in the struggle for what is better, and against that which separates him from Christ or what reduces him to spiritual mediocrity.

What is it that gives God's servants the right to remind Christians of their duty to strive for holiness and commitment? Maybe it sounds inconceivable or disjointed but that is what the Bible says: the privileges of apostles arise from their ministry, they are serving a holy cause and that makes them holy.

Reflections

The temple of a new people

To serve Christ, to strive to pass on and show forth the Gospel is a work of two-way communication. In both cases that communication is with God and our neighbors. One of those channels of communication could be depicted like this: God sends the Good News; the messenger receives it; the messenger passes on the Good News to all the other recipients. The other channel doesn't look so natural, but it nevertheless exists: God reveals Himself directly to men; the Holy Spirit enlightens the recipients; they seek the messenger; the messenger advises men of what they should accept.

Under the influence of the Good News, those who have received it change. They become an offering accepted by the Lord. That is how people outside the fellowship of believers come into the family of God's children and share in building the temple not made of human hands.

Men are called and sanctified by the Holy Spirit. If Christian witness is inspired by human desires it will not win souls. But if it is inspired by the Holy Spirit, it will bear fruit. New Christians rush in.

Is the temple a place of mysterious phenomena? In scriptural terms, no. Of course miracles will happen in the temple. But holy places are not theatres. They are stages but they are not theatres. Real events take place on that stage, the smashing of illusions and a common sharing in the transformation of individuals and whole societies.

A Spiritual House

A temple is also a building site. Every person present is having something built into him. Many of those who are not present are

Aleksandar Birviš

also experiencing something for the first time. God is planting something into men for whom the fellowship has been praying. The spiritual building has its building works, its building regulations and maintenance, its models and — its dangers.

The apostle Peter (1 Pet. 2:5) urges Christians to be built like living stones into a spiritual temple. That temple is of course a house, that is, a holy place for the nurturing of spiritual life. The Apostle preserves other aspects of the temple not built by human hands. The priesthood is one, not as a class of people, but as a holy nation. Each individual is committed to God's service. At the same time their service is to bring a sacrifice. Whatever they do, Christians do it as a service to God, functioning as priests.

The priests of the Lord Jesus Christ are a temple. They reveal to the world the nature of the true holy place. God is pleased with their service and He rejoices that He has such sons and daughters.

Such a concept of the temple focuses the minds of Christians. The man-made temple was the center of spiritual and national life. The temple not made by human hands has the effect of making Christians more composed and stable people. The Savior has accomplished a great victory so that every brother and every sister know who and what they are. They do not need anyone to tell them who they are. God has revealed to them the makeup of their personalities and all their good points and bad.

The temple not made by human hands is unambiguous in defining what is not Christian. A Christian man or woman knows what he or she is not and must never be. The holiness of the temple demands honesty. The conscience is the guardian of honesty. What does the conscience prevent? What does it oppose? It stops the child of God from becoming what it should not become.

Reflections

The living temple comprises a single whole. Christians fit into it through what they are: faith, hope, love and other virtues, through their confession, their deeds and achievements. They fit into this temple not made by human hands through what they have rejected too. Like stone, the Christian is shaped in such a way that pride, unbelief, hopelessness, evils of the flesh and the baggage of fleshy unspirituality are cut away.

A very important task in the spiritual house is the introduction of righteousness into everyday life. Holiness is not set apart or fenced round; it just tries not to get polluted. It comes among men, influences the social awareness of this world and this age, as well as conduct of people who believe. In countries where the Gospel is more prominent, the economy is stronger, the legal system more consistent and the defense of the weak, underprivileged and the socially marginalized more fully developed. On top of that those countries have more freedom and more readiness to serve all those who do not threaten it.

The temple and its court

I am not talking about the decaying temple. We are talking about the place where God dwells.

The courtyard of the temple not made by human hands is inhabited by the God who performs miracles. He instructs, corrects and heals. He gives fatherly advice. Everyone comes into the courtyard just as he is and each one brings joy to the Heavenly Father simply by being there. In the courtyard the prodigal sons meet with the Father. They have been wandering for a long while, they have suffered much, they have lost everything, but they have come to their senses and gone back to the one who came out to meet them.

Aleksandar Birviš

In the courtyard is the older brother. Each one of us can become like the son who reproached his father for rejoicing at the return of his long-lost son. In every man there is some sort of feeling of contempt and revulsion towards repentance and the repentant sinner. The courtyard is at the same time both attractive and repulsive — both in the individual as well as in the fellowship. At the level of the courtyard the carnal has not yet been separated from the soulish and the spiritual, nor the soulish from the carnal and the spiritual, or the spiritual from the carnal and the soulish.

After the courtyard of the temple in Jerusalem you went into the Holy Place. Only priests were allowed to enter it. The temple not made with human hands also has its Holy Place. It can be entered by priests or rather Christians who have been built into the holy priesthood. At that level what is carnal can be discerned. Carnality is separated from the soulish. Carnality is separated from the spiritual. The difference between the soulish and the spiritual is not clear, but service to God is more open and sincere.

The level of the Holy Place is the place where the altars are located. The whole prayer life is brought as a sacrifice. It is similar to the incense altar in the man-made temple. Holiness is first distinguished by separation. What does that consist of? It consists of separation from worldliness and a deeper prayer life. In the Holy Place the cross of Christ is intertwined with the cross of each individual Christian.

In the Holy Place, Christians accept Christ's sacrifice. It redeems them and sets them free, teaches them forgiveness and heals them, makes them better and equips them, brings them into a closer bond with the Lord Jesus and separates them more fully from sin. Every drop of Christ's blood, from the hour of His suffering on Calvary right up to today, cleanses, corrects, renews and protects. That is why the Holy Place is a precious place and a higher level of blessing.

Reflections

At the level of the Holy Place the personal sacrifice comes to the fore. A Christian submits himself to Jesus with all-embracing love: with all his heart and all his soul and all his mind and all his strength (Mark 12:30). As this sacrifice is made, many personal attributes and achievements will fall away. At the time when the man-made temple still existed, all the refuse was burnt outside the settlement. In the temple not made by human hands the Lord takes it on Himself and tosses it into oblivion. He promises, *I have blotted out, as a thick cloud, thy transgressions, and, as a cloud, thy sins: return unto Me; for I have redeemed thee* (Is. 44:22).

The Holiest of Holies

I must not leave out the Holy of Holies. In the temple in Jerusalem the High Priest went into it only once a year, on the Day of Atonement. It should be similar, but without any restriction (at least, that is how it should be) with the people of God and each individual. At the level of the Holy of Holies, life in the Spirit is accomplished. Christ's love opens up for those Christian men and women who are prepared, who are sufficiently humble, who are transformed into ash and enlightened by the wounds of Christ.

As the Savior was dying on the cross, the curtain of the temple was torn in two. The temple not made by human hands was open. That which was unapproachable became accessible thanks to Christ's intercession. By His sacrifice He opened the temple, and by asking the Father made the Holy Spirit available to His disciples and followers who were to come after. By perseverance, self-denial, love towards God and love towards his neighbor each Christian man and woman can enter the Holy of Holies not made by human hands.

Aleksandar Birviš

What is there to do in the Holy of Holies? To bring a burnt offering. To allow the Holy Spirit to completely take over oneself, so that nothing remains of man's intellect and will and feelings, but for God's mind and God's will and God's love to live and move and have its being in all things.

One thing remains — never to leave the Holy of Holies not made by human hands, but to remain in it for ever and to always worship the one, living and life-giving God: Father and Son and Holy Spirit. Amen.

Belgrade, 16th February 1992

THE RICH FOOL

Indifference towards the time that we live in

And He spake a parable unto them, saying, The ground of a certain rich man brought forth plentifully: And he thought within himself, saying, What shall I do, because I have no room where to bestow my fruits? And he said, This will I do: I will pull down my barns, and build greater; and there will I bestow all my fruits and my goods. And I will say to my soul, Soul, thou hast much goods laid up for many years; take thine ease, eat, drink, and be merry. But God said unto him, Thou fool, this night thy soul shall be required of thee: then whose shall those things be, which thou hast provided? So is he that layeth up treasure for himself, and is not rich toward God (Luke 12:16-21)

What happens when a train is late? One day the station guard came on duty. He was informed that the train that should arrive at 11.10 was arriving at 11.05. He was surprised that the train was arriving five minutes early. They explained to him that the train was running 1,435 minutes late, i.e. that it should have arrived at 11.10 the day before.

We read about a man who got rich – richer than he already was. But he was running very late. God told him that he would die that same night. He thought he had made for provision for the future by amassing enough for the next fifty or maybe sixty or seventy years. In fact he had totally missed the boat. It is dangerous to be late.

Aleksandar Birviš

I am not going to speak against rich men (you can get that in other places from other speakers). Instead I want to talk about the dangers associated with being late, of putting things off, of indifference towards the time in which we all find ourselves in. I am afraid that we do not have a sufficiently well-developed sense of time.

Take, for example the subject of being late for church services. The Church is not a business, nor a school; we don't record absence and lateness. Men who are used to coercion see freedom in the Church and they are surprised that they need to be on time for the start of services. But when you look at time as a gift of God, as a precious thing which can't be stored away and used when you feel like it, to waste such a gift is a sin against God who gives the gift, and also a sin against our neighbors who have understood the value of time, and are disrupted by others in receiving those gifts of God.

It's a similar sin when we say more than we should in our prayers or we repeat what the brother or sister before us prayed. I don't want to shorten our prayer meetings but I am all for shorter and more succinct prayers. It is not good to take time from those who would prayer better prayers but can't get in. It is impolite to repeat to God something that He undoubtedly knows — and our neighbors know as well. You don't need me to tell you that it is possible to be dishonest in this way by stealing time from others.

The most important time is when we meet with God. If we miss that moment, eternity will be lost. No one will lose their eternal existence but they will spend it where the worm does not die, and the fire is not quenched (Mark 9:44).

Reflections

"This night" but not unexpectedly

In 2 Corinthians we read, *I have heard thee in a time accepted, and in the day of salvation have I succoured thee: behold, now is the accepted time; behold, now is the day of salvation* (2 Cor. 6:2). Although we are struggling to reach eternity, we must be focused both on the present and on the time that is coming. The Lord was very wise in not telling us the day or the hour when He will come. Otherwise our indifference would show itself to its full extent. As it is we are more careful and we use the present hour wisely.

Let us think, work, and study as if everything will last for a very long while. But our moral and spiritual state must be such that, if the Lord comes now, we can say, "Here we are, Lord."

When men live through times of adversity they begin to think of the end of the world. Men lose their wealth and think, "If I am ruined, the village will be ruined — if the village is ruined the whole world is ruined."

At the time of the end of the First World War, many men's plans were wrecked and many values both material and spiritual were shattered. Two friends meet in New York and one says to the other:

"The prophecies are being fulfilled. Do you know that the Lord will come soon?"

"I know," replied the other, "but even He knows that I live on 17th Avenue."

The Lord can come when He likes. It will not catch me by surprise. But I want to be ready for it in a worthy manner, since it can be at any time, and my heart must be ready, all my relationships right. Let Him come right now and let us rejoice that He is coming.

If this state of affairs does not exist, all our so-called preparations are upside-down, because we are not prepared where it is most

Aleksandar Birviš

important, we are not prepared in this time that we live in — that is now. Now is the accepted time, now is the day of salvation – do not delay, because this may be your last night.

Think "today"

And so we need to think about the following things:

First, our way of life. The large majority live just to survive. For many, the important thing is not what they will do nor how they will do it but how they can reach retirement. Conversely there are those who work all their lives and we just can't imagine how they have managed to achieve all that they have.

Look, for example at Spurgeon. Not much of his work has been translated into Serbian. And so we are more familiar with him from quotes and conversations than from his written works. He lived from 1834 to 1892. At that time London was one of the largest cities in the world. He had no car because there weren't any. He had no carriage. He had a horse, not a very special one, but a useful one. At one point he was forced to sell it in order to cover the costs of the orphanage that he had founded. He served a church in the middle of London and the thousands of people around it. Apart from that he led a preacher's school (it still exists today and functions as a training center for pastoral care and preaching). He also helped a number of fellowships, and cared for the underprivileged. On top of all that Spurgeon wrote books. Each year he published a book of sermons. He wrote the "Treasury of David", a work in several volumes in large format in which he interpreted all the Psalms, listed important quotations on every verse which had been written up to his time and gave outlines for sermons on every verse of the Psalms. He published

Reflections

his lectures and a long series of other works. How did he find the time to do all that?

Second, use of time. Amongst the parables that He told, the Savior told one about the barren fig-tree.

A certain man had a fig tree planted in his vineyard; and he came and sought fruit thereon, and found none. Then said he unto the dresser of his vineyard, Behold, these three years I come seeking fruit on this fig tree, and find none: cut it down; why cumbereth it the ground? And he answering said unto him, Lord, let it alone this year also, till I shall dig about it, and dung it: And if it bear fruit, well: and if not, then after that thou shalt cut it down (Luke 13:6-9).

God has been waiting for you until today. Maybe He will wait another year. What if this moment is your last opportunity? If you knew that this was your last year, how would you use it? Would you say, "He doesn't have to come today? Maybe tomorrow?"

How many people are there in this city who will not see tomorrow? They will simply die. How many individuals will say that tomorrow they will do this and that, only to be prevented by circumstances beyond their control? And they will have lost the opportunity to hear the news of the Lord Jesus.

In the Epistle to the Hebrews (2:3-4) the writer asks, *How shall we escape, if we neglect so great salvation; which at the first began to be spoken by the Lord, and was confirmed unto us by them that heard Him; God also bearing them witness, both with signs and wonders, and with divers miracles, and gifts of the Holy Ghost, according to His own will?* We are offered such a great and precious salvation and we run away from it. There is no running away.

Do we not incur God's wrath? By running away from salvation we insult God and reproach Him for not adapting Himself to suit the times we live in. Salvation doesn't come when we want it to or

Aleksandar Birviš

when it suits us. The Lord has set the accepted time. Our task is to grasp that time and not miss it.

Third, cooperation with the Lord. We often have a way of telling God what to do, of course, ever so politely. Let's get this into our heads once and for all: You can't tell God what to do. He is the one who gives the orders.

We can cooperate with God. We thank Him that He has made that possible. We are grateful to Him for allowing us to be called His fellow-workers and to actually act as such. He cooperates with those whom He needs to and in the things that are necessary. That is one of the great achievements. God loves man. Love does not like to be alone. It strives to have someone to love. God involves man in everything that we call development and growth.

It is our fault if we don't get involved in that growth. The Almighty gives us the most wonderful opportunities to share in that growth and development. Of course, we get involved by entering into salvation and being made right with God. The Lord justifies the sinner. He wants to blot out every unrighteous act of the sinner, every sin, and every lawless act, so that the sinner can be remembered before Him. God wants to say, "Look, here in the Book of Life is the name of My servant". But He also expects His servants to serve worthily, and to be the ones who are always prepared to welcome Him and to be with Him.

Fourth, the cautionary example. In Noah's day men were busy with their everyday tasks and long-term planning. They were born, they married, struggled and died in different ways. They passed their time in friendship and enmity with others, in work and recreation, in varying frames of mind.

The people saw Noah making the ark. He was building something exceptionally large to their way of thinking. This caused some of them to wonder, "What is it for? What a waste of time and effort!" Others mocked him, "What are you up to, Noah? You reckon there's going to be a flood. No chance. Heaven and earth have stood firm since the creation. There's no chance of downpours and floods!" There were probably those who came every day and watched their neighbor working and said to him, "What are you wasting your strength for? Relax, take it easy, and enjoy yourself. You've married off your sons, so you've got someone to help you and take over from you. Forget it, man!"

Noah carried on working. Conscientious work is a sermon in itself. Men discovered that the Lord intended to punish the human race for their sins. They needed to repent. They kept putting it off. They thought, "If this is really serious, we will wait until Noah is finished, to see whether his prophecy comes true, and then we can stop sinning and seek refuge."

But the ark was finished. Those who were appointed went in. The animals went in too. The deep waters rose. The floods came and the water rose up the mountains. It was too late. It was no good crying for help – Noah couldn't hear, and he couldn't open the ark.

They should have thought and obeyed. They should have grasped God's warnings. That was nothing new; they had heard it many times before. In Proverbs we read: *He, that being often reproved hardeneth his neck, shall suddenly be destroyed, and that without remedy* (Prov. 29:1).

We all need to consider this: God has allowed wars, hunger and all sorts of disasters. He wants to tell us something through them, and that is, "Start thinking you people! Stop being pig-headed and deceiving yourselves! Time is passing. The best days are coming to an end. Thank God that He is still waiting, but His time is now."

Aleksandar Birviš

Belonging to Christ — now

Blessed are those who do not hesitate. Blessed are those who throw off everything that prevents them coming close to the Lord. Blessed are those who instead of being ashamed before the Holy One have the courage to say, "Here I am, God. You are the only God, the only hope to whom I can turn, the only one whom I can lean on. You and only You."

The Lord is the only joy, the only one who will take me in His embrace, the only one with whom I can stay. He has been waiting right up to this day. As long as He waits, that is good. A day will come when He will no longer wait. The doors will shut whether the waiting room is full or not.

You don't need much wisdom to join your God and to take every step according to His will. He will lead you and you will be His now and for eternity.

Belgrade, 16th February 1992

IN THE SCHOOL OF BLESSING

Teaching and missionary aspects of blessing

Main reading:

The LORD shall command the blessing upon thee in thy storehouses, and in all that thou settest thine hand unto; and He shall bless thee in the land which the LORD thy God giveth thee. The LORD shall establish thee an holy people unto Himself, as He hath sworn unto thee, if thou shalt keep the commandments of the LORD thy God, and walk in His ways (Deut. 28:8-9).

God wants to show us that all these blessings have one purpose. They are very specific and relate to the fruitfulness of the land and the holiness of descendants. But they are focused on the following: the people of God must be a missionary people, and an apostolic people. They will shine before others. Where there is no light they will cause it to shine and will enable the light to be carried to where little is known of it.

There is a great need for the light to be carried forth. Men are often not aware that there is a conditional relationship between what God has given to us and what we must give to others. We cannot offer what we don't have; only what we have.

We differ significantly from the world by our calling. The writer is saying: "The Lord will command. You won't have to do it, it won't be possible on the basis of your possessions or your personal goodness or the things people make such a show of. This is something different: the Lord Himself will do it if you hold to His will."

Aleksandar Birviš

I must make a comment here. When He says commandments, that doesn't just mean the Ten Commandments (Decalogue). There are many places where we hear God giving commandments and asking people to keep those commandments. On the other hand there are the wider requirements of God's will which go further than the Commandments. For example, there is no commandment that says, "Do not envy!" but the New Testament teaches us in very many places not to envy. The same is true of many other things connected with the human heart. They are all expressions of God's will.

Thanks to these promises we have something to approach people with, if we have enough love to understand how the Lord directs us and to whom. We are sent as individuals, and as a fellowship. This is the great task of the people of God. We live with one conviction: all the blessings that we receive in life make up something that this world must be told about, and must see. God's great mercy must be proclaimed. It is becoming visible and must be made known to those around us. Imagine a doctor who knew the cure for a serious disease, and who had cured himself, but kept it a secret from others who needed the same treatment. We would regard him as a criminal.

The world must come to know Christ. Each person has to decide whether to accept the Savior or not, but it would be a crime not to tell people that the Savior is here and that He is the one who can reveal Himself. The Lord Jesus is a teacher (John 13:13). We come to Him as Savior and Lord, but we also come to Him as Teacher. He teaches us how to live a life of blessing. What use is the gift of life to a Christian if he has not been taught how to live? Life is full of distractions and people can lose sight of their goal and the blessings.

We don't think that it is always something to cry about. We don't have to keep complaining. Just specific people, things and ways of thinking irritate us. They irritate us not because they cause trouble,

Reflections

but because they prevent us from seeing what the real hindrance to blessings is.

God gives His promises on condition that we faithfully obey His will. The true hindrance to the blessing being fulfilled is disobedience. If I don't want to be a lamp and shine forth the light of Christ, I am a hindrance; I prefer to hang on to my darkness. It is an interesting fact how much people are in love with what they should reject and how difficult it is for them when they need to get rid of something. Such people keep wandering into mazes, and getting trapped in dead-end streets, instead of heading in the direction that God has given.

Christ instructs us how to have a life of blessing. Each step that we take is the step of a learner. We know that Christ's disciples didn't comprise only the twelve apostles. All the others who followed the Lord were disciples. The disciple of Christ spends all his life learning. A Christian learns how to receive blessings and how to pass them on to others. It is good for Christians to receive light and to become new sources of light.

There are people all around you. They need God's help. They need your help too. In what way can you help them? You can help them to know the light. It is dangerous to know the Scriptures and not to know what their purpose is, to desire blessings but not to know what they are for. There are people who would like blessings for themselves but God gives blessings in the expectation that we will live for those who need to hear about Christ. That is still to happen and it should happen. The Lord is equipping us for that.

Such a life is not without its pitfalls. The question is, how great an enthusiasm do we have for a life with Christ and for Christ? How much does the Holy Spirit lead us like a new light? Many people replace the true light with an artificial light. In place of joy they make

Aleksandar Birviš

do with elation, in place of songs of joy they have loud voices that they can shout with. That isn't the same.

A new question: how much is Christ truly reflected in us, in our hearts, in our innermost being? How much can our salvation be seen? How much love is there for our neighbors, towards those who are around us, towards those who are with us and those who are against us? In every house there are those who hate us. With some people, that hatred is the result of difficult and unsuitable living conditions, but some people hate simply because hate lives in unregenerate men.

Let us learn to have the right attitudes, the Christian approach to things.

When God promises He will give us blessings, He looks for obedience from us. Obedience in what? In everything - in our work, in our struggle for our neighbors and those further off. We are here as the bearers of news as well as of reconciliation and of righteous deeds, for we carry the love of God. God will help us, He will equip us. He, in fact, has every power and all glory belongs to Him.

Final reading:

> *God is the* LORD,
> *Which hath shewed us light:*
> *Bind the sacrifice with cords,*
> *Even unto the horns of the altar.*
> *Thou art my God, and I will praise Thee:*
> *Thou art my God, I will exalt Thee.*
> *O give thanks unto the* LORD; *for He is good:*
> *For His mercy endureth for ever* (Ps. 118:27-29)

Belgrade, 23rd February 1992

ABOUT FOREGIVENESS

The art of small steps

Then came Peter to Him (Jesus), and said,

Lord, how oft shall my brother sin against me, and I forgive him? till seven times?

Jesus saith unto him,

I say not unto thee, Until seven times: but, Until seventy times seven. Therefore is the kingdom of heaven likened unto a certain king, which would take account of his servants. And when he had begun to reckon, one was brought unto him, which owed him ten thousand talents. But forasmuch as he had not to pay, his lord commanded him to be sold, and his wife, and children, and all that he had, and payment to be made. The servant therefore fell down, and worshipped him, saying, Lord, have patience with me, and I will pay thee all. Then the lord of that servant was moved with compassion, and loosed him, and forgave him the debt. But the same servant went out, and found one of his fellowservants, which owed him an hundred pence: and he laid hands on him, and took him by the throat, saying, Pay me that thou owest. And his fellowservant fell down at his feet, and besought him, saying, Have patience with me, and I will pay thee all. And he would not: but went and cast him into prison, till he should pay the debt. So when his fellowservants saw what was done, they were very sorry, and came and told unto their lord all that was done. Then his lord, after that he had called him, said unto him, O thou wicked servant, I forgave thee all that debt, because thou desiredst me:

Shouldest not thou also have had compassion on thy fellowservant, even as I had pity on thee? And his lord was wroth, and delivered him to the tormentors, till he should pay all that was due unto him. So likewise shall My heavenly Father do also unto you, if ye from your hearts forgive not every one his brother their trespasses (Matt. 18:21-35).

Forgiveness, the ability to show mercy, is a blessing that can easily be passed on. If we forgive others small things because God has forgiven us the biggest things that can ever be forgiven, then we will demonstrate how we fulfill our duty as new creations. We will demonstrate something else too: that we are capable of living like those whose sin has been forgiven.

This is the art of small steps.

It seems to me that we suffer from a major problem. But there are small steps we can always take. We get enticed into attempting big things by the very fact that they are unattainable and we overlook what we can achieve. Begin by forgiving someone for some everyday deed, begin with a small step. Later on it won't be difficult to progress to something bigger.

I heard someone say that Tolstoy has a story about two women who came to an old man to make confession. One of them said that she had committed a great sin, whereas the other said she didn't know if she had done much sin at all. He sent them to a stream: the first woman was to bring two large rocks from the bank and the other to bring a sack of small stones. When they had brought the stones, he told the women to put the stones back where they had taken them from. The woman had no problem in putting the two big rocks back where they came from. Two depressions were clearly visible in the ground. But what was to be done with the small stones? How could the woman put every one back in its place?

There are many people today who don't take care of the small things. By overlooking the small details large errors are made. We read in the Psalms (112:5): *A good man sheweth favour, and lendeth: he will guide his affairs with discretion.* Blessed is he who is able to do the small things. Not because small things are important, but because by doing them we can prepare ourselves for doing something bigger, and for something really significant.

Our ability to forgive should be growing. This is how we become big-hearted. This is how we make progress. As a rule Satan offers us what we don't have. Boastful people are similar: they say they have things they don't have, and make out they are different from what they really are (for example, men who buy books by the yard).

That's a false image. The true image is something else. We read in 2 Corinthians 9:8: *And God is able to make all grace abound toward you; that ye, always having all sufficiency in all things, may abound to every good work.* We don't need to have an abundance of property or all sorts of worthwhile and beautiful things, but to abound in good works. This includes generous forgiveness.

Big-heartedness can have an effect on others too. Then it is a blessing for them too.

In our local press (Ilustrovana Politika) there was a story not long ago about a man who lent money to his whole village. People kept borrowing and not paying back. Whenever they met him in the street they would be embarrassed. They avoided talking to him, disappeared indoors when he went down the street, and moved away from their windows when he was standing beside their house or nearby. When he was waiting for the bus, people would disappear and delay their journeys. No one would sit at his table in the bar.

The man had had enough of this so he put a notice up on the public notice board to the effect that he was canceling all the debts.

Aleksandar Birviš

Everybody suddenly changed. They all became friends again. People began to be helpful again. No one was ashamed to greet him and ask after his health. The man no longer felt like he had the plague.

That's what generosity did. Forgiveness restores life to its smooth course.

Generosity of action and of heart is able to bring people true blessing and to teach them a high standard of Christian faith.

The Savior says in the Sermon on the Mount: *Ye have heard that it hath been said, Thou shalt love thy neighbour, and hate thine enemy. But I say unto you, Love your enemies, bless them that curse you, do good to them that hate you, and pray for them which despitefully use you, and persecute you* (Matt. 5:43-44). Why? *That ye may be the children of your Father which is in heaven: for He maketh His sun to rise on the evil and on the good, and sendeth rain on the just and on the unjust* (Matt. 5:45). We are somehow selective: we do good to the good, and bad to the bad; better to the better, worse to the worse. We are afraid that we will lose out. We should rely on God's promises. He will enable us to forgive and not to fear loss.

God's promises are true grace, like rain in season. We can rely on them without fear, as that is the basis of our faith: total reliance on the Lord. At the end of his teaching about the resurrection, the apostle Paul instructs us, *Therefore, my beloved brethren, be ye stedfast, unmoveable, always abounding in the work of the Lord, forasmuch as ye know that your labour is not in vain in the Lord* (1 Cor. 15:58).

Faith can be achieved and that is done by reliance on God's promises. Be steadfast. Why? Because God knows our needs. He will sustain us. We need never fear that the Lord will forget us and that the Almighty will not carry out His word. His promises are steadfast and unchanging.

Reflections

Let us take one of the Savior's promises as an example, *Verily, verily, I say unto you, he that believeth on Me, the works that I do shall he do also; and greater works than these shall he do; because I go unto My Father* (John 14:12). Here is one work that is greater than any that Jesus did: the Lord never preached to such great masses of men, women and children. Today it is possible to transmit a sermon via satellite link right across the world. Christ becomes accessible to parts of the world that have never heard of Him and that have never wanted to hear.

No one is preventing us from trusting in God, who is equipping us for great works. Step by step, maybe hardly noticeably, Christians are ever closer to works of glory because they themselves are drawing near to the glory of God.

This does not mean that everything will run smoothly. Someone will not be able to forgive, just as others are unable to repent. There is also a need for new teaching and new experiences. Dositej Obradovic[12] in the preface to his autobiography (*Life and Events*) says, "My eyes shed sweet tears of recognition and gratitude whenever I think on the great mercy of heavenly Providence. How often has she come to my aid in misfortunes, how much suffering and trouble has she delivered me from, and how often has she turned my plans and intentions, which would have been harmful and fatal to me in my folly and stupidity, to good and has, like a loving mother, led me by the hand and brought me to a good conclusion!"

All men will not be good nor will all of them be equal to the task God has set them. There will be those who are not up to the misfortunes and troubles. But that should not discourage you. Nothing must be allowed to divert you from the path on which you will be a blessing to others. If you learn to forgive, the Lord will help you not to give up in the face of obstacles.

Aleksandar Birviš

We must remember that Paul in fellowship with others often talked about something that Christ frequently referred to: suffering for the sake of the Lord Jesus. If you want to be a blessing to someone, you must reckon with Satan, the evil one, who opposes every blessing. He hates Christ and is seeking to spread hatred and damnation. The Good News is an obstacle to him; he hinders it, stifles it, and releases frightening news amongst men. Today there is more and more of such terror, not only terror of what is happening, but of the news about what is happening or is likely to happen. Fear of the unknown is on the increase.

All psychiatrists will tell you that the conditions in which we live, the fear and uncertainty that surround us, are the causes of much mental illness. People suffer less from what is happening and more from the world which has become unbearable. Satan's main strategy has been to make the world as attractive as possible in order to win over as many as possible to his side. In this the main role has been played by enjoyment and entertainment. But there are now so many means of enjoyment and entertainment that a man cannot find the time for proper recreation. He is becoming more and more dependent on the television, around which the whole household gather, so that Satan no longer can destroy the family as aggressively as he used to.

Today the evil one snatches his victims in another way. He piles on the fear of the unknown. Everyone asks himself what tomorrow will bring. Man is neglecting eternity. He has become feeble and is just trying to live one day at a time, a week at a time, a month, a quarter, a year. If things go well for him he lives in fear from one tax assessment to the next. And that puts him back amongst the fearful.

Christians are free from both of these attempts to enslave them that Satan uses. Not because they have found some middle road as

Reflections

children of God, but because they have found Christ's road. That is a totally different way. Faith goes on into glory. The faithful followers of Christ are full of that glory. Others may share this glory if they will just have faith.

Small acts of forgiveness, small steps, just a small readiness — all this builds great faith and leads to the greatest treasure: the glory of God. That is our way to eternal life, as we come before the face of the living God.

Belgrade, 26th February 1992

CHRIST THE HEALER

The eighth Sunday before Easter

Introductory reading: Ps. 69:29-33
Main reading: Luke 14:1-6

Let us make our prayers today prayers for health. Let us remember that the Lord Jesus is the friend of the sick and the Healer. Right up to this day His disciples and followers believe in God's power to heal. That is an integral part of our spiritual life.

And it came to pass, as He went into the house of one of the chief Pharisees to eat bread on the sabbath day, that they watched Him.

The Savior exposes Himself to the public gaze. There were times when He would withdraw into solitude, but we see Him most often amongst people. He meets other people and He never avoided meeting people. It was no problem for Christ to enter anyone's house. And He was certainly not afraid of people watching Him.

The Christian life needs a public. We won't go into the reasons why people watch Christians. Let us show how much we are committed to Christ.

And, behold, there was a certain man before Him which had the dropsy.

The Savior encounters a sick man. The two men come face to face: The God-man and an ordinary man. The Almighty Name stands before a nameless individual. The Lord gives, and the sick man receives. It is not important what the Son of God said or what

Reflections

the sick man said — that is not recorded. What we do have recorded is the fact that a man stood before Christ, and what is important is that God loves man.

The Savior encounters sickness. Health and sickness seem like two separate worlds. But no one is so healthy that not even a little seed of some illness is not at work in him, nor is anyone so sick that there is not a grain of health in him. We all need health. Christ knows precisely the man's illness. He cures it in the most effective way.

And Jesus answering spake unto the lawyers and Pharisees, saying, Is it lawful to heal on the sabbath day? And they held their peace.

The Savior talks to the representatives of the Old Testament Law. All the onlookers know that healing is a difficult and complicated task. They all know the fourth commandment that says:

Remember the sabbath day, to keep it holy. Six days shalt thou labour, and do all thy work: But the seventh day is the sabbath of the Lord *thy God: in it thou shalt not do any work, thou, nor thy son, nor thy daughter, thy manservant, nor thy maidservant, nor thy cattle, nor thy stranger that is within thy gates: For in six days the* Lord *made heaven and earth, the sea, and all that in them is, and rested the seventh day: wherefore the* Lord *blessed the sabbath day, and hallowed it* (Ex. 20:8-11).

What were they missing here? Firstly, that the Lord Jesus is the Son of God. No one and nothing can set itself up in authority over Christ. Secondly, that the new covenant between God and man is not sealed by commandments (at Sinai), but by Christ's sacrifice (at Calvary). The sign of the covenant is no longer the Sabbath but baptism. Thirdly, that it is important to the Savior that the man is delivered immediately.

The teachers of the law and the Pharisees could not answer Jesus. We shouldn't expect anything different in the future - may all God's enemies be silenced.

Aleksandar Birviš

And He took him, and healed him, and let him go;

A simple action. The Savior saves. Not many words, no ceremony, no big scene.

The Lord does not set many conditions. He is deeply and intimately involved with every man. Healing is the natural outcome of a supernatural cause: the presence of almighty God. He came to do good and He did only good. One of those good things is health.

And answered them, saying, Which of you shall have an ass or an ox fallen into a pit, and will not straightway pull him out on the sabbath day?

Those present learnt something that they didn't know. The New Testament is something different. Certain relationships are changed: God is amongst men, and men can approach Him without a go-between. Christ demands salvation. Nothing must be omitted, nothing glossed over, for people are more important than animals, even the most useful domestic pets.

Salvation is an urgent task. Any hesitation, doubt or procrastination will lead to destruction.

And they could not answer Him again to these things.

Let us repeat: may God shut the mouths of all his enemies.

★   ★   ★

All Christians have the right to expect healing. The Sinai era is past.

Let us approach the new mountain, as it is written, *For ye are not come unto the mount that might be touched, and that burned with fire, nor unto blackness, and darkness, and tempest, And the sound of a trumpet, and the voice of words; which voice they that heard intreated that the word should not be spoken to them any more: But ye are come unto Mount Sion, and unto the city of the living God, the heavenly Jerusalem, and to an innumerable company of angels, To the general assembly and church of the firstborn, which are written in heaven, and to God the Judge of all, and to the spirits of just men made perfect, And to Jesus the Mediator of the new covenant, and to the blood of sprinkling, that speaketh better things than that of Abel* (Heb. 12:18-19, 22-24).

Don't be in two minds, come to Him. Jesus Christ is the same yesterday, today, and forever. (Heb. 13:8).

Belgrade, 1st March 1992

WITNESSING

Our part in God's work

The main general task of Christians is to witness. What does that mean? It means to make known the truth about the living God. But there is something here that could lead us astray. We are trying to explain something that we can't explain to ourselves, define, or put into words or thoughts. We cannot explain to men who God is.

God is God. That is all that we can really say, without violating His glory or any other of His characteristics. We cannot reduce God to our own human concepts, nor can we contain Him within our definitions.

Witnessing about God and man

There is something else we need to explain to people. It's important for our testimony that people learn who man is. That's the first thing. Thanks to man, creation has been subjected to futility and decay. The Apostle Paul describes the sadness of creation because of the existence of sin, and because of the consequences of man's sin. The bondage of corruption is a fact both for those who believe and for those who do not (Rom. 8:19-25).

There are many forms of evil in nature. They all entered into it when man sinned. But man was and remains the main object of

Reflections

God's love. Creation enjoys that love because of man. When man is delivered from sin, creation will be set free from its bondage and the danger in which it obviously is today more than ever before.

The creation of man himself shows God's love. God said as He was creating man, *Let us make man in Our image, after Our likeness: and let them have dominion over the fish of the sea, and over the fowl of the air, and over the cattle, and over all the earth, and over every creeping thing that creepeth upon the earth* (Gen. 1:26).

Man was made intentionally, not by chance. God had clear intentions. The Lord gave a purpose and a task in life to every son and daughter of man. The purpose is to praise God; and the task is to help others to praise God. Let us not run away from what the Almighty intends for each one of us. Behind each human life stands God's purpose.

The other thing that we need to witness to is the fact that man is made in God's image. Man is similar to God in his makeup. Man is made of three parts: he has a body, a soul and a spirit. They are inseparable. If one of the three is missing, man ceases to be man.

This triune nature is a great advantage of man's. He is different; he stands out from all other created beings. This advantage is especially important in communicating with God. Only man can engage in two-way communication with the Lord — men are the only creatures that are able to pray (or to curse and swear) that is, to talk to the Almighty.

His Godlikeness obliges man to define his relationship towards God. Only man can ask himself, "Do I belong to God or not?" Only He knows the answer to that question. (Of course, the Creator knows the answer too, but the Creator is not the creation). The moment man ceases to belong to his God, the human spirit loses its strength, and becomes paralyzed. To put it another way, *The Spirit itself beareth witness with our spirit, that we are the children of God:* (Rom. 8:16). If that testimony ceases, our main bond with the living God and even with life itself ceases.

God has enabled triune man to be totally conscious of himself. The son of man knows who and what he is, who and what he is not, and he grasps what his being should comprise and what it should not comprise and should not be. Man lives with that completeness: the more he discovers it and realizes it the more complete and mature he is.

We need to tell people that they are God's creation (no matter how evil they are). If we tell them that, we open the doors for the blessings intended for every man, for God loves every man. If we don't have the words or we are unable to speak, it is enough that those around see that God's image and likeness is being created in us.

It ought to be the case that everyone who takes a step towards a Christian takes as many steps away from sin. And so, let us make every effort to have the image of God created in us. Let us encourage virtues and holiness and people will understand that the Lord is calling them.

The third thing that we witness to is man's privileges. God has set man as lord over His creatures. Man is described as lord over the living creatures because that is the more difficult part. It's much easier being lord of the plants. They don't revolt or rebel against us. (Who ever saw a carrot running away from a man or trying to stab him?). A master rules over that which wishes to escape from his control.

I draw your attention to God's promise in Deuteronomy (28:13): *And the* LORD *shall make thee the head, and not the tail; and thou shalt be above only, and thou shalt not be beneath....* Here is the solution to our personal problems, and here is the way out of the situation in which we find ourselves: Let everyone go back to fulfilling God's

Reflections

will. The dizzy spiral of price rises and poverty will cease, politicians will agree, armies will be cut back and see reason, education will improve, business become more secure, people will come to their senses. God does not want to ruin man, He wants to renew him and put him in a place where he can reign. We need to pray with the Psalmist: *Restore unto me the joy of Thy salvation; and uphold me with Thy free Spirit* (Ps. 51:12).

Of course when God talks about authority, and man's authority and rule, He means authority that will not be to the detriment of others, that will not cause hardship to others. In these destructive times I must add: nor cause damage to the environment. The problem is that men strive for power without regard for what it does to things around them: people, animals, plants, water, the soil and the air.

There are, needless to say, lots of nice phrases used to cover up this damage that is being done. It is done for people's good and it justifies plunder and greed for fame.

It is easier for Christians. God is the ruler. He is the Supreme one. It is true that He appointed man to be lord over all creation, but He also appointed man to be obedient to God and to belong to God. There is never any difference of opinion between the Creator and the creation. We know who the Creator is and who is the creature.

The enemy wants to shake man

An unshakable believer is a thorn in Satan's eye. He gets angry and loses his temper as soon as he sees that a person's heart has become the Lord's stronghold. And so he sends unbelievers. The godless are the devil's assault troops, warriors sent to attack Christians. They do their job. They are often very conscientious, and their attacks are very skilful, cunning and well-planned.

Aleksandar Birviš

The first thing that the godless have always wanted and still want is to shake the believer's faith in his Creator. They usually say something like, "Man created gods to drive away his fear, to get rid of some of his problems; God didn't make man." The aim of such an attitude is to isolate man, so that he is left without any way out and to separate him from the one who has all decisions in His hands.

The Scripture clearly shows that God created everything, including, of course, man. The creation must honor its Creator just as a child must honor its father. The human race did not show much inclination to honor God, and so the devil appeared in order to stir things up. That is sin.

But there will come a time when the Lord Jesus will cast sin and all that goes with it into the lake of fire (Rev. 20:14, 21:18). The Scripture calls this the second death.

After the second death the Lord Jesus will establish His order where the creation will be in harmony with the creative will of God. Man will know who he is before the Lord, because only by a clear and honest realization of who he is can man stand before the living God. The eternal order begins with Christ, and such limits as beginning and end will disappear.

Eternity is necessary and we should get to know it here on the earth in everyday life. Man is ruining his environment, nature and his fellow men. It is no longer a question of what we shall leave our children, but in what sort of mess we will be in a couple of years. We have shunned the eternal order of things to such an extent that we have become not just temporal creatures but creatures for whom time is running out.

The second trap of the godless is to trick us into thinking that negligence and disorder are the natural state of affairs. Is that because man despises God's creation? That is partly the reason. But a more important reason is poor stewardship. Man has ignored the Creator and His instructions about how to work and preserve what He has created. Men try to find ways of getting into the corridors of power, but they despise service. Nobody has the slightest intention of changing. Everyone wants to change the world, and even God if it suits them.

But the Lord constantly works at changing man. He brings men to repentance, that is to change their way of thinking, feeling and their wishes, and to redirect human desires towards the Almighty and that which is above — where Christ is sitting at the right hand of God (Col. 3:1).

Sin does not reduce just because the number of those who do not believe has fallen. Deep-down repentance is required. The world must see the signs of disintegration which indicate how much everything has been corrupted and how necessary it is that God begin to sort out everything that is not in its rightful place. In nature as in human society circumstances that should be clearly defined have become confused.

How are we to achieve that in our difficult circumstances? We shouldn't get involved in anything that does not bring salvation. Let us establish order amongst ourselves. We are all different. We are not equal, but that doesn't mean that we don't have equal rights. Each one needs to know where his place is and to understand why he is here and what he should be doing in that place. Then he won't despise others, or envy others, and the cooperation will be according to God's will.

That is why we need God's Word. It is a two-edged sword (Heb. 4:12). It pointedly establishes what is what and who is where. We learn from God's Word how to behave in the different levels of light

Aleksandar Birviš

and darkness about us, as well as how to invite others to come into glory.

★　★　★

Men are at different levels in their knowledge of God. Whether it will be easier or more difficult to accept the Good News of Christ depends on how well we know God. It is even more difficult for someone to understand time and eternity as they arise before him.

Christians have an obligation to explain to men what awaits them and who is waiting for them. Each one of us must know who he belongs to and with whom he will spend eternity and whom he will leave behind. It is difficult for the individual to remain unshaken. Let him join the fellowship of Christ's people and become His faithful disciple.

We are in God's glory, maybe just at the first dawn. Maybe we can just see it coming, but it is an eternity intended for all those who believe. We point out God's glory to others, because men are hungry to appear before the true glory. Let us instruct men to praise the One who should be praised, for all glory, honor and dignity belong to Him.

Final reading:

I will praise the LORD with my whole heart, in the assembly of the upright, and in the congregation. The works of the LORD are great, sought out of all them that have pleasure therein. His work is honourable and glorious: and His righteousness endureth for ever (Ps. 111:1–3)

Belgrade, 4th March 1992

PARDON AND WITNESSING ABOUT PARDON

Text for study

1 Tim. 1:12-17

And I thank Christ Jesus our Lord, who hath enabled me, for that He counted me faithful, putting me into the ministry; Who was before a blasphemer, and a persecutor, and injurious: but I obtained mercy, because I did it ignorantly in unbelief. And the grace of our Lord was exceeding abundant with faith and love which is in Christ Jesus. This is a faithful saying, and worthy of all acceptation, that Christ Jesus came into the world to save sinners; of whom I am chief. Howbeit for this cause I obtained mercy, that in me first Jesus Christ might shew forth all longsuffering, for a pattern to them which should hereafter believe on Him to life everlasting. Now unto the King eternal, immortal, invisible, the only wise God, be honour and glory for ever and ever. Amen.

Study

When the apostle Paul wrote his first epistle to Timothy, he had already had many experiences of life with the Lord. One experience that left a deep impression on his was that of being pardoned. God had pardoned him. He was guilty before the Lord, but He was not condemned. Instead the Almighty Judge had acquitted him.

Aleksandar Birviš

The Apostle has every right to believe that Christ came to save sinners of whom he was chief. He has the right to believe, but believes he has the right to salvation through the Lord Jesus. The apostle Paul doubtlessly committed less sin than other people, both people of his age and of ours. But he still looked on himself as the chief sinner. He sees the pardon that he has received as a sign of God's immense mercy.

The thought of sin and of the sinner depresses us. But the knowledge of a God who forgives and allows us to live with Him sets us free. Unearned acquittal or pardon amazes each of us when we encounter God's mercy.

I cannot come to God without the conviction that I am a sinner and that sin is enmity towards God, as well as enmity between man and man. I won't go into what sin is here. God willing, we will talk about sin another time, because we must: we struggle against it, and it is essential to know one's enemy

No one should return to his sin. God does not like that: *Remember, and forget not, how thou provokedst the* LORD *thy God to wrath in the wilderness: from the day that thou didst depart out of the land of Egypt, until ye came unto this place, ye have been rebellious against the* LORD (Deut. 9:7). The Almighty advises caution. It is dangerous when someone is lulled by temporary pleasure and forgets that he was a sinner.

When a man lives a shallow, insufficiently serious life it seems easy for him to do something without thinking much. Many hide behind the excuse – "everybody does it". But God doesn't address Himself to everyone as an impersonal crowd. He talks to each individual and gives the same message: "Remember how you used to lose your temper, how you use to oppose me; I offered you the hand of friendship and you rejected it."

Reflections

The Law of God was tough on ordinary enemies, that is enemies in the physical sense. Joshua was entering the Promised Land. He was a first-class general and he didn't miss an opportunity to assert that he would not fall short in anything that the Lord would ask of him. And his countrymen, honoring the command of man as if it were from God, replied, *According as we hearkened unto Moses in all things, so will we hearken unto thee: only the* LORD *thy God be with thee, as He was with Moses. Whosoever he be that doth rebel against thy commandment, and will not hearken unto thy words in all that thou commandest him, he shall be put to death: only be strong and of a good courage* (Josh. 1:17-18).

If they honored the word of man in this way, the word of their general, then we need to see how much greater is the enmity which men show when they strive to oppose the living God. That is enmity which is forced upon God. He does not want to be anyone's enemy.

But men insist on provoking God through their disobedience. They do all sorts of things that look nice and seem worthwhile, but they are not pleasing to God and so God's anger is aroused. God hates such deeds. Sin is enmity towards the Lord and the Lord hates sin. *For all that do such things, and all that do unrighteously,* says Moses, *are an abomination unto the* LORD *thy God* (Deut. 25:16). If sin seems attractive to man – for it is not just a crime that is sin, it is sin that is a crime – then it must be stopped even if it seems unpleasant or even cruel to do so.

Some sins have taken over, much lawlessness has become legitimate. Men abolish one lawless act by putting another in its place. Man is an expert at devising ways of opposing God, because he can't stop opposing Him. The old nature, whose reins Satan holds in his hands, easily sending him in the wrong direction, lives in human nature.

Aleksandar Birviš

Solomon says in Proverbs (6:16-19), *These six things doth the* LORD *hate: yea, seven are an abomination unto Him: A proud look, a lying tongue, and hands that shed innocent blood, An heart that deviseth wicked imaginations, feet that be swift in running to mischief, A false witness that speaketh lies, and he that soweth discord among brethren.* God lists the things He hates. He gives a whole arsenal of sins, enough to show that God has a deep revulsion towards all that is wrong and opposed to His will. For example, what is a proud look? We might say, "Who doesn't have a proud look? Why do we buy things that we don't need? Why do we sometimes try to dress smartly and cross the boundaries of decency? Why do we try and get some important honor by dubious means if not for the sake of a 'proud look'? Why are some people so obsessed with the idea of their children getting masters' and doctors' degrees etc.?" It is difficult to give up a proud look. Why do men today fight over borders and why are so many people dying as a result? There is a lot we don't know. No one can define what a Serb is, or a Croat, a Macedonian or any other nationality. But men do all this because of proud looks.

This all has a deadly effect. God hates that. We have no idea how lost we are in the maze of evil. How many lies people speak today! How many people today say "Good day", but don't wish you any good! How many people say, "Good night", and at the same time think to themselves, "Wouldn't it be good if he didn't sleep very well"?

How many lies are being spread about unrestrainedly? We call them compliments, politenesses, etc. but they are lies. It is just such lying language that the Lord hates.

What can we say about hands that shed righteous blood? About a heart that gives birth to evil thoughts? Try and catch your thoughts for a moment. You will see that here and there will appear some evil

Reflections

thought. What evil have we wished someone else? What wicked thought has appeared? Haven't we perhaps tried to make fun of someone? Why? Because we think evil, and evil thoughts are the source of many other evils. Put another way, for a man to achieve something he must first have the idea to do so.

Many wicked thoughts are just the beginning. After them come wicked words, and after them wicked deeds. God hates that. That is what is blackest: a sinner is not a sinner because he has to sin, but because he has embraced such thoughts and carried them out. In our language we call that "feet that run for evil". Many men are quick when they need to do evil, but slow when they need to do good.

The Word of God talks of the false witness who tells lies. There is a reason why this is put like that. It can happen that a false witness tells the truth. Because of that truth God will not punish him, for God loves man. The Lord expects even of a false witness that he will acquire a love for the truth and no longer be a false witness. This is where the key problem lies: God hates sin, although He doesn't hate the sinner but wants him to be saved.

He who causes arguments amongst brothers is repulsive to God because He loves all the brethren whether they argue or whether they love one another. The Almighty loves men. That's the well-known verse from John's Gospel (3:16). We should talk about it often. God loves that world, that wicked world, that bloody world that is doing stupid things. The world freely and willingly elects unsuitable people to lead it. It is just such people that Christ loves. It was for that world that He died.

This is the reason why there are men who preach Christ, the lover of man. God's goodness and love for man is proclaimed. It is proclaimed to man and he needs to grasp how much that love towards man is needed by every man and woman.

Aleksandar Birviš

"The Word is the truth and worthy to be received". Pardoned men have the Word of God, they have the Gospel. It tells us who the one who saves us is, who the friend of sinners is. Christ became the friend of fallen man, even when that man insulted Him and killed Him, because He is the Good Shepherd.

It can happen that someone offers us salvation without Christ. That has become fashionable today. We talk about how people are turning again to religion, but they are really returning to a political system. There is very little real belief. Faith isn't intended for show, it is intended to bring sinners to God. Christ came to save sinners, which means to save me too.

Each individual needs to respond to that personally.

Belgrade, 11th March 1992

ABOUT OUR TESTIMONY

Some aspects of our testimony

Witnessing is the task of every Christian. What is it that we need to tell others? A witness does not speak his own opinion or assessments, but he presents a range of facts.

Firstly, all men are in sin

Men generally avoid this fact. Instead of sin they make learned speeches about guilt complexes, neuroses and the like. No one wants to use the simple word: *sin*. However, sin exists and it can be found wherever there are people. Where there are people, there is sin. In this context we must repeat what it says in Romans (3:23): *For all have sinned, and come short of the glory of God.* Why did this happen? Because, *There is none righteous, no, not one: There is none that understandeth, there is none that seeketh after God. They are all gone out of the way, they are together become unprofitable; there is none that doeth good, no, not one* (Rom. 3:10-12). The third chapter of Romans is to the soul what an X-ray is to the body. It shows us just as we are.

a) All men are in sin *by their very nature.* This is what King David meant when he wrote a good thousand years before Christ, *Behold, I was shapen in iniquity; and in sin did my mother conceive*

Aleksandar Birviš

me (Ps.51:5). Someone might say, "That's Old Testament thinking," but we also find written in the New Testament: *Among whom also we all had our conversation in times past in the lusts of our flesh, fulfilling the desires of the flesh and of the mind; and were by nature the children of wrath, even as others* (Eph. 2:3). So we are nothing else except sinners, like the rest of the world which we would like to separate ourselves from.

b) All men are in sin *by choice*. Man is able to choose and more often than not he gives preference to sin; maybe consciously, maybe unconsciously, but nevertheless freely. That is why the Lord Jesus says: *And this is the condemnation, that light is come into the world, and men loved darkness rather than light, because their deeds were evil* (John 3:19). There is nothing new in that. Sin has burdened and restricted man. The multitude of human wickedness has reduced man's ability for discernment, and increased his persistence to continue in evil. That is why it says in the Old Testament: *All we like sheep have gone astray; we have turned every one to his own way; and the LORD hath laid on Him the iniquity of us all* (Is. 53:6). Each person has committed his sin of his own will and volition. Man had a desire to sin and has carried that wish out.

c) All men sin because sin has become a *habit* with them. In Matt. 12:30 we read that the Savior said: *He that is not with Me is against Me; and he that gathereth not with Me scattereth abroad.* In practice there are two camps: one which commits sin and the other which wants to turn from sin and to be with Christ. Both groups pass through the everyday experience of sin. Those who desire sin persist constantly in it until sin becomes a habit. They don't have to directly commit evil. Many will answer before the Lord because they have become

Reflections

insensitive. They know what is right, but they have become accustomed to evil and they fail to take the opportunity to do good. The Word of God says about such men *Therefore to him that knoweth to do good, and doeth it not, to him it is sin* (James 4:17). It seems to me that the apostle James had very clearly seen some of the qualities that ordinary people do not see or do not intend to see. Man lets the opportunities to do good go by and thinks that in that way he will live his life to the full. He is not at all worried about it, and that also is sin.

Secondly, sin has its consequences

Our testimony shouldn't stop with the simple conclusion that all men are sinners. We must stress that sin has consequences. In the words of Scripture, *for the wages of sin is death* (Rom. 6:23). Death undoubtedly came into the world because the first men sinned. This is a consequence we are all subjected to.

Since God has placed in every man the ability to believe, and to believe in Christ, for the Savior is ... *the true Light, which lighteth every man* (John 1:9), it is impossible to escape the consequences of unbelief. That is why we believe that ... *he that believeth on Him is not condemned: but he that believeth not is condemned already, because he hath not believed in the name of the only begotten Son of God* (John 3:18).

a) The first consequence of sin is that sin — and the unrepentant sinner too — *is already condemned.* In the words of the apostle Paul, *for as many as are of the works of the law are under the curse: for it is written, Cursed is every one that continueth not in all things which are written in the book of the law to do them* (Gal. 3:10). The word curse does not mean so much 'damnation', but more 'a sentence'. The Lord has surely passed sentence, for His court is not like human courts where neither judges nor prosecution nor defense are perfect. That sentence was passed when justice was first created and when the whole order of creation was established on the basis of justice.

b) The second consequence is: man is under God's wrath. We read: *He that believeth on the Son hath everlasting life: and he that believeth not the Son shall not see life; but the wrath of God abideth on him* (John 3:36). When we read this it is not clear whether it is John the Baptist speaking or whether they are the words of John the Evangelist. For the purpose of our discussion that isn't important. The important thing is that wrath abides on the man who does not believe. Today it is fashionable to believe in the reappearance of the same personality in another being, man or animal. After paying for their sin they expect they will have a new and more blessed life. This is called reincarnation. However the Word of God clearly says: *"shall not see life."* Wrath remains and there are no further opportunities. Blessed are those who repent now and turn to God. We mustn't delay, for sin is no joke. *Or despisest thou,* says the apostle Paul, *the riches of His goodness and forbearance and longsuffering; not knowing that the goodness of God leadeth thee to repentance? But after thy hardness and impenitent heart treasurest up unto thyself wrath against the day of wrath and revelation of the righteous judgment of God; Who will render to every man according to his deeds* (Rom. 2:4-6).

c) The third consequence is *death*. One man (Adam) sinned. Through his sin death came, firstly to him, and then to his descendants (Rom. 5:12). But this is not the whole problem. Death itself would be a blessing if everything ended there. But

Reflections

God is not so unrighteous: He doesn't leave debts unsettled. Christ Himself says that if they are not reconciled with God, sinners will go *where their worm dieth not, and the fire is not quenched* (Mark 9:48). Death is continual separation from God and continual torment of the consciousness and the conscience. This consequence can be avoided by avoiding the enjoyments of sin, for *when lust hath conceived, it bringeth forth sin: and sin, when it is finished, bringeth forth death* (James 1:15). The people of God must be aware of that because the pitfalls are all around us and it is so easy to fall into them. Many fall every day and do not seek Christ to deliver them. These are the ones who will have torment, *everlasting destruction from the presence of the Lord, and from the glory of His power* (2 Thess. 1:9). The verdict, the sentence and the eternal punishment will come from the presence of the Lord and His glory. That is one meaning. The other meaning is: where the presence of the Lord and His glory are absent, a worse hell is not necessary. Every man will suffer the terrible torment and hardship of eternity without anything glorious, honest, good or positive to relieve it. God has punished him through the awareness that he is lost which is worse than being lost.

Thirdly, no one can save themselves

Man must believe. There is no other way apart from faith. We read that … *without faith it is impossible to please Him: for he that cometh to God must believe that He is, and that He is a rewarder of them that diligently seek Him* (Heb. 11:6). Faith is the factor by which we can know and define whether God exists or not. All our efforts are in vain if we do

Aleksandar Birviš

not have that assurance. It is not something that man uses to exchange or acquire knowledge, but an ability innate in every man.

a) Good *works* do not save. The great apostle warns: *For by grace are ye saved through faith; and that not of yourselves: it is the gift of God: Not of works, lest any man should boast* (Eph. 2:8-9). God pardons the sinner, not because he is no longer a sinner, but because God is so good and He does not want the sinner to perish. Whoever believes in that pardon, receives the gift of salvation. The sinner does not win or earn salvation — God gives salvation to him as a gift. In this way the Lord puts a stop to all boasting. I don't need to found a church in order for the Lord to save me. The Lord has already saved me and if I believe, I will do all I can out of gratitude and a desire to help others to experience salvation too. Many would prefer it not to be like this. They would rather sacrifice all their possessions in order to somehow redeem themselves before God. That presupposes, firstly, that God is corruptible and, secondly, that only those who have the means, that is the rich, can be saved. We need to tell people clearly that their good works will not save them. Blessed is he who does good, but does it because he has become a different person: not because he is big-hearted or generous, but because he has become like that through the merits of the Lord Jesus Christ.

b) Religious rituals cannot save. Priestly acts, the sacraments, are of no value if they are not based on faith in the all-sufficiency and supremacy of the Savior's sacrifice on the cross. *Almost all things are by the law purged with blood; and without shedding of blood is no remission* (Heb. 9:22). The writer of the Epistle to the Hebrews was thinking here of Christ's blood as the

Reflections

fulfillment of the type of the blood of animals that were brought as a sacrifice. I may take part in the most solemn and most mysterious ceremonies. I may grasp the meaning of all signs and symbols. None of that can save me. My salvation is in Christ's blood shed at Calvary. When He was crucified nineteen hundred years ago on Calvary, I was saved. The sacrifice that was made on Calvary's cross was for all who believe at any time and at any place. That is the shedding of blood without which there is no salvation for anyone. Our actions, ceremonies, deeds and sacrifices only have any worth alongside Christ's sacrifice.

c) Good *behavior* or good *conduct* does not save. For example the prisoner who is released early for good behavior did it in the prison of his body: his spirit wasn't imprisoned. The prison called sin doesn't award such early release. Why? Because it is a prison of the spirit. How ever well I behave or control myself, sin won't release me. On the contrary, the well-mannered criminal is even more necessary to the devil. The evil one holds on to his captives. Release comes when one understands God's pardon (grace, mercy). As it says in the Scriptures, *Knowing that a man is not justified by the works of the law, but by the faith of Jesus Christ, even we have believed in Jesus Christ, that we might be justified by the faith of Christ, and not by the works of the law: for by the works of the law shall no flesh be justified* (Gal. 2:16). The Law prescribes behavior, but the great truth that we have learned demonstrates that behavior is not a cause of salvation but a result of being saved. The Law sets out very clearly defined rules: from holidays and festivals, through rights and punishments, to medical and

Aleksandar Birviš

military rules, and rules relating to the treatment of plants and animals. None of that can save.

What then can save us? Only God, who has pardoned you personally, can save you. This seems to be beyond our normal way of thinking but that is just what the apostle Paul stresses in his sermon in Antioch in Pisidia: *And by Him* (that is by Christ) *all that believe are justified from all things, from which ye could not be justified by the law of Moses* (Acts 13:39). I would like to underline the word "everyone". Salvation is intended for all men. No one has an excuse. No one can say, "That doesn't apply to me". Salvation is for everyone.

Salvation is for you.

Belgrade, 11th March 1992

TRIALS — THE TEST OF THE KINGDOM OF GOD

The sixth Sunday before Easter

Subject: The King and the Kingdom — trials

Introductory reading:

As for me, I will call upon God; and the LORD shall save me. Evening, and morning, and at noon, will I pray, and cry aloud: and He shall hear my voice. He hath delivered my soul in peace from the battle that was against me: for there were many with me (Ps. 55:16-18).

Main reading:

Be sober, be vigilant; because your adversary the devil, as a roaring lion, walketh about, seeking whom he may devour: Whom resist stedfast in the faith, knowing that the same afflictions are accomplished in your brethren that are in the world (1 Pet. 5:8-9).

We can count on there being trials and that Satan will be at work in many different ways. Each of these is an attack in itself. The Devil knows nothing else but to oppose the children of God.

The same things happen to others too, not just to us. There are those who thought that if only they could get to the free West then their spiritual problems would just disappear. Here they were confused and their lives were made difficult by those who do not believe and those who hate Christ, while over there in the West there

Aleksandar Birviš

is freedom and they will become more spiritual in no time. But Satan is at work there too. Nothing changes as far as he is concerned; he just changes his approach, his methods or tactics.

Let us not forget that our Lord was tempted. Only after His temptation did Christ begin to preach the Gospel and The Kingdom of God. When we read the account of His temptation, for example in Mark's Gospel (1:12-15), we see that the devil tempted Him in the wilderness and only after that did the Savior begin to preach, *The time is fulfilled, and the kingdom of God is at hand: repent ye, and believe the gospel* (v. 15). First testing and then the Kingdom.

This order of events is based on the Gospel. So we should adhere to it. We will progress if we successfully confront temptations. It is useless to expect Christians to growth healthily and to mature without testing. What sort of school is it that has no exams and no grades? Christian discipleship would be of little worth without examinations, and that is what trials are.

We need to repeat the New Testament answer to the question: What is the Kingdom of God? The answer is: *For the kingdom of God is not meat and drink; but righteousness, and peace, and joy in the Holy Ghost* (Rom. 14:17). The temptations of the Kingdom of God, then, are temptations relating to righteousness, temptations relating to peace and temptations relating to joy.

Righteousness in the Holy Spirit —what are the temptations of righteousness?

Righteousness in the Holy Spirit is not the righteousness of this world. Such a righteousness adheres to the terms of the worldly, that is that which is without Christ or which hates Christ.

Reflections

The first temptation in connection with this is the danger that righteousness is reduced to the letter of the law instead of dependence on the Holy Spirit. The Apostle Paul writes as follows: *And such trust have we through Christ to God-ward: Not that we are sufficient of ourselves to think any thing as of ourselves; but our sufficiency is of God; Who also hath made us able ministers of the new testament; not of the letter, but of the Spirit: for the letter killeth, but the Spirit giveth life. But if the ministration of death, written and engraven in stones, was glorious, so that the children of Israel could not stedfastly behold the face of Moses for the glory of his countenance; which glory was to be done away: How shall not the ministration of the Spirit be rather glorious? For if the ministration of condemnation be glory, much more doth the ministration of righteousness exceed in glory. For even that which was made glorious had no glory in this respect, by reason of the glory that excelleth. For if that which is done away was glorious, much more that which remaineth is glorious* (2 Cor. 3:4-11).

There is a great danger of reducing righteousness to legalism. In this case where men serve the letter of the law they are in fact serving something that has passed away. It all had a glory of its own, but it can no longer survive.

Secondly, the temptation of righteousness in the Holy Spirit is when people talk about righteousness, but don't think about God's will. People sometimes think that what is beneficial is right. They fight for justice, but only when it affects their pocket; up until then everything is fine. But the Lord Jesus says, *Therefore take no thought, saying, What shall we eat? or, What shall we drink? or, Wherewithal shall we be clothed? (For after all these things do the Gentiles seek:) for your heavenly Father knoweth that ye have need of all these things. But seek ye first the kingdom of God, and His righteousness; and all these things shall be added unto you* (Matt. 6:31-33). Don't worry about what is beneficial to you, or about what is necessary. The world seeks those things.

Aleksandar Birviš

Your Heavenly Father knows all that. The Heavenly Father wants us to strive for heavenly righteousness. Righteousness isn't just when we all have something to eat, when we all have something to drink and something to wear. That is good, because an unjust society takes from one group of people and gives to others: it makes the hungry go hungry, and those who have had enough to eat gain weight; it lets the thirsty become parched with thirst, while those who have had enough to drink get more; it takes the clothes from the naked to dress up those who have full wardrobes. But righteousness is when we are primarily focused on the Kingdom of God, when God shows His justice, when Christians accept it as the supreme law, and the Lord resolves everything else in the best way possible. There is another damaging temptation, and that is the temptation of self-righteousness. Vuk Karadzic[13] in his translation of the New Testament used the phrase "those who think they are righteous" for this type of person. And the Savior specifically pointed out that danger. He told a striking story (about the Pharisee and the tax-collector): *And He spake this parable unto certain which trusted in themselves that they were righteous, and despised others: Two men went up into the temple to pray; the one a Pharisee, and the other a publican. The Pharisee stood and prayed thus with himself, God, I thank Thee, that I am not as other men are, extortioners, unjust, adulterers, or even as this publican. I fast twice in the week, I give tithes of all that I possess. And the publican, standing afar off, would not lift up so much as his eyes unto heaven, but smote upon his breast, saying, God be merciful to me a sinner. I tell you, this man went down to his house justified rather than the other: for every one that exalteth himself shall be abased; and he that humbleth himself shall be exalted* (Luke 18:9-14). Christ's parable is one of those things that you don't forget even though what He said was nothing extraordinary. His contemporaries encountered such things at every step. They knew the attitude of the Pharisees. They knew

Reflections

about the tax-collectors: these were sinful men whom no one liked. But the interpretation of the parable was unusual: it is dangerous when someone thinks he is infallible and sinless. The tax-collector was justified because he realized that he was a sinner, and not because he was sinless. The Pharisee believed that he could justify himself before God, and that is where he made his mistake by comparing himself with our sinless Lord.

The Savior's teaching points us to a God who forgives. Only He can justify. The precondition for justification is repentance. Only a repentant sinner can count on the Almighty to justify him. God forgives him and transforms him into a righteous man.

Peace in the Holy Spirit — what are the temptations of this peace?

Peace is an important quality which is being jeopardized before our very eyes. And what is more, even those who live by war and earn huge profits from it, are beginning to feel apprehensive about what they have done. Those who hate men are searching for peace. But it is a peace without the Holy Spirit. God-given peace is constantly being put to the test.

Men want peace without righteousness. This is the toughest trial that peace is going through just here and now where we are. Men say: "Just let peace be established, and then we will see where we go from there". That's what people think who do not know the Gospel. When Christ was born the angels greeted him, singing (Luke 2:14):

Glory to God in the highest,
And on earth peace,
Good will toward men.

Aleksandar Birviš

It seems to me that the angels weren't speaking to the shepherds but to politicians: "Gentlemen, first do all you can to glorify God — pray, be honest, shout His praises. Then make peace: make your peace with God, make peace with men, make peace with your own consciences. Only then seek goodwill, consensus, etc. Stop doing it the other way round: trying to achieve goodwill first, and then peace, and what's left over give to God's glory".

Peace is the result of righteousness and justice. Spiritual life establishes such an order and spiritual men must adhere to it. Let us remain honest in dishonest times. Without that there can be no peace in the Holy Spirit.

The Kingdom of God has been established on the earth in order to declare that honesty is possible and is in fact the only proper way of doing things for all men. We cannot expect the world to submit to God's order of righteousness, peace and joy in the Holy Spirit. God expects Christians to know how precious peace is and what leads up to peace. Followers of God know very well where they are and why and for what purpose they are appointed.

Christians don't expect the world to know what true peace is. But the world can see and should be made to realize, that righteous peace is possible and righteous peace is the only correct form of peace for all men.

Peace without righteousness is an even tougher trial. We can for example say that there is always peace in a cemetery. Nobody argues, nobody complains that someone else is in a better or larger grave, nobody is jealous of the large number of visitors another one has or complains about the disturbance. All are at peace, but they don't live in peace, because they simply aren't alive.

Many yearn for such a peace. They set out to kill other nations so that their nation would live in peace. Then they are surprised that

Reflections

even in that homogeneous nation there is no peace. So they get rid of those who disturb them. But men can agree a truce out of fear, but still there is no peace. Why? Because there is no righteousness.

In the Epistle to the Romans (12:21) we read, *Be not overcome of evil, but overcome evil with good.* Evil tries to overcome at any price. For the evil one it is important that all should be obedient and keep quiet. The best discipline is that which exists amongst gangsters. They know who obeys whom. But amongst gangsters there is no righteousness.

God's people think of the peace that God gave, and not about the temporary truces that men impose or agree. The peace of God overrules men's narrow aspirations for peace which cover up their secret wishes and longings for their own interests and gain. Christ gave us and left with us a peace based not only on justice but also on other virtues. Then God is present amongst men. He gives them the power to overcome evil with good, so that goodness triumphs even when it seems that all is lost. This inspires hope: God is the victor.

The third temptation related to peace is making righteousness without peace. Men make laws, exert pressure, and take reprisals, in order to force men to do something which can blow up in their faces at any moment. God's servant writes, *Recompense to no man evil for evil. Provide things honest in the sight of all men. If it be possible, as much as lieth in you, live peaceably with all men* (Rom. 12:17-18). This teaches us that we must first of all give up any thought of retaliation, and then avoid what all men strive for, in other words, we must do good to all men without exception. The general good takes precedence over the good of the individual not because it must be so, but because individuals are committed to it. Only then can we talk about peace as an idea. In order for peace to become a reality there are obstacles to be overcome. Peace is a possibility and righteousness must not stop

Aleksandar Birviš

at being righteousness without peace. Only peace tried and tested in line with God's Word is the peace which the children of the Lord can call peace.

Joy in the Holy Spirit — what are its temptations?

Joy is a gift of God and the ingredient of the Kingdom that follows righteousness and peace. Christianity is filled with joy much more than many other faiths. It is not surprising that Easter and Christmas are the most joyful days on the planet.

The temptation that many encounter is the temptation of false joy. That is when a man pretends to be joyful or he rejoices that he can pretend to be joyful— there is obviously no natural and unaffected joy in that. Along with this temptation goes imposed joy. Some other person forces a man to be joyful, even though he has no real reason to be joyful. In order to create such joy these men resort to forced laughter and mass control of people in so-called outpourings of enthusiasm at the presence of their favorite leaders or the stars of this world.

There is a whole industry of artificial and enforced joy. The life of the world is in essence empty, but there are many different forms of entertainment. They all lead to sin and heap burdens on to men. It is true that they give him some form of happy feelings, and for some that is enough, as no one has ever pointed them to genuine spiritual joy. In actual fact, joy should be studied and nurtured. It is better for a Christian to check out himself how genuine his joy is. If he does that he will be able to consistently oppose everything that is not joy in the Holy Spirit.

By neglecting good taste and well tried spiritual criteria the children of God are in danger of forfeiting their joy and making do

Reflections

with being entertained. When we talk about this we usually mean modern music, modern dress and modern behavior in general. But there are other forms of bad taste: desire for making a display of oneself, I mean the theatre.

Many Christians would like to be seen. They like people to see them, for example on TV. They get more pleasure from that than from the Holy Spirit. Instead of joy in the Spirit they have joy in themselves. The Church has a hard time with the "priests of show-business". They create their own entertainment, and offer these performances to God and the community.

The Almighty teaches us that joy in the Holy Spirit is the result of something that has happened inside a man, but which doesn't depend on man. It depends primarily on God. In the Psalms (Ps. 30:5) we read,

For His anger endureth but a moment; in His favour is life:

Weeping may endure for a night, but joy cometh in the morning.

In the same Psalm (v. 11) King David puts these thoughts into a prayer:

Thou hast turned for me my mourning into dancing:

Thou hast put off my sackcloth, and girded me with gladness.

We shouldn't be discouraged if someone tries to inhibit spiritual joy. That is a temporary annoyance. Joy overcomes because it comes from Christ, and He is the victor and sustainer of all. The Savior changes our difficulties and sadness into true joy.

The second temptation is joy for joy's sake. It is not good for joy to be an end in itself. Joy flows from the presence of God. If the Lord departs from us, our joy recedes. When that happens, we need to find out why God has taken away our joy.

The great prophet Isaiah is speaking in the name of God when he writes (Is. 16:10):

Aleksandar Birviš

And gladness is taken away, and joy out of the plentiful field;

And in the vineyards there shall be no singing, neither shall there be shouting:

The treaders shall tread out no wine in their presses;

I have made their vintage shouting to cease.

Who has stopped them singing? Who has put a stop to the party? If men want joy, they need to be more seriously-minded. Spirituality is not for the frivolous. God does all things according to His purpose. If he causes grief to someone, there is a reason — and we need to find out why.

God promised the church in Philadelphia, *Because thou hast kept the word of My patience, I also will keep thee from the hour of temptation, which shall come upon all the world, to try them that dwell upon the earth* (Rev. 3:10). The book of Revelation is a book of hope. It is also a book of perseverance. But often people who read Revelation become impatient. They would like to hurry the Lord up. The book of Revelation is often used wrongly: men tell God to stick to the timetable that they have discovered in Revelation.

God Almighty promises each one of us that He will protect us from testing. There will be tests but they will be individual tests and only partial setbacks. Christian men and women, families or fellowships or tribes and nations will be tested. It is not possible to reject the temptation but you can reject the tempter.

Our King and Lord, Jesus Christ, was tempted and was victorious in the struggle with the tempter. The Son of God put Satan in his place. The evil one will continually put pitfalls and traps in the path of Christians, but victory remains in the hands of our Lord. If you belong to the Lord, you are a conqueror in fellowship with Christ.

What can you expect? Don't worry. God promises to protect those who live according to His will. The future is tough, uncertain

Reflections

and frightening only if you refuse to obey God's will. If you continue to honor God's will, the future can do you no harm. You are focused on the eternal Kingdom. In the blessed presence of the King of kings eternity has already begun. All temptations cease, pure serenity begins.

Thank God that the promise is for each one of us.

Final reading

I said, O my God, take me not away in the midst of my days: Thy years are throughout all generations.

Of old hast Thou laid the foundation of the earth: and the heavens are the work of Thy hands.

They shall perish, but Thou shalt endure: yea, all of them shall wax old like a garment; as a vesture shalt Thou change them, and they shall be changed:

But Thou art the same, and Thy years shall have no end.

The children of Thy servants shall continue, and their seed shall be established before Thee

(Ps. 102:24-28).

Belgrade, 15th March 1992

FROM CONFLICT TO CONFLICT – CHRIST

The fifth Sunday before Easter
Subject: The King and the Kingdom — conflicts

> *These things I have spoken unto you, that in Me ye might have peace.*
> *In the world ye shall have tribulation: but be of good cheer;*
> *I have overcome the world.* (John 16:33)

Jesus Christ is talking about peace. Christians are men of peace. Peace is not found in agreements but in Christ. The Savior has the right words which bring genuine peace. The Son of God is speaking. He is telling us what is going to happen. His words instill peace even when He announces unpleasant times, sufferings and wars.

In contrast to Christ, the world is in constant upheavals and conflicts. We can't call the world anything but a hater of Christ. If the world were to stop hating Christ, is would cease to be what it is.

That is why the Kingdom of God is in continual conflict with the world. The follower of Christ is not warlike; instead he tries to be a peacemaker in a world of constant unrest. A Christian tries as far as he is able to be at peace with all men, because that is what the Scripture teaches him (Rom. 12:18). But the world does not want peace.

1.

There are conflicts in marriage. However the marriage was entered into, for love, from self-interest, or out of obedience, marriage

Reflections

is a communion is which one of the partners is closer to Christ, while the other one may be far from the Savior or even hostile. If there is no oneness in commitment to the Lord, the result is intolerance. Satan causes enmity towards Christ. He instills it into the very being of those who are opposed to the Savior.

Each one of us knows that when we did not live in fellowship with Christ as we should have, many of us were completely at peace. But, when we became believers, our nearest and dearest suddenly remembered that they too have their faith and began to oppose us. Up until then they didn't care a jot, but then they were jolted out of their indifference. They became concerned. All of a sudden they had something to say and something to do. And what did they do? – all sorts of things, but not God's will.

2

Family relationships are more complex and conflicts are more common. The problem is not that some have become believers, but that others are unbelievers. Difficulties arise because there is a lack of tolerance. The modern way of life deludes the youth of today. Politicians who give the impression of being serious get the high-schoolers behind them. And what's more, they think they will bring the government down with their help and establish a new order. Discord creeps into families unnoticed.

The youngsters are also being tempted by the shops. Expensive, fashionable items are on sale, intended for those who have money to waste. Children start to brag, and make their friends want better things and spend more money. Conflicts are inevitable, because no one can earn enough for those who have the spending bug.

You will say that this applies to the families of non-believers. God grant that that is the case. But this desire for show and fashion

Aleksandar Birviš

is infecting believers as well. Parents are poisoned by the desire for their children to make a good impression on the world. Many of them have never taught their children about simplicity.

But something more harmful is becoming the norm: the family is becoming a means of imposing goodness and religious values. Many parents look like Christians to the world, but there is no Christianity in the family. In order to maintain a good impression in front of others, their children are forced to be religious. Instead of loving to pray they pray so as to be loved. This leads to them becoming little hypocrites, a new type of Pharisee. This process gathers pace — little Pharisees become big Pharisees, — big hypocrites who do not know how to tell lies from the truth. They soon find fault with the world around them that does not show them the respect that they would like. In the course of time a lack of goodness and religious values comes to the surface. Those around them think that the Pharisees have lost something, whereas in fact they never had anything. What is left? Conflicts and more and more dysfunctional families.

3

The wider the community, the more likely conflicts are. Today we no longer know the meaning of the word 'commune'. We usually mean an agricultural or trade commune, or a productive or consumer commune. But the real commune is a gathering of families who have the same ancestral origins, who live together and help one another, share the work and organize their life under the leadership of one elder and his fellow leaders (usually brothers or cousins). The community is managed by the most capable person (father, widowed mother, brother, or more rarely an unmarried sister). They remain together for two or three generations, and when they do split up they still stay closely linked together. The possibilities for conflict

Reflections

are much greater and there are always many squabbles. That is why the commune is falling out of use. It is considered an old-fashioned, backward way of life. Who today would force someone to live with his grandfather and grandmother, uncles and aunts, sisters-in-law? But it is from one such commune that one of the most successful companies in Serbia has emerged — the Karic Brothers[14].

Believers in general do not live in communes. Some of our large families succeeded in keeping all the family together until life overseas offered a more comfortable way of life. The young rushed off to get rich. They are still members of churches in the countries they have gone to, but to what degree they are still believers and to what degree they have become modern idol-worshippers — only God knows, and probably they themselves.

4

As the community expands, conflicts become more complex. On the other hand stronger and stronger appeals for unity are heard: louder and louder but less and less successful. Satan is not stupid. He likes unity, but only amongst non-believers. Against Christians the evil one uses every means at his disposal to disturb them, and to cause dissention and conflicts.

This is nothing new. It is just that it is assuming much more horrendous proportions.

5

The world will talk of peace. But there will still be no real peace, peace in the Holy Spirit. Each occupying force wages war and then asks for peace from the nations it has conquered. The world is full of disturbances and disagreement, but the main thing it wants is for the children of God to be submissive, to mind their own business, not

Aleksandar Birviš

to get involved in politics and, of course, not to increase in number. So every new conversion is a source of conflict with the world. For the evil one that is an attack and a defeat.

The devil knows that he doesn't have much time (Rev. 12:12). And so he is upping the tension. Today men are openly saying that we need to forget friendship amongst the nations and just get on with our own thing. The time is coming when the same situation will exist between individuals: a friend is worth having while he is useful, but when he is no longer of any use, I will get rid of him. The devil will instill that same way of thinking into the family. Everyone will take advantage of everyone else for as long as they can. When a man is no longer useful he will be rejected. (This can be seen in the attitude towards old people).

There will be less and less talk of what is now considered inhumane. Humanism and humanists are something that we don't like to talk about in the Church today.

Genuine spirituality was never hostile to men. Why did Christ come to the earth? In order to save mankind. In other words, for the sake of men. Christ had serious conflicts with the Pharisees, the teachers of the Law and other defenders of the status quo. They excluded man from the work of God. They forgot that man may be sick or hungry, possessed and tormented. To them man was good as long as he kept all the rules and regulations and respected them and remained in their debt.

The same conflicts exist today. If we don't resolve them, there is not much hope of a blessed eternity for us. The Apostle James teaches us in his Epistle (2:12-13), *So speak ye, and so do, as they that shall be judged by the law of liberty. For he shall have judgment without mercy, that hath shewed no mercy; and mercy rejoiceth against judgment.* We are advised to practice freedom and mercy. Arguments can be

Reflections

settled with their help. Instead of resorting to complex lawsuits, the Christian can retain his humanity in any court by using the methods of freedom and mercy.

I am not going to explain what we mean by freedom and mercy on this occasion. If God grants us the health, strength and ability to meet again according to His will, there will be a time for that too.

I would rather attempt to explain what the law of freedom is, that is the law which sets men free. Before Christ there were laws and legislatures. All those laws, including the Law of God, set out restrictions. Every legislator — the Lord included — starts from the bitter knowledge that if man is left with no restrictions, he will commit one evil after another with nothing to stop him. Remember the Tower of Babel: men joined together in order to reach to the skies, to build a tower in order to depose God.

With Christ has come the time of birth from above and new life in the Spirit. Earlier laws have become useless. The Old Testament law is especially beneficial, important and inspired because it is the Word of God. But a Christian is a changed man. He needs a different law.

Let me give you an analogy. Before it is born a baby is perfectly protected. It has everything it needs: its mother breathes for it, she feeds it, and she makes many sacrifices for it. The baby doesn't have to know anything, nor take notice of anything in particular, because all its needs are met. But one day the baby is born. It is no longer perfectly protected, but neither is it limited to the confines of its mother's body. New rules come into force for it: independence, learning, movement and many other things that come with life. The child belongs to its mother and will do all its life, but it will slowly stop being a baby and become more and more a man. If it had not come into the world it would not have achieved any of that.

Aleksandar Birviš

So it is with life in Christ. The difference is that people enter that life by their own choice. In that life they breathe the Gospel. That is the law which sets them free, as the Lord Jesus said, *And ye shall know the truth, and the truth shall make you free* (John 8:32). You have come into the world of truth, and freedom has come with Christ. The conflict between slavery and freedom doesn't concern you any more because the Savior is freedom, the Spirit is freedom, and you are free.

★   ★   ★

The world and its troubles can't be overlooked. Christians are right to be concerned. But there is no need for fear. The Savior encourages us: *Be of good cheer; I have overcome the world* (John 16:33). Jesus is victorious. The world has been overcome. The world opposes every effort on the part of Christ's followers, but to no avail. We have a stronger one on our side, we have the Conqueror.

About the time of Lenin's death (1924) the authorities put a group of Baptists from southern Russia into a cattle wagon, sealed it up and transported them for days without giving them any information or giving them anything to eat or drink. People were dying of hunger and suffocation, the roof let in the rain, so that they were able to collect the rain water and drink it. Bodies were rotting in one corner — it was horrific, but at least it kept the temperature up, and the cold stopped the bodies from decaying.

All of a sudden the Red Army soldiers opened the doors of the wagon and threw them all out into the snow. The believers asked for the bodies of their dead. Surprisingly, the army agreed. So the pile of bodies was left beside the railway track and the train departed.

When the men's eyes got used to the light they realized that they were somewhere in the snowy wilderness of Eastern Siberia. There

Reflections

was no sign of life. Just forest, with all the dangers that lurk in it and the unknown situation in which they found themselves.

In such situations men become savages. They resort to cannibalism in order to survive. Some commit suicide. Sometimes whole groups.

But in the case of these believers it was different. First they thanked God. Then they set off into the forest and found roots, and dry twigs and fallen branches. The cooked some of the roots to build up their strength. They made crosses out of the branches and some sort of shovels. They buried the dead as their faith and human decency required. Then they made a sort of hut out of some more branches. They covered the branches with snow and spent the night there. As they only had two boxes of matches, they took turns to watch the fire.

At evening prayer they said: "Lord, you have overcome the world. Teach us to share in your victory." In the morning they set out to work. They had two axes. They cut down some trees. Then they made something they could use to clear the snow, and something to use as spades and other tools. At first they ate roots and drank tea made of pine needles. They found some plants that had salt in their roots. They managed to catch some game, and so had meat to eat.

Some of them died but the community survived. They soon built better living accommodation and began to have children. They found people who lived in that area, not very close, but near enough to exchange goods, services, experience and assistance with them. They witnessed to them and some souls were saved. They built churches. They constructed roads, dug wells, and found springs.

The Soviet authorities found them some ten years later. They wanted to forcibly resettle them. But they changed their minds. They sent them people's representatives. They set up a police force and tax officers and built a local town hall, a prison, a statue of Lenin and

Aleksandar Birviš

a Hall of Culture — with their forced labor. That indirectly meant that these unbelieving officials recognized their right to be there.

The Gospel has its own way of making itself felt. Conflicts and obstacles only reinforce the news of the Savior and salvation. Let us proclaim the Victor and the victories.

Christ is victorious! Christ reigns! Jesus Christ is King!

(Final reading: Ps. 24:7-10).

Belgrade, 22nd March 1992

I LOVE MISSION

We are talking about mission as work based on God's promise. There are many places in the Scriptures where God promises that His Word will be spread; the Church has its apostolic function, its mission.

A passage from the book of Isaiah comes particularly to mind (60:11):

> *Therefore thy gates shall be open continually;*
> *They shall not be shut day nor night,*
> *That men may bring unto thee the forces of the Gentiles,*
> *And that their kings may be brought.*

This is a word from the Bible. God has spoken it and He will fulfill what He has promised.

Mission is based on faith.

We can base mission on some missionary organization. But we must begin from above. We believe that God promises that His people will be able to take responsibility for all the other nations, and that they will be open to receive them. Such openness will have its consequences. It will be displayed in the very life of the people of God, because it will breathe new stimuli for life into that same people. They will have not only open doors but a special power.

In fact people have lost their way. We see more and more so-called negative definitions (We don't want this! We don't want that!

Aleksandar Birviš

Down with this! Down with that!). Nobody will say what they <u>do</u> want. Where is a man to turn? That is just why the Gospel comes as the only affirmative power that teaches people what they want, whom to turn to and how to show those many nations that the power of God is alive, and that God's promises are being fulfilled and that they need to have a completely different approach to everything that they are so worried about these days. We shouldn't see things from the point of view of men but with God's eyes, and see things as God sees them. He sees nations that still have not heard of Christ, and whose hearts are still closed. He sees us and our doors that were once closed. He sees our apprehension, our inability to take the first step and open ourselves up to great blessings. That is what the Lord is offering us. In this way our faith should become stronger. We pray as the apostles did: Give us faith. Lord, give us faith for missions, for we believe that you are God and that you can do all things.

Mission is a question of love

The Son of God came to the earth out of love towards men. And that is how He motivates us to reach out to those who we did not know and haven't loved. We go to those whom we haven't seen. Our intention is to do good to those who do not do good to us. We rejoice for those who today close themselves up to us, but we must bring them new life whatever happens.

Only life can bring life. The living God has given us eternal life and only those who have eternity can bring eternal life to others. That is the normal consequence of our way of life: every task that is not superficial, and that leaves permanent results, which is not just a desire to be entertained, to enjoy ourselves and to have a good time and which in some way contributes to some additional new life. If

Reflections

somebody at some time in the past erected a drinking fountain for people to drink from, by doing that he made a positive contribution to the lives of those people. There used to be a reservoir in Belgrade between Hotel Moskva and Hotel Balkan which supplied the old parts of the town (Stari Grad and Savamala) with water. Such a system of water pipes was called 'terazije' in Turkish and that name is still used for the central part of Belgrade. The drinking fountain of Terazije was also erected for thirsty people to drink from and to keep people alive. Someone had the desire to give life to those who came after him. The same applies when someone writes a book. The writer makes a contribution to the lives of some of us. Even today we still benefit from people who lived who knows when, and who did something that has an impact on our life today.

In the spiritual life lasting work and values are inspired by a special love. There is a desire for life to go on and be richer. Mission makes life different, it makes it eternal. That was the purpose of Christ's life. He didn't say: "I have come to do miracles", even though He did perform great inimitable miracles. He doesn't say: "I have come to tell you beautiful words", even though He spoke words which totally surpass all literature. What did He say? *I am come that they might have life, and that they might have it more abundantly* (John 10:10).

For this very reason that He came to bring a special unique quality of life, life is of no worth unless it is renewed and multiplies. Christ has left us as heralds of that life. Christianity is the bearer of life in Christ. Christians bring the love of God to all who are prepared to understand and accept the glory of God and His mercy and salvation.

Aleksandar Birviš

Mission is the work of the Holy Spirit

Whose work is mission? We usually talk about great missionaries. But mission is the work of the Holy Spirit. He is at work in the fellowship. He gives believers the inspiration to get up and start witnessing. In the Acts of the Apostles we read that the Holy Spirit told the believers to set apart individuals for service in order to win new souls and new regions for Christ.

Mission is a great work. We must take it seriously. How can we take our part in mission? Should we get involved as a fellowship? Should we get involved individually? Should we give ourselves wholeheartedly?

We say we love God with all our heart, with all our soul, with all our mind and with all our strength. Doesn't that mean that we should love all the things of God and all His works just as fully? We are focused on other people. We must love them. We must feel the same sufferings that they are going through. We must feel the pain of their wounds and share their poverty, and their ignorance of Christ should prompt us and bring us to our senses: men need the news about Christ, about the Savior who loves them and sacrifices Himself for them.

There are many who will live in hell. They go there by rejecting salvation. Can we say about them: "God, I did all I could for them!"? We haven't done everything we can. Each one of us must stop there and think to himself: "What else is there we can do?" Maybe just some little thing. Maybe just forgive them some small thing. Maybe pull back some mental or spiritual curtain that stands as an obstacle between me and my neighbor.

Reflections

The Holy Spirit directs us to examine our own consciences. We have been entrusted with a job, a great shared job to help the Kingdom of God to be established and to function.

We are not alone

The Lord Jesus says that in the world we will have tribulations. We cannot expect that everything will go smoothly just because we have set out on God's path. There will be difficult moments. There will be seemingly insurmountable obstacles. We will think that we can't go any further. We will ask: "Lord, what else can we do?" This was the experience of the prophets and apostles. And all serious-minded Christians will have it too. There will be moments when the people of God will ask: "Lord, I am doing the best I can. Where is that wall? Why won't you let me break through, and why don't you break through it? Why is it in the way? Break it down, Lord! Why are you waiting?"

But Jesus says, *These things I have spoken unto you, that in Me ye might have peace. In the world ye shall have tribulation: but be of good cheer; I have overcome the world* (John 16:33). Don't be afraid. Maybe things aren't going as we would like, but things are working out for the best in accordance with God's plans. God is with us because He loves those who contribute to His glory. We rejoice when we see people thinking about mission, that is, how to proclaim God's word.

Apart from the Lord we have with us many people, some whom we know and some whom we don't. Many who came before us are cooperating with us in their own way. They cleared the way and made it easier for us. With us now are those who will take over from us. The work of God has been going on since the beginning of time. Ours is a task for the long term.

Aleksandar Birviš

The Lord Jesus told a parable of a man who entrusted his wealth to his servants and said, *Occupy till I come* (Luke 19:13). Jesus expects us do business efficiently, professionally and with love. We must increase His wealth. We will see the joy that it will bring us.

★ ★ ★

God's mercy brings us nearer to eternity with each passing moment. Everything that occurs is for His glory. Christians enter into the glorious life when they multiply it.

No one need miss out on the glory of God. Christ came in glory. Christ went away again in glory. Christ will come again in glory. Blessed are those who live in that glory right now.

Final reading: Ps. 67

Belgrade, 25th March 1992

BEFORE THE THRONE AND BEFORE THE LAMB

Fourth Sunday before Easter

Subject: The King and the Kingdom — suffering

Introductory reading: Ps. 103:19-22

Main reading: Rev. 7:9

Great troubles are upon us. Afterwards the world will be peaceful again, and many things will be resolved, but truth-loving and Christ-loving men will not be able to compromise with a world of treachery, self-deceit and lies. The world will become ever more skilful at this, so that many will think they are serving God consciously and wholeheartedly, but they won't really be serving Him.

Where there is less of the Gospel, there are more troubles. The more troubles there are the more martyrs there are too. We mustn't shrink from martyrdom. The Lord has a special place for martyrs in His glory.

After this I beheld, and, lo...

Martyrdom isn't something to boast about. Suffering is not a performance or an opportunity for someone to make a show.

God's criteria are different. He sees even the most well-hidden thoughts and events. All is open before Him. What comes before Him is visible to the angels and the prophets. The Lord quite readily illuminates skillfully perpetrated injustices and troubles. Unspiritual people think they can successfully hide evil and violence through pretense and shrewdness. But that is no good, the Lord can see through it all.

There is little point in trusting in human rights commissions. They are staffed by ordinary people. They may be inspired by noble aspirations. The situation on the ground only partly makes use of those noble intentions. They are ensnared in webs of self-interested and unscrupulous power-hungry men. They use them as far as suits their aims in grasping power.

Christians trust in the Lord who comprehends, sees, knows and understands everything. He shows everyone what troubles are coming and what to expect and when, and what to do at all times, for He says: *Occupy till I come* (Luke 19:13).

A great multitude, which no man could number, of all nations, and kindreds, and people, and tongues…

Martyrs are not in the minority among Christians. There is a large number of them. Each age has those who have laid down their lives for Christ.

Persecutors and their methods come and go. In some cases they are the results of intolerance towards everything that comes from the Lord. Some people are fearful: Christians question some of their supposed values. Others are just not prepared to believe in the living God. That is why the enemies of Christ resort to violence. Satan changes his tactics from day to day, but his aim is the same: to kill men in hell.

Christians don't let themselves be tricked by the evil one's offers of retreating before the world. Victors do not retreat. And so persecution and rejection of Christians goes on. The world cannot bear those whom it cannot compel to hate the Savior or at least to be indifferent towards Christ.

Reflections

Martyrs can be found and always will be found in all nations, nationalities and tribes. Martyrdom doesn't respect national borders, languages or dialects, social structure, or the level of development of the area in which a man lives. There will always be those who persecute and hate, and sow fear and suffering.

This should not alarm us. Let us not lose faith and courage. Our freedom is not threatened just because our service is threatened. The world is showing its true face: horror, hopelessness and violence. There will be trouble and suffering in the world even when it looks attractive. Christians are tolerated, but they are not welcome.

Stood before the throne, and before the Lamb ...

God has found those wretched ones worthy. They have appeared in the presence of God. God is pure and worthy. Nothing could stand before Him. If nothing can stand close to the sun without melting or evaporating, what can it be like in the presence of the one who made not only the sun but also the stars which are much more powerful than the sun.

But martyrdom has enabled the martyrs to stand before the Heavenly throne, that is, before the exalted and incomparable authority of God. How is that possible? We don't know. But we know something else: it is possible for each one to be a martyr and to appear before the Lord. Martyrdom is not a privilege. It is a blessing, a gift of God which overcomes time and space.

The most wonderful thing that can happen to anyone is to appear before the throne of God and before Christ who was sacrificed for the sins of the word. God loved the martyrs so much that He enabled them to have close and direct participation in glory.

Today we appeal to human rights and we are blessed because they do not torture us for Christ's sake. What self deception! Someone or something is always tormenting us. If Christ is in any way the cause

Aleksandar Birviš

of troubles arising in the Christian life, then that too is to a large extent a participation in witnessing if not witnessing itself.

The crucified Christ (the Lamb) is a special honor and blessing for all who glorify the Lord. Martyrdom and witnessing are focused on Christ. Witnessing and preaching must not omit the cross and the resurrection. The good news of Christ is only fruitful when it leads to a life-and-death decision, when it leads through martyrdom to the throne of God.

Clothed with white robes …

The white robes represent righteousness. The martyrs were killed for the sake of justice. They are also justified through the blood of Christ. Suffering and torment are not a badge; they are a part of spiritual growth. Those who are not martyrs needn't be sorry; they needn't feel like second-class Christians. The Lord surely has something prepared for them. If they consciously, willingly and enthusiastically make a stand for the Lord, the task is there, the opponents are ready, but the white robes are ready— the Lord gives justification and access to glory.

Christian righteousness is visible to men and to God.

Men can see what righteousness contributes to society: improved legislation, improved law-enforcement, security of the individual, property and freedom, the implementation of human rights and lack of restriction of personal freedom etc. This includes the reduction of crime and the improvement of the social standing of those who need to be protected. In short: what can be seen is a faultless society (if such a thing exists?) — the aspiration of all men who are not burdened with prejudices and evil (if such people exist?).

God sees something else. The Scriptures declare that in Christ each of us has justification. The precondition is faith in Jesus Christ. We believe that the Savior saves me. My chances of being justified

Reflections

before the Heavenly Father are nil in the light of His perfection and righteousness. But still the Almighty declares me righteous on the basis of Christ's sinlessness. Man does not obtain righteousness before God, he receives it from God.

The martyrs were amongst the first to realize this and in the best possible way. The world does not understand them. They are an enigma to the world: why do they suffer and what do they hope for if God does not immediately deliver them from their torment; why don't they abandon Him? The world forgets — and the same thing happens to some who are weak in faith — that God is not Lord just in the pleasant moments. He is God when the going is tough too, and when it seems that it's all too much to bear.

And palms in their hands …

Palms are a sign of great joy and a greeting to God who is about to appear. The martyrs are welcoming the Victor and so they are not sad. Many of them went off to their deaths singing and praising God. Their suffering could not quench their joy. Heavenly enlightenment doesn't depend on the darkness of this world. It will not be extinguished by cruelty.

What is the nature of the martyr's joy?

It is certain that martyrs are not greedy. They rejoice because they do not receive their reward in return for what they have invested or in accordance with an estimate, but as the Lord decrees. Those who suffer have submitted to God's will, not leaving anything to their own will. And so they have lost nothing, everything is gain and everything serves to increase their joy.

Joy includes uninterrupted serenity. The martyrs were not frivolous, neither were they depressed. Their oppressors and tormentors were furious that they couldn't force the followers of the Gospel to behave and become excited as if they were of the world.

Aleksandar Birviš

No one can accuse Christians of indifference, but likewise no one can impose the mood of this world upon them.

Joy also contains freedom and independence. Martyrs are living proof that there is no true freedom in the world until men are prepared to die rather than to submit to evil. Slavery is not just being in the power of foreign military forces. (Even our own military service is compulsory so there is no freedom there either. It is a great delusion to think that an army can protect freedom. It protects itself, and freedom and peace are by-products of its desire for a comfortable and privileged life). Slavery begins where people least expect, for example, in the free market place: man is so obsessed by the freedom to acquire goods that he becomes a slave of money, mainly the money that he wants to get. And so he imagines that he is liberated and independent, while all the time he is enmeshed in the shackles of still unrealized financial gain. The shackles may be of gold, but they are still shackles and this type of slavery is no less than enemy occupation. (Come to think of, there is no such thing as friendly occupation).

We mustn't think that poverty of itself brings freedom and independence. Even the poor man has his desires. Since he finds it very difficult to fulfill his desires then his slavery is very burdensome. The enemy, the slave driver, not only cannot be seen, he doesn't exist. But such slavery is a reality.

★　★　★

We pray for men and women who are being martyred today. The enemy clearly knows that there is no place for him in the hearts of those who are committed to Christ. That is why he tortures them. Thank God that there are those men and women who suffer for Christ and whose love for Christ is more precious than life itself.

Reflections

In our efforts we must stand up for human rights, and for a world without martyrs. But we mustn't be deceived: not until Christ finally binds Satan will there cease to be martyrs. We struggle in prayer for Christianity to be made up of the right people who are not prepared to compromise.

Christ is coming. We all need pure white robes. We have all been given a branch to wave joyfully. Let us wave it in our prayer meetings. Let us cast off every obstacle. Let us seek the power to live a consistent life of faith.

May the Lord grant us the strength to love those who torture us, and not to seek revenge, but to pray for them. May they too learn the truth about Christ and the truth about themselves, and may they believe for salvation.

Glory to the living God, who lives in heavenly glory, and who saves and guides. He knows the blood of the martyrs and the tears of those who suffer. Let us worship Him, the God who has justified us by faith and given us peace in Him.

Belgrade, 29th March 1992

ETERNAL KING — ETERNAL KINGDOM

Fourth Sunday before Easter
Subject: The King and the Kingdom — suffering

Main Reading: Dan. 4:2-3 (the statement of King Nebuchadnezzar)

I thought it good to shew the signs and wonders that the High God hath wrought toward me. How great are His signs! and how mighty are His wonders! His kingdom is an everlasting kingdom, and His dominion is from generation to generation.

God has for His part always made use of signs and wonders. The words of men are sometimes very poor. Everything we say about God is a poor reflection of the reality. Our words are limited since they are the product of limited men. Men's minds can extend a long way but they cannot reach infinity. Our words spring from our feelings of amazement and wonder before infinity that are never able of full comprehension.

The Apostle Paul says, *For we know in part, and we prophesy in part* (1 Cor. 13:9). We are all incomplete. We would like to be complete and whole, but there is always something missing.

Each one of us is missing something, we have a shortcoming. Some have larger some smaller shortcomings. Likewise, all our knowledge, especially our knowledge of God, is partial and we have to continually add to it, revise it and correct it.

Reflections

This bible study is just part of this process of increasing our knowledge. We started with what God has given us, what He has revealed to others, which they then wrote down in their enthusiasm and transformed into words and music. In this way we have been able to discover God's signs and wonders, so that we can give glory to God and declare His Kingdom.

There are three characteristics of the Kingdom of God that we can recognize in Nebuchadnezzar's statement in the Book of Daniel:

First. The Kingdom of God is powerful. Man needs to think about this. We usually link power with violence. There are no well-intentioned bullies. When we say that something is powerful, we think of violent imposition or compulsion. But God's power is energy (to use a concept from physics), the ability to do work. God does what has not been done; He travels the road that others cannot travel and carries out a task that looks difficult if not impossible. Because of God's omnipotence we should know that His Kingdom cannot be conquered by any other power. It is above all other kingdoms, and does not depend on so-called politics or military might. God is completely independent and no one can impose himself upon Him.

It is difficult for men to believe such a thing. How many demands do we hear today that religious education be taught again in schools! Does God need pupil-power or any other power? Does the minister of education need to tell children to believe? People don't realize how silly they are and how they reduce their faith to the level of something that isn't faith and insults the Almighty. We must realize that God doesn't need people to carry out His plans. Man should be honored to work with God, because the Lord is able to do everything on His own.

The supreme school of wisdom is here, in the Church. This is where we should direct people. In the fellowship of God's children all the blessings of God's love can be received, not only wisdom but

Aleksandar Birviš

the free gift of salvation too. Only in the house of God can peace and joy and God's righteousness in the Holy Spirit be learned.

The Almighty gives us the power to be justified so that we can stand before Him without fear and anxiety and be joyful.

Those are all great gifts which God gives through His power. He gives them on all sides. We just need faith, not great faith, not miracle-working faith, but simple acceptance. We believe in the wonderful truths that are heard here right through the year from one service to another, year after year. Here we receive the special gifts of the Lord's Kingdom.

Second. The Kingdom of God is eternal. The kingdoms of the world are temporary. Men lay down their lives for them. Whole nations are sacrificed for the sake of empires, or even small countries. But countries and nations live and die just like people, just like every other organism. They spring up, make their appearance and then disappear. Only traces remain. Where is Babylon today? In museums. Where is ancient Egypt today? It is just a tourist attraction. Where is our glorious medieval Serbian state? In territory that has now been taken over by other peoples and other nations. At one time it did exist but now it is no more. All sorts of things have happened, now a new thing is taking place. People used to live in a certain way which is no longer the way people live.

But God's Kingdom lasts for ever and ever and will never end. God is king. He rules on His throne from generation to generation. He will not cease to rule. All those who belong to Him will not stop coming before Him to bow down and to live with Him and to remain in His presence.

That is what God's Word teaches us. We need to submit to the requirements of God's will. But in spite of that His Kingdom is not a Kingdom of force. Anyone who wants to and who believes can enter.

Reflections

Anyone can leave whenever he wants. Blessed are those who willingly and of their own free will follow Christ as free individuals, in the desire to please God in that Kingdom just as He teaches them. We can please God by our faith (Heb. 11:6). The person who believes strives for the good things that the Lord offers. Then he does not take account of what the world will say and even less about how the world will behave towards him. The world and the glory of this world pass, but God's glory endures. The Apostle Peter writes, *For all flesh is as grass, and all the glory of man as the flower of grass. The grass withereth, and the flower thereof falleth away: But the word of the Lord endureth for ever. And this is the word which by the gospel is preached unto you* (1 Pet. 1:24-25).

The eternal Kingdom of God is established on the eternal Word of God. These are the important points from this teaching about eternity as it is set out here:

1. In the Kingdom of God there is only one King. There is no other and no one will ever replace Him or depose Him. There is no heir to the throne. There are no other kings that will come to take God's place. The Kingdom is eternal and the King is eternal.

2. The Kingdom is unlimited in space. It does not depend on any borders. Borders are erected by men, or at least men are obliged to recognize the existence of natural borders. God's Kingdom is the only one that will not impose itself upon your will and your faith. There is no need for passports, visas, customs inspections, nor anything else. God accepts you and lets you come to Him.

3. God's Kingdom is a Kingdom of blessed progress. Blessing — doesn't that sound strange? Man does not realize that God's Word is good, and that God fulfills His promises. He is the

Aleksandar Birviš

only one who can keep His promises no matter what the circumstances. That is what He wants.

We stand before that Kingdom. We live in it. For many it is an enigma. But Christ has David's key (Rev. 3:7). He opens the gates of the Kingdom. Everyone can live in that Kingdom.

Third. The Kingdom of God is a Kingdom of the most perfect authority. The word authority is not one that people readily accept. Authority is often abused. There are not many who retain their integrity when they seize power, and there are even fewer rulers who have not seized power by force. Do people realize what authority is? When we say authority we usually mean the police, the courts, the prisons, the army and so on. Men find it difficult to understand what it really means when we say that God rules and has His Kingdom. Why?

Firstly, because we are used to such thinking. No one has ever offered us a more correct or different approach to authority.

Secondly, men also have a very superficial understanding of what God offers us in the Scripture. But the words of Scripture are very unusual. The Lord destroys our habits, for most of them are not in accordance with His will.

Thirdly, God rules because He is irresistibly appealing. He doesn't resort to compulsion or force. His love is perfect, His beauty is perfect, His mercy is perfect, His goodness is perfect, His generosity is perfect. All God's qualities are perfect.

Fourthly, there is no other choice for the Christian man and woman. There is one God. It is a great mistake which leads to all kinds of complications when man rejects the only God, and devises gods of his own, that are very unsuitable and troublesome: people, things, ideas, handiwork, intellectual work — and none of that is God.

Brothers and sisters,

Reflections

We have accepted God's Kingdom. We have made up our minds to receive it. He is our ruler from beginning to end.

There is a question game that Jews play at the end of their ceremonial Passover supper. I will recount it to you just as I heard it in their company:

Number one. Who knows what one is? — I know what one is: Our God who is in heaven is one.

Number two. Who knows what two is? — I know what two is: there are two tablets of the Law. Our God who is in heaven is one.

Number three. Who knows what three is? — I know what three is: There are three patriarchs. There are two tablets of the Law. Our God who is in heaven is one.

And so on up to thirteen. Then someone says:

Number thirteen. Who knows what thirteen is? — I know what thirteen is. Thirteen is the number of God's characteristics. There are twelve tribes of Israel. There are eleven constellations. There are ten Commandments. Nine is the number of months it takes for a baby to be born. Eight is the number of days before a child is circumcised. There are seven days in the week. There are six parts of the Mishna. There are five parts of the Torah. There are four mother patriarchs. There are three patriarchs. There are two tablets of the Law. There is one God who is in heaven".

★ ★ ★

Our God who is in heaven and on earth is one God. He rules, He reigns and He is calling you. Do not remain deaf to His word. Seek His Kingdom. It is the only Kingdom prepared for you; not only to your measure but also to meet all your needs.

Belgrade, 29th March 1992

HOW TO DEEPEN YOUR FAITH

Third Sunday before Easter

Subject: The King and the Kingdom — transformation

Introductory reading:

The law of the LORD *is perfect, converting the soul: the testimony of the* LORD *is sure, making wise the simple. The statutes of the* LORD *are right, rejoicing the heart: the commandment of the* LORD *is pure, enlightening the eyes. The fear of the* LORD *is clean, enduring for ever: the judgments of the* LORD *are true and righteous altogether. More to be desired are they than gold, yea, than much fine gold: sweeter also than honey and the honeycomb. Moreover by them is Thy servant warned: and in keeping of them there is great reward* (Ps. 19:7-11).

Main reading:

And after six days Jesus taketh Peter, James, and John his brother, and bringeth them up into an high mountain apart, And was transfigured before them: and His face did shine as the sun, and His raiment was white as the light. And, behold, there appeared unto them Moses and Elias talking with Him. Then answered Peter, and said unto Jesus, Lord, it is good for us to be here: if Thou wilt, let us make here three tabernacles; one for Thee, and one for Moses, and one for Elias. While he yet spake, behold, a bright cloud overshadowed them: and behold a voice out of the cloud, which said, This is My beloved Son, in whom I am well pleased; hear ye Him. And when the disciples heard it, they fell on their face, and were sore afraid. And Jesus came and touched them, and said, Arise, and be not afraid. And when they had lifted up their eyes, they saw no man, save Jesus only. And as they came down from the mountain, Jesus charged them, saying, Tell the vision to no man, until the Son of Man be risen again from the dead. And His disciples asked Him, saying, Why then say the scribes that Elias must first come? And Jesus answered and said unto them, Elias truly shall first come, and restore all things. But I say unto you, That Elias is come already, and they knew him not, but have done unto him whatsoever they listed. Likewise shall also the Son of Man suffer of them. Then the disciples understood that He spake unto them of John the Baptist (Matt. 17:1-13).

The followers of Christ live by faith. All Christian knowledge is acquired by faith. Faith is a virtue, a force and a precious treasure from heaven.

That is why we need to deepen our faith. Shallow faith is not real faith. Shallowness is not allowed even in worldly matters. Is a doctor allowed to be superficial? Can a builder work carelessly? Superficiality causes harm to the economy, money and goods are lost, the education system deteriorates and traffic accidents happen.

So our faith has even less justification for being superficial. I pray that we will see step by step from the Savior's transfiguration how we can deepen our faith.

Let Christ set us apart. Not every Christian will be privileged to be present at Christ's transfiguration. Some will be expected to be obedient and accept responsibility in one specific area. Others will be given some other work of obedience and responsibility.

Each task requires a certain level of separation. School children are not allowed to copy written work. Each one has to work on his own, as if he is the only person in the world.

God gathers us together in the fellowship of Christ. There we help one another and we minister to God, to one another and to the world. But God makes every effort to get us on our own in order to bring us into His presence. The deepening of our faith is achieved in our shared services and commitment to Christ, but it is above all the fruit of our willingly getting on our own with God. The fellowship brings individuals together with the express purpose of teaching them how to become and remain followers of Christ, how to avoid eternal suffering, and how to set off on the road to blessed eternity.

Christ has certainly set you apart for a specific task. It is good for you to examine how far you have understood your relationship with the Savior and salvation. At the same time that the Lord Jesus called you to be saved He called you to a task. If it is not apostleship, maybe it is prophesying. If it is not prophesying maybe it is teaching, teaching work aimed at building up God's people. If it is not teaching, maybe it is intercessory prayer. In any case it is a specific task. The Son of God sets you apart.

Don't leave out Moses. Shallow faith can hardly wait for a life without responsibility. "We are not under the law," say some Christians, "we are under grace, and we have been pardoned. We don't recognize any law".

Such statements can be backed up by biblical quotations, but there is something missing in them: a readiness to understand and obey God's will. Just as if such people have never prayed: "Your will be done on earth as it is in heaven".

Christians must be reasonable. It is not a question of knowing the commandments, but of knowing what God wants. The Almighty assuredly has His own will and that will must be honored. Our job is to discover all God's demands. Christ also has His commandments. If He is talking to Moses, why should we be intolerant towards him?

Reflections

Faith cannot be deepened without obedience. Shallow faith knows nothing of obedience. The deeper faith is, the greater obedience is and the calmer our behavior.

Pay attention to the prophet Elijah. Prophecy comes from the Lord and is intended for the strengthening of our faith. God raised up prophets when faith declined. Elijah prophesied at a time when idolatry was widespread. He was persecuted, they tried to kill him, and he was pursued by the authorities, so that he had to flee. But the Almighty brought him back in power, and he accomplished the great and awesome work of restoring faith.

Prophecy is an inspired word about God's will and a revelation about God of life. Deeper faith is a deeper knowledge of God. How to bring your life into line with the provisions of God's will is the subject of all our teaching. We also have His voice. God speaks through selected men.

Prophets don't need people to worship them, nor do they need anyone to build a tabernacle or an altar to them. The prophetic word does not come to exalt man. Its first task is to call us to a life in the presence of God. There is no room for momentary enthusiasm. The only thing that is important is to accept and obey God's word.

Elijah confronted the people with a choice. A true prophetic word is unrelenting, incorruptible and unobtrusive. A prophet is a prophet because he cannot resist the impulse he receives from the Lord. But the prophet's words are not words of constraint, but a choice presented to responsible people.

Faith will not deepen without the acceptance of responsibility. Responsible prayer, responsible obedience, responsible speaking, responsible work and responsible relaxation. Christians should examine their consciences every day as they cast off the past and set their sights on the future. Believers don't live by history but history

Aleksandar Birviš

lives by them. Why? Because they have lived responsible lives, and have taught others how to live responsibly.

Obey the Son of God. There is no transfiguration for individuals or fellowships if we don't set our minds to be obedient to Christ. I am shocked to think how little desire there is to study and obey the Christ of the Gospels. The Heavenly Father doesn't talk much about change and success. He talks about love for the Son and obedience. How can people neglect the more important and better thing and dash after the unimportant and evil? It's not that they are ignorant. Many of them have had plenty of time to discover only too well what is waiting for them if they turn from the way of righteousness. But they still fall spiritually, mentally and physically, because knowledge by itself isn't enough.

We honor and obey the Son of God because He is the true God and eternal life. Before Him we are contrite because no one can compare with Him. We receive everything from Him and we are thankful to Him for it all. We are especially thankful for His sacrifice on the cross. We especially think about that in the period coming up to Easter.

The Lord's Supper has special significance on these terms. We are in fellowship with the Savior who has experienced death and victory over death, life and loss of life, the giving of himself and the return of life.

Be careful of words. The Savior charged the disciples not to talk about the glory that they saw during Christ's transfiguration. To witness is not to use many words but to use the right words and to confirm them by deeds. Deep faith is more about being quiet than about talking. Those Christians who realize in time that not all experiences are to be passed on will deepen their faith. May God grant power to each one of us to know when to be quiet as well as

Reflections

giving us the ability to choose the right words. What should we be silent about? We read in Proverbs (25:27): *It is not good to eat much honey: so for men to search their own glory is not glory.* Many people would just love to enjoy the glory of God and to boast about their special knowledge and revelations. We are drawing near the time of Christ's second coming. Our Lord taught us to be patient in the days leading up to His coming. He says, *In your patience possess ye your souls* (Luke 21:19). But the majority of Christians have got heavily involved in research. Instead of patience, vigilance and perseverance, they are obsessed with dates, frightening events and study that do not bring them serenity.

How long should we keep silent? Until the glory appears. When we see Christ and when He draws us to Himself, then we will join the choir of those who celebrate. Then our lips will be opened to speak wondrous things. We will be united in desire, united in joy and united in glorifying God. There is one God and only one glory.

Glory to the one God: Father, Son and Holy Spirit! Amen.

Final reading:

O the depth of the riches both of the wisdom and knowledge of God! how unsearchable are His judgments, and His ways past finding out! For who hath known the mind of the Lord? or who hath been His counsellor? Or who hath first given to Him, and it shall be recompensed unto him again? For of Him, and through Him, and to Him, are all things: to whom be glory for ever. Amen (Rom. 11:33–36).

Belgrade, 5th April 1992

WHO BELONGS TO CHRIST?

It's the fashion today to talk about identity crises. It's something like when a man or a nation doesn't know who they are. There aren't many people who realize that nobody fully knows who they are, for the simple reason that no one can foresee their end.

But not only is it a fruitless exercise to talk about the end, no one is entirely sure about his beginning either. We often meet people (not just young people) who introduce themselves by stating only their first name. Consciously or not they are saying that they are reconciled to the fact that there is much they do not know about their own origins and that many things relating to their identity are a secret.

There is no such thing as an identity crisis for Christians. They know who they are, they know who they are descended from and they know whom they belong to for the future and for eternity. As a contribution to our awareness of our Christian identity I would like to quote an account from the Gospels, taken from Mark's Gospel (3:31–35).

There came then His brethren and His mother, and, standing without, sent unto Him, calling Him. And the multitude sat about Him, and they said unto Him, Behold, Thy mother and Thy brethren without seek for Thee. And He answered them, saying, Who is My mother, or My brethren? And He looked round about on them which sat about Him, and said, Behold My mother and My brethren! For whosoever shall do the will of God, the same is My brother, and My sister, and mother.

These words seem clear enough. It means that the teacher (in this instance the Lord Jesus) was talking specifically and in an easily understood way. The teaching was successful, because more than nineteen and a half centuries later the Teacher has been successful in getting His disciples to understand Him. In order to understand the text better we need to consider some of the background.

Some time before the Lord Jesus spoke these words we find recorded in the same Gospel: *And when His friends heard of it, they went out to lay hold on Him: for they said, He is beside Himself* (Mark 3:21). Christ's relatives thought there was something wrong with Him and that He had gone mad. Were those the same people who now appeared in the company of Jesus' mother? If they weren't the same people, then weren't at least their intentions the same? I have no right to attribute evil intentions to anyone, but neither do I have the right to ignore what the Gospels teach us by attributing good intentions from pure politeness or a desire to give a better impression.

Measures of closeness

There is a story about the Italian composer Verdi who was walking down the street one day when he saw a blind organ grinder. He was performing some tunes from Verdi's operas. The composer stopped him and said:

"My friend, that one should be a little faster. You're playing too slow."

"How do you know, Sir?" asked the organ grinder.

"I ought to, I wrote it. I am Giuseppe Verdi."

Aleksandar Birviš

The blind man started to play a little faster and continued to walk up and down the same street. The next day, when Verdi came by again, he was pleased to hear the blind man playing his tunes at the correct tempo. When he caught up with him the composer stopped in amazement. The organ grinder was carrying a placard which said: "Student of the famous composer Verdi".

In the same way all those who sat and listened to Christ could have boasted that they were the Lord's disciples. The very fact that they were sitting down indicated that it wasn't a political meeting but a teaching session. Such was the custom: the teacher would sit on a chair or tree stump or stone and his disciples would sit at his feet, that is, around him on the floor or grass.

They could all claim to be disciples of Christ. A good number of them really were. We know that His listeners were amazed when the Lord Jesus spoke. As soon as they sat down near Him, they would decide not just to be curious onlookers but to learn something. And so they came closer to Him. Close in terms of space, but close in Spirit too. As they received the Savior's teaching, the people absorbed something, and they all received something in common. The Great Teacher explained the truths about their common Father in heaven. This increased the closeness between Him and His listeners even more.

For their part, Jesus' mother, brothers and sisters based their connection with Christ on family ties. Family ties grant rights of a kind. That is why Jesus' relatives wanted Him to come to them, so that they could stop Him talking to His disciples and make Him see and listen to them instead. We don't know how many of them there were, but it's obvious that they thought they were important enough to make such a demand.

Reflections

Did the Savior pretend not to know them? No. He just demanded that the criteria for closeness be changed. This is not the only place where He spoke about what was more important and what was less important; what was nearer, and what was not as near as people thought.

Fulfilling God's will

According to Christ's words, those who fulfill God's will are the closest to Him. Closeness in space is just ordinary nearness if there is no obedience. Not every listener becomes a disciple. What is required is obedience and not just listening. Relatives can also count on nearness if they do God's will. Family, family ties and other close relationships can be very strong. But those sorts of tie can be broken. Whole tribes have disintegrated - brotherhoods, communes, and many families too. There are whole nations that have disintegrated. Not only have many of the biblical nations disappeared (Assyrians, Acadians, Babylonians, Edomites etc.), but such disintegration of nations has occurred in the not-so-distant past. At one time the Paulicians lived in Romania and Hungary, on both sides of the border separating the two countries, a Slavic people whose language had similar sounds to Macedonian, and words and sentences similar to Bulgarian. They used the Latin alphabet. They probably used to belong to the Paulicians from Asia Minor and the Balkans, from whom the Bogumils got some of their teachings. They got the New Testament in their own language as late as 1927, thanks to an unusually gifted and hard-working teacher of Slovak nationality and an evangelical believer, Jan Horvat. That people no longer exists today. They were not forcibly wiped out, they just died out.

Aleksandar Birviš

For this reason our persistence in fulfilling God's will has a far wider significance than just the welfare of individuals, even their personal salvation. Obedience to God shows us that the criteria of this world, whether noble and lofty or less noble and more mundane, cannot even sustain us as people let alone before God. The key to true identity is belonging to Christ, and not family ties, nationality or religious ceremonies or traditions.

It is interesting to note that the Lord Jesus is not talking here about faith. However this missing element is only lacking superficially speaking. Faith is a vital factor without which it is impossible to imagine the events of the gospel. In several earlier accounts the Gospel writer Mark tells us that not only do people believe but that evil spirits do too. We are talking about true faith, which can only be realised through obedience. What good is it to Satan that he knows better than most of the human race who Christ is when he refuses to obey the Lord? God sets out His demands, and true disciples are those who conscientiously meet those demands not because they are compelled to but because they are excited about their Savior.

What sort of man do God's requirements demand? God's demands require a person who will fulfill those demands personally, who will be fully committed to those demands and for whom they will become an on-going part of his experience.

The fulfillment of God's demands is *personal*. When I am obedient to the Lord, it is me doing it. I don't need any deputies or mediators. I don't look at others, and above all I don't use the imperfections, shortcomings and failures of others as an excuse. Others may try to convince me not to go over the top but to live as the world lives, but that is what I want to avoid and I am looking for those who believe that if they are not the best they can be before God, they will not be good enough. The Lord does not seek more, He just seeks me.

180

Reflections

The fulfillment of God's demand is *comprehensive*. God's will does not just grip my spirit or my soul or my body. It is with all my being that I fulfill what God wants. I am certain that when the Almighty wants something that is His full and rounded will. The fulfillment of His will is the best thing that has been given to me. That is why I submit to Him in that way. His will isn't something that relates just to our behavior and conduct towards God. It relates to computing and building and commerce and medicine and, of course, to the study of the Scriptures and prayer. There is no area of life where the will of the Almighty is superfluous. That is why the man of Christ continually endeavors to discover God's will and rejoices at every opportunity to fulfill it.

The fulfillment of God's demands is *experiential*. Life from above – that is, life according to God's will and inspiration – is not just a story. Rebirth and radical changes in a man's life have to be experienced and men live in them continually and consistently only if they want to. This experience leads us into new experiences. The consecrated life begins. The will of God demands separation from worldliness and the cultivation of spirituality. Sin attacks us from all sides but it does not defeat us. The Lord wins the victory and that is one more experience in the life of every faithful believer. Experiences become truer and more real. Just as a workman does his job better and better if he works to the best of his ability every day, so the spiritual man comes a step closer to God every day if he truly takes that step in the best possible way. The ultimate experience is when God's glory comes. Every Christian man or woman may become worthy of that experience if he or she fulfills God's will in a worthy manner. Of course this requires patience and consistency. God's glory is not available to order.

Aleksandar Birviš

Authentic belonging

By serving Christ we reestablish our shattered and lost identity. By fulfilling God's will we become Christ's. We know whose we are. By living a consistent life in conformity to God's will we continue to belong to Christ. Our allegiance to the Savior will not be lost. There is no danger that we won't know whose we are.

Whole-hearted fulfillment of God's will does not depend on external factors, just as it does not depend on temporary factors (thoughts and feelings). It cannot be achieved by our possessions or our servants. The most important factor in man is the will. We must want what the Lord wants. The Lord Jesus teaches us that. Whoever wants to can become a brother or sister of Christ permanently and without hindrance. God has so ordained and arranged things that His plans will be fulfilled. He is waiting for the other side to make up his mind. The other side of the agreement and covenant is man. Will man recognise the role he has to play?

CHRIST HAS RISEN FROM THE DEAD!

Easter

(1 Cor. 15:20-28)

Christ has risen from the dead!

Let every atom, every molecule, ever mineral, every grain of sand, rejoice. May the plowed land and the soil shout for joy. Let the unfertile, weed-infested land, covered with thorns and brambles, exclaim. Let the stony and sandy wastes, the glaciers and eternal snows, the polar ice and the jagged mountain summits, roar and resound. The rule of the corruptible has ceased, the hope of the incorruptible has been revealed.

Christ has risen from the dead!

Let all the water, water vapor, every liquid and every gas, wherever they are, rejoice. Let the running waters shout: the springs, streamlets, streams, rivulets, rivers great and small, the mighty seas, and the raging torrents. Let the rains, the showers, the mists and fogs exclaim. Let the snows, the hail, the hoar frost, blizzards and snow-storms, the drizzle and the scattered snow-flakes, roar and resound. Christ is preparing a new age where there will be no grief and no destruction. The risen Savior has overcome the natural limitations and has regenerated nature. A time is coming when there will be no more floods, as the glass sea awaits us.

Christ has risen from the dead!

Aleksandar Birviš

Let every blade of grass and every flower-head, from the heights of the mountains to the deepest depths, rejoice. May they spring into life and burst into flower. Let the flowers, both large and small, multi-colored and single-colored, bright and pale, shout out. Let the prickly plants and the wild barley exclaim, no one will rebuke them or despise them. The Savior is ushering in a time – eternity – when nothing and no one will upset anything or anyone else. Let the thistles and ferns, vines and fruit trees, climbing plants and upright trees, deciduous and evergreen, scrub and forests, solitary trees and bushes, rustle, roar and resound, for God is already giving them special voices to praise the Lamb who was slain and sacrificed from the beginning of the world. All things bow down to Christ and all will bow down to Him because of the advent of the new creation and new life and because of the new brightness that is dawning: after the resurrection of the dead, plants will no longer wither, nor die from drought, or rot from damp, for there will be no more death.

Christ has risen from the dead!

Let the ants and ladybirds and all creatures that swarm on the ground, through the leaves, tree stumps, rubbish heaps, over or under clumps of grass, rejoice. Let all the little creatures that dwell, unnoticed and unobserved, in the depths of the caves and mine shafts, shout out. Let the fish and birds, and all that flies, jumps, swims, dives and hovers both in the water as well as in the air, rejoice. Let all the dumb reptiles and hissing snakes, large and small amphibians and the other creatures that live with them, amoeba and protozoa, shout for joy. They are not without a voice. Their voice is incomprehensible today because it doesn't reach our human senses, but one day they will become approachable and no one will find them repulsive. Let many bugs and butterflies, caterpillars and larvae, metamorphosed or not, beetles with hard wings, with soft wings and with no wings at

Reflections

all, worms and slugs, snails and crabs, roar and resound even if they are hidden and inaudible. The Savior will rescue them and save them when He transforms nature.

Christ has risen from the dead!

Let all the creatures both large and small in the fields, woods and deserts, in the mountains, in the valleys and under the valleys, rejoice. Let all the wild and domestic animals, man's friends, companions and fellow sufferers, pets and enemies, that are nevertheless always lively and interesting, resourceful and attractive, shout for joy. Let the overabundant and common breeds, as well as the rare and threatened varieties cry, roar, howl and resound, for the days are coming when their cries and howls will no longer be discordant. Everything that is alive will have a song and its own music and all will rejoice at the harmony of the composition and the bright sounds and colors.

Christ has risen from the dead!

Let men be glad. Easter is joy. Every man, woman and child should rejoice at it. Let the inhabitants of the North Pole and the South Pole and every meridian shout. Let forgetful, polluted, aging Europe be glad, for Christ has made her the leading continent and led her a step further forward than the rest of the world. Let both Americas shout for joy, for if it were not for the Christian spirit of enterprise we might not know about them even today. Let Asia and Africa resound, for we all arose from their voices, and from them came fire, literacy, the decimal system, the basis of technology and science. Let Australia be joyful and New Zealand too, and let the numerous islands in all the oceans be glad. They were the last to be discovered, but they will not be last when the Word of the Lord wakes those who have long ago passed away. People are the special love of the Almighty. That is why He has given them the right to resurrection and eternal life. Because of them He is restoring

Aleksandar Birviš

incorruptibility to nature. He Himself raises up in men the awareness of eternal glory in which the new creation will be included.

Christ has truly risen from the dead!

For your sake and for your salvation He suffered torture, death and the grave. But He also rose again for your sake. What should you do at this solemn time?

First. Thank the Lord for all He has done and is doing for you, your neighbors and acquaintances and the whole human race. Thank Him too for what He is going to do.

Second. Ask the Lord to give you the true joy of the resurrection, the true commitment of the resurrection life and true life in the risen Christ. Christ is our life and only through Him will we come to that life of perfection in eternity.

Third. Promise that you will never neglect anything that the risen Christ has taught you. Tell it to others so that they too can march into eternity without being hindered by evil, superstition or lack of faith.

Fourthly. Acknowledge your doubts, lack of faith and ignorance of true life with God. Lose yourself in an examination of your own spiritual treasure-house, and see what you are missing and obey God's advice. The Holy Spirit will give you the right word and the right course of action at the right time.

Fifth. Don't miss an opportunity to glorify God. It isn't Easter just today. Easter is every day for as long as you live, provided that you live in accordance with God's will.

Christ is alive!

The resurrection began with Him, and continues with you and on into eternity. Amen.

Reflections

Let us pray.

> Glory to Christ, the risen Lord,
> The most righteous and undisputed One,
> The Alpha and Omega of all that we have learned
> and all that we know not,
> and all that cannot be known.
> Christ, You are Lord, King and God,
> None can be compared with You.
> The darkness fled before You,
> Death fell back and the devils fled
> Everything will pass, but You remain
> Reigning on Your throne.
> I am unworthy to appear before You,
> But I believe in Your resurrection power,
> And know that You will renew me and all of us
> to a victorious life in glory.
> And so we praise You, worship You and exalt You
> As we bow down to Your Holy name:
> The one God –
> Father, Son and Holy Spirit.
> Amen.

Belgrade, 26th April 1992

BREAD FROM HEAVEN

First Sunday after Easter
Subject: Bread of life

Introductory reading: John 6:25-53
Main reading: Ex. 16:11-18

Meditation for the Lord's Supper

As the Israelites were traveling through the wilderness, they came across a strange dew. How can you have dew when there is not even any water? They didn't have time to think about that. Events were moving ahead, things were happening much faster than they had time to think about them.

The dew evaporated. But something even more puzzling was left. There was something small, white, round, similar to hoarfrost, like coriander seeds, and sweet like cakes made with honey.

The questions came thick and fast. What was it? (In ancient Hebrew the word is "Man hu" — the origin of the word manna). They didn't know what it was. The question remained in the air. Yet somehow it took root in the language and a special word for it was adopted.

God did not leave His people without an answer. He inspired Moses. He made the unclear clear. We learn from Moses' answer that it was heavenly bread. It was given by the Lord so that the Jews

Reflections

would have something to eat in the wilderness. It lasted until they entered the Promised Land and began to feed on the fruit of the land.

The second interesting thing here is that they didn't have to plant and cultivate the manna. They just had to gather it. Thirdly, the manna was given in equal quantities for each person. Fourthly: the people had to gather it according to set rules. They weren't complicated rules, but they were strict. Whoever infringed the rules incurred God's wrath. Additionally, they kept some manna in a pot in remembrance. It stood in the Ark of the Covenant in the Holy of Holies. Why? Because the rule had been established that the Israelites should remember what God had done for them.

Let's examine all this in relation to Christ.

Day dawned on the human race when the Lord Jesus came to the world. An amazing day dawned. The prophets had already foretold the events. The people were amazed and asked for an explanation. The shepherds said, *Let us now go even unto Bethlehem, and see this thing which is come to pass, which the Lord hath made known unto us* (Luke 2:15). But events unfolded quicker than men could think. Everything was well-known. The official court interpreters knew where Jesus was to be born. But it was not yet time for all to be revealed. Something had to happen first. Something new.

And that something did happen. Jesus proclaimed that He was the bread of life (John 6:47-51). Those who were present did not understand. They wondered: What does He mean "bread of life"? All bread gives life. The question should have been phrased differently: Who is the bread of life? Jesus' answer was: *I am that bread of life*. In that case the next question should have been: Who is this Jesus? What sort of food is He?

The Lord Jesus is speaking in illustrations, but His language nevertheless illustrates reality. Each picture, each sign, each word, has

Aleksandar Birviš

a corresponding meaning in everyday life. Food is essential in order for life to be sustained, and for organisms to function. We know that when our body is in order then our spiritual life is also stable. Spirit, soul and body are connected. We can't say: "I am spiritual so I will live without physical life." Physical food affects the soul and the spirit. Conversely, Christ is food for the spirit, but He also maintains our souls and our bodies.

Christ is food for every Christian. He is first and foremost the food which enables our Spirit to live. In practical terms that life begins with prayer and repentance. The Savior explains Himself. He is able to lead us from prayer and repentance up to and into eternity itself.

The Lord's sacrifice on Calvary has cosmic significance. The Lord Jesus transformed that sacrifice into a reality that no one can remain indifferent to. He talks about Himself as food on the basis of specific life accomplishments.

First: Christ is the Son of God and He will be our food for the future and into eternity.

Second: we have done nothing for Christ. He freely makes Himself available to all. We just need to receive and accept Him. That is something we do every day. Each prayer is in fact a receiving of heavenly food.

Third: the Savior has not delivered some people more than others. His gift is full salvation, just like with the manna, which was sufficient for all.

Fourth: we must come to Christ according to certain rules. Whoever does not keep those rules will incur the Lord's wrath.

Fifth: just as some of the manna was left in remembrance, so Christ is the eternal God and we must always remember Him.

Reflections

Part of that remembrance is the Lord's Supper. It is an amazing meal. It is not like ordinary meals. The bread and the wine are present with their special significance. While we meditate on the significance of the bread and wine, pictures of Christ's sufferings and torment appear before us. We ask: Lord, why did You suffer? The answer is not a riddle. But it is a mystery. My sin took the Lord Jesus to the cross. We ask again, being simple people: Couldn't it have been done another way? Did He have to go through such suffering? But let us try and keep our eyes on Christ instead of asking all these questions. Look to Him and you will be saved. Christ was, in fact, one of many whom the Roman authorities crucified on a cross, but His was the only sacrifice that was holy and redemptive. That is the answer that saves. Christ is food.

In conclusion:

First: the Lord's Supper was established by God. It will continue until the Savior comes again, that is, until we enter the promised Heavenly Kingdom.

Second: we don't look on the Lord's Supper as the fruit of the farmer's or vine grower's labor. We don't have to work for it, but we have to receive it regularly in purity, decency and simplicity.

Third: The Lord's Supper is not bread for our hunger and wine for our thirst. The small, approximately equal amount that we take meets our various needs, which differ greatly and are far from equal. Christ meets every one of your needs through that same small piece of bread and that same mouthful of wine.

Fourth: The Lord's Supper must be taken according to certain rules and on God's terms. Whoever does not adhere to God's will is subject to the wrath of the Almighty. The Apostle Paul says, *For he that eateth and drinketh unworthily, eateth and drinketh damnation to himself, not discerning the Lord's body* (1 Cor. 11:29).

Aleksandar Birviš

Fifth and finally: The Lord's Supper is a wonderful and precious remembrance for us. No one has the right to take that remembrance from us or to change it. Each one of us takes part in that act of remembrance without hesitation and doubt.

And each one of us has the same rights to take part and to be exceptionally grateful.

Final reading: Ps. 78:23-25

Belgrade, 3rd May 1992

CHRIST — THE GOOD SHEPHERD

Second Sunday after Easter:
Subject: The Good Shepherd

Introductory reading:

I am the good shepherd: the good shepherd giveth His life for the sheep. But he that is an hireling, and not the shepherd, whose own the sheep are not, seeth the wolf coming, and leaveth the sheep, and fleeth: and the wolf catcheth them, and scattereth the sheep. The hireling fleeth, because he is an hireling, and careth not for the sheep. I am the good shepherd, and know My sheep, and am known of Mine. As the Father knoweth Me, even so know I the Father: and I lay down My life for the sheep. And other sheep I have, which are not of this fold: them also I must bring, and they shall hear My voice; and there shall be one fold, and one shepherd. Therefore doth My Father love Me, because I lay down My life, that I might take it again. No man taketh it from Me, but I lay it down of Myself. I have power to lay it down, and I have power to take it again. This commandment have I received of My Father (John 10:11-18).

Main reading:

A Psalm of David.

The Lord is my shepherd;
I shall not want.

Aleksandar Birviš

He maketh me to lie down in green pastures:
He leadeth me beside the still waters.
He restoreth my soul:
He leadeth me in the paths of righteousness for His name's sake.
Yea, though I walk through the valley of the shadow of death,
I will fear no evil: for Thou art with me;
Thy rod and Thy staff they comfort me.
Thou preparest a table before me
In the presence of mine enemies:
Thou anointest my head with oil;
My cup runneth over.
Surely goodness and mercy
Shall follow me all the days of my life:
And I will dwell in the house of the LORD *for ever*
(Psalm 23)

What do I expect from the Good Shepherd?

I expect from the Good Shepherd that I shall want nothing. He gives me all I need. I also expect Him to provide refreshment, so that my life does not become stagnant. His refreshment is not unrest. So I expect the Shepherd to give me calmness.

My life is pulled in all directions. The Shepherd will restore my soul.

The Good Shepherd will lead me in the path of righteousness no matter what this world of injustice declares to be righteousness. He will release me from the little things that compromise my Christian integrity.

Reflections

The Good Shepherd takes away fear by His presence. He will enable me to stand before my enemies, without fear. He is here, while fear is over there somewhere.

I expect the Shepherd to provide me with order and government. That is the meaning of the rod and staff in the Psalm that we just read.

Naturally I expect the Good Shepherd to defeat and subjugate my enemies. Where enemies raise their heads, the shepherd has not done his job properly.

The Shepherd will give the anointing, by adding to my outpouring of joy and spiritual mercy. He pours out His abundance on me, from the cup that runs over. He will bless me with His special blessing and continue to bless with mercy which is new every morning.

But the expectations of Christians do not stop there. Each one of us has the right to hope. Christians hope for eternal life in the presence of the Lord and a long blessed life both in heaven and on the earth. The Shepherd contributes to this in two basic ways: (a) by explaining and demonstrating life and eternity, on the basis of the revealed truths of God, and (b) through prayers, life and sharing in His sufferings.

Christ has fulfilled all our expectations

1. Salvation in Christ is perfect salvation. In Christ nothing is lacking. Neither is there anything lacking in the work of Christ. Justification in Christ is perfect justification. No one can make any objection to His justice. Sanctification in Christ is faultless sanctification. Only in the Lord Jesus is it possible to live a true and perfect spiritual life. He is the only one who leads into perfect glory, and only He can maintain

Aleksandar Birviš

and keep us in that glory. He is holy and glorious and so places His holiness and glory in us.

2. As a Shepherd, Christ is always new. He gives refreshment. With Him and in Him we have continual spiritual renewal. The Savior is never boring. Preachers can sometimes become boring. And so people just stop caring and are not renewed. But where the Holy Spirit is, everything is dynamic and mysterious as if blowing in the wind (John 3:8).

3. The only true peace is found in Christ. The Scriptures say of Him, *For He is our peace... for to make in Himself of twain one new man, so making peace* (Eph. 2:14-15). That peace is both peace with God and peace with men and peace with ourselves. Christ radiates peace. All true serenity originates from that peace.

4. Christ restores life. Sin is the destroyer of life. The Savior came that each of His followers might have a special kind of life. The Lord Jesus gave the meaning for His coming, His purpose, as: *I am come that they might have life, and that they might have it more abundantly* (John 10:10).

5. Christ leads along the narrow way. He says, *Enter ye in at the strait gate: for wide is the gate, and broad is the way, that leadeth to destruction, and many there be which go in thereat: Because strait is the gate, and narrow is the way, which leadeth unto life, and few there be that find it* (Matt. 7:13-14).

Righteousness is the main precondition for such a life. That is why the Shepherd draws our attention to what is of prime importance for our life: *But seek ye first the kingdom of God, and His righteousness; and all these things shall be added unto you* (Matt. 6:33). Where there is no righteousness there is no Kingdom.

Reflections

6. Christ releases from fear. He often greeted people with the words, "Fear not!" Christians need not fear for their church. It is small, but it is in accordance with God's will (Luke 12:32). The Savior promised that He would never leave His own. He will be with them to the end of time (Matt. 28:20). That was His promise and we believe Him. It can happen that our faith fluctuates because we are mere mortals and susceptible to all kind of weaknesses, or even fear. But the will of the Father remains. The Father wants us to exist as a Church to live and overcome the world. The local church is small and under attack, but it belongs to Christ.

7. There is no need to fear because the Scriptures bear witness that the Lord Jesus is the Almighty. John writes in Revelation, *I am Alpha and Omega, the Beginning and the Ending, saith the Lord, which is, and which was, and which is to come, the Almighty* (Rev. 1:8). Christ's order of things is the best. It is intended for all men. Our Shepherd is both King and Ruler at the head of the most exalted Kingdom. The Savior is in perfect control. Only the Lord knows what is right and carries it out. In Christ we have the lamb who is Lord of Lords and King of Kings (Rev. 17:14).

8. Satan fell like lightning before Christ. The Lord Jesus saw it and bore witness to it (Luke 10:18). The Savior is the victor. Let us praise Him as the victor, as the One who has defeated the evil one. He has humbled Satan and all the evil spirits, for all demons love to boast, but Satan has nothing to be proud of since the death and resurrection of our Savior. Satan was the first to lose out at Calvary.

9. The Lord Jesus asked the Father to give the Holy Spirit to His disciples. The Holy Spirit has come to dwell in Christians. He

is the sure promise of Christ Himself (John 14:16-17). Even the poorest Christians have become a nation of plenty, also according to the Savior's promise. (John 7:37-39).

10. We receive abundance from Christ. The Apostle Paul explains this using the example of the church in Corinth, *Moreover, brethren, we do you to wit of the grace of God bestowed on the churches of Macedonia; How that in a great trial of affliction the abundance of their joy and their deep poverty abounded unto the riches of their liberality. For to their power, I bear record, yea, and beyond their power they were willing of themselves; Praying us with much intreaty that we would receive the gift, and take upon us the fellowship of the ministering to the saints. And this they did, not as we hoped, but first gave their own selves to the Lord, and unto us by the will of God. Insomuch that we desired Titus, that as he had begun, so he would also finish in you the same grace also* (2 Cor. 8:1-6). Christ will not stop giving us every good thing (grace). Men are sometimes ungrateful and dissatisfied. But the Lord still gives His gifts.

11. Our Shepherd is good. He gives us His goodness. It is passed on to the people of God and it multiplies in us. Whenever we look on someone in trouble, when we ourselves are set free and we help others to find that freedom, we pass on God's goodness to others. We do it because we are aware of the role that God's goodness has had in our lives and salvation: none of us could stand before God if he were not made acceptable by the Savior's goodness.

12. The Shepherd is our Savior. He has delivered us. He promises that goodness and mercy will follow us. Salvation will follow us, because evil has never saved anyone. Saving goodness has been revealed in Christ. We look on Christ's sufferings as an

Reflections

expression of the love of the good Father. On the other hand, the cross of Calvary shows the impotence of human evil. The Savior is good in and of Himself. No one can impute any evil to Him. We remember that at Christ's trial, Pilate demanded they cite at least one of the Savior's evil deeds. But His accusers could only shout. *And they were instant with loud voices, requiring that He might be crucified. And the voices of them and of the chief priests prevailed* (Luke 23:23). We all know that there were no good reasons for Christ to be put to death (John 10:32).

13. The Lord Jesus is preparing eternal homes for His disciples at this very moment. The Son of God Himself says: *In My Father's house are many mansions: if it were not so, I would have told you. I go to prepare a place for you. And if I go and prepare a place for you, I will come again, and receive you unto Myself; that where I am, there ye may be also* (John 14:2-3). This is Christ's promise and this is the work of our Shepherd. Only He can do it. The works of men, their achievements and effort cannot do it.

14. The Shepherd promises undisturbed and unending life in the Lord's house. Salvation is eternal salvation, and not just a temporary deliverance. Christ is the eternal Savior and our obligations towards Him are eternal obligations. Let us not fear the times in which we live. All of time and the whole of eternity belong to Christ.

The Shepherd — our confidence

Our confidence in Christ is never brought into question. He leads us and He is the only reliable guide.

Aleksandar Birviš

One of my friends used to believe in reincarnation. That was the dominant religion in his country. When he heard the Gospel, he was so excited, and he repented, turned to God and joined the Church. But he was still worried about the question of the meaning of life: if there are no new and better incarnations, he thought— what is the point of life? As he was reading the Psalm about the Good Shepherd he remembered his people who were cattle breeders. Suddenly the thought came to him: "I have someone who leads me faultlessly. Christ will surely lead me to the true understanding of the truth. It is my duty and my aim in life to praise God." And so he continued. Being set free from the baggage of his old life he was able to fulfill the purpose of life: to praise God and to serve Him in all that He asks.

Final reading: Psalm 89:1-14

Belgrade, 10th May 1992.

WRITTEN IN THE BOOK OF LIFE

Third Sunday after Easter
Subject: The Resurrection and the Life

Introductory reading: 1 Cor. 15:19-24
Main Reading: Rev. 20:11-15

God has His own books, and His own way of recording our works, desires and feelings. He also records the way He will reward us for it all. This record is directly linked with the resurrection.

The resurrection is directly linked with the Book of Life. The dead will rise up. How it will happen is recorded in detail. Everything will come before God's judgment seat. Everything will come because everything will be resurrected with full awareness of what has happened and what there is to answer for. Take the apostle Paul for example: he forgot the things he could boast of, but not the things that he was indebted to others for. (Worldly people have it all the wrong way round. They would like their good deeds to be remembered, but they are very quick in forgetting their mistakes and oversights). The Lord Jesus says, *Verily, verily, I say unto you, The hour is coming, and now is, when the dead shall hear the voice of the Son of God: and they that hear shall live. For as the Father hath life in Himself; so hath He given to the Son to have life in Himself; And hath given Him authority to execute judgment also, because He is the Son of Man. Marvel not at this: for the hour is coming, in the which all that are in the graves shall hear His*

Aleksandar Birviš

voice, *And shall come forth; they that have done good, unto the resurrection of life; and they that have done evil, unto the resurrection of damnation* (John 5:25-29).

We eagerly await that time. We should be looking forward to it, if we have spent all our time as we should have, if we have settled all our business with Christ in time, and if all our personal relationships are in order.

Christ raises the dead. He has the authority and the judgment. He doesn't talk about changing governments but about changing people. A completely different judge has appeared, a completely different representative of authority with completely different attitudes from the usual ones. He will come and bring the dead to life by the power of His voice. Then He will judge. His judgment is the final judgment. There is no appeal, just the second death, the lake of fire into which death and hell will be thrown. The scriptures use the language of pictures, but behind every picture there is a specific meaning, a definite reality. We must consider that reality, because the Savior is the one who keeps the heavenly books. He rejoices over those whose names are written in the Book of Life. He urges His followers to have that same joy. When His disciples went out among the people, healing and performing miracles, they were certainly joyful. They came back full of excitement and explained how the evil spirits had submitted to them. Then the Savior replied to them, *I beheld Satan as lightning fall from heaven. Behold, I give unto you power to tread on serpents and scorpions, and over all the power of the enemy: and nothing shall by any means hurt you. Notwithstanding in this rejoice not, that the spirits are subject unto you; but rather rejoice, because your names are written in heaven* (Luke 10:18-20).

Today we rejoice at every advance of the Gospel and every breakthrough against the powers of darkness, and so we should. But

Reflections

that is not the most important thing in life. The most important thing is that the names of men and women who live and work with the Savior are written in the heavens. That is a greater thing than working miracles, greater than victory over evil spirits, because it is a sign of a guaranteed eternal life.

Whoever believes in Christ and follows Him is recorded in heaven, in the Book of Eternal Life. Everyone would like to be in the lists of the privileged, but the Book of Life isn't just an ordinary piece of paper, it is God's record. As the people of God we are happy that the record has been kept. Jesus has written us in it with His blood and is still doing so. His blood redeems and it has the power to accomplish all things.

The Apostle Paul explains who the people are whose names are recorded in the Book of Eternal Life in a special way. He writes, *And I intreat thee also, true yokefellow, help those women which laboured with me in the gospel, with Clement also, and with other my fellowlabourers, whose names are in the Book of Life* (Phil. 4:3). Who is the apostle talking about? He is talking about real friends who are prepared to lay down their lives for the Gospel. This is what we should encourage: true discipleship, true fellowship, friendship in the unspoilt meaning of that word.

The apostle mentions his helpers or co-workers. The Book of Life records work done in the service of the Good News in cooperation with others. God has given the Good News. It is spreading throughout the world. All such works of cooperation are recorded in the Book of Life. All other types of assistance are recorded too. When Paul and Clement came to the Greek part of the Balkan Peninsula, those courageous apostles met with stiff opposition. But they also encountered people who helped them carry out their mission. All

Aleksandar Birviš

such support is a visible expression of the invisible record in the Book of Life.

Our moral and material responsibilities extend to our feelings as well. We help one another in this way too. How? By our ability to take an interest in both our own salvation and that of those around us. As the Word says, *Or despisest thou the riches of His goodness and forbearance and longsuffering; not knowing that the goodness of God leadeth thee to repentance? But after thy hardness and impenitent heart treasurest up unto thyself wrath against the day of wrath and revelation of the righteous judgment of God; Who will render to every man according to his deeds* (Rom. 2:4-6). Let us help each other not to become hard of heart, and insensitive to God's goodness, patience, and judgment. Let us seek the glory of God no matter what we may have to go through. Let us find out what we will stand for: for destruction and shame or for the glory of God, for the honor of the work of the Lord, for incorruptibility.

Eternal life is a great gift. Blessed are those whose names are written in the Book of Life.

Final reading: Ps. 115:9-18

Belgrade, 17th May 1992

BROTHERS AND DISCIPLES

Third Sunday after Easter:
Subject (extra to the normal schedule): Putting things in order

Main reading:

But be not ye called Rabbi: for One is your Master, even Christ; and all ye are brethren. And call no man your father upon the earth: for One is your Father, which is in heaven. Neither be ye called masters: for One is your Master, even Christ. But he that is greatest among you shall be your servant (Matt. 23:8-11).

The Jews had a specific class of people who were responsible for their spiritual state and who had the task of making known the truths of God. These were the rabbis. The word rabbi is similar to the word for a teacher. But in the Jewish world of that time and of today the rabbi was not just a teacher, he was a man with a whole range of jobs. He had to be prepared to teach people about all sorts of things, and to work with them, and especially to encourage the knowledge of God and the truths of God.

God then has given some people a special task of revelation, or of opening up revelation and instructing people in it. The task of the rabbi was to always be amongst the people, to organize things and apply these revelations to life.

Aleksandar Birviš

Over the course of time the rabbis forgot what their real task was, and were more and more attracted by the honor that the people wrongly afforded them by expecting them to be something like pagan priests: mediators between God and men. That is why the Lord Jesus speaks out against this kind of honor and this kind of role.

Christ is our true rabbi. The mode of address is not important. A true rabbi is one who cooperates with God and with the people of God. He is prepared to give of his utmost to contribute to brotherhood between the followers of God. Christians are all brothers and Christ teaches them how to remain such in everyday life. All that the Lord reveals to our brethren, everything they discover, everything they apply in specific circumstances, this they share with others and help them to come to a saving knowledge. There are no such things as private revelations — they all belong to the people of God. Every Christian man or woman has something that they can use to help others and they must make it available to their brothers and sisters.

The Savior expands the truths that He is teaching to encompass the Father. *And call no man your father upon the earth: for One is your Father, which is in heaven.* We are all sons of the heavenly Father and therefore brothers one of another. That is a great privilege of being a Christian: Christians know their true Father. There are other monotheistic religions which do not know about the Heavenly Father. The Jews are only vaguely aware that God is their Father, whereas Muslims do not have that understanding at all. They quote the 99 beautiful names of God, as set out in the Koran, but the word Father is not among them.

On the other hand the title Father has become a sign of respect among many people. The Jews had this too. So we find disciples of the prophets who called their teacher and prophet, My Father! (2 Ki. 2:12; 13:14).

Reflections

The Lord Jesus puts it differently. There is only one Father in heaven, nobody else has the right to that name. Why? Because even the oldest men, the best educated, most authoritative and reliable cannot lay claim to having even a general revelation. They can make revelation known to us, and show us beautiful things. But the things that are direct and most meaningful come from the Father in heaven. He sent us His Son in whom is all the fullness of the Godhead, so that we can experience the fullness of revelation here on earth. Whenever we think about revelation we must think about Christ through whom God has revealed Himself. Men are just helpers and co-workers. They are the agents of good works. In no way does man alone reveal God; only the Holy Spirit does that.

The Savior continues, *Neither be ye called masters: for One is your Master, even Christ.* The ministry of teaching is respected among Christians. The highest levels of education and instruction have been reached in the Christian world. Everyone tries to copy Christian education.

The Lord Jesus said on one occasion, *Ye call Me Master and Lord: and ye say well; for so I am* (John 13:13). He Himself is the supreme teacher, the role model for all education.

Not many people know that in the ideal teaching situation teachers learn as much from their pupils as pupils learn from their teachers — and we all learn from Christ. Jesus exhibited a special aspect of the science of teaching. Later on Protestant teachers developed it and gave it to the world.

Study has become a way of life. That is why study meets with opposition. We need to acquire the habit: a student can't manage without a teacher, nor without books, nor without pondering and processing what he has learnt. In our situation that is primarily the study of the Scriptures and the understanding of what they give us.

Aleksandar Birviš

At the same time we and our teachers are brothers; titles and positions become insignificant. We get university degrees for ourselves, but we use our knowledge for the benefit of our neighbors.

The Lord promised through the prophet, *And they shall teach no more every man his neighbour, and every man his brother, saying, Know the LORD: for they shall all know Me, from the least of them unto the greatest of them, saith the LORD: for I will forgive their iniquity, and I will remember their sin no more* (Jer. 31:34). This is not talking about abolishing teaching and discipleship, it just means that the need for people is reduced and the need for the Lord is increased. That is what John the Baptist said, *He must increase, but I must decrease* (John 3:30). I hope that by our study we enable the glory of God to grow amongst us, and serve one another humbly and meekly. We are here to marvel at what God has shown us.

Almost three thousand years ago the Psalmist said that the heavens tell the glory of God (Ps. 19:1). Some thousand years after King David, the apostle Paul wrote that amongst the Gentiles their thoughts sometimes defend and sometimes accuse them, and their conscience bears witness (Rom. 2:15). The idea of looking to heaven and to our conscience has become one of the foundations of European philosophy. Emanuel Kant (1724-1804) held that the only true evidence for God's existence was the starry sky above and the conscience within us. The people of God knew that before Kant and before the whole of European philosophy. The Almighty revealed it.

Our position as learners is proof of our powerlessness. But it gives us power. We are powerless to discover God, but we are powerful because He has revealed Himself to us. With each lesson that we learn God transforms us. We serve one another with more and more conviction and commitment and we praise the Lord in a more worthy manner.

Belgrade, 17th May 1992

THE BIBLE HAS COME TO US FROM THE JEWS

What advantage then hath the Jew? or what profit is there of circumcision? Much every way: chiefly, because that unto them were committed the oracles of God (Rom. 3:1-2).

We are indebted to another nation. We are indebted to that nation for many unquestionably magnificent advances and achievements. All humanity is in their debt.

I am talking about the Jews: an exceptional people with exceptional gifts.

The main advantage that the Jews have, which is our main benefit too, are the Scriptures. If the Jews had not left anything else to humanity apart from the Bible, they would still be a people above all others. Through them we have received the pinnacle of literacy and literature. All other writings of this world are mere literature, law, philosophy and science. They exist, have their period of relevance and then cease to be important. Most of them have been committed to history. Those which are valued today will have their rise and fall, and will eventually remain powerless, since they have no power in themselves.

Aleksandar Birviš

The Word communicated

God has spoken. He spoke His words to the Jews. The first people to hear and collect the Word of God, to put it into book form and leave it to the descendants of every nation, were the Jews. The Lord did not reveal Himself in this way to the Syrians, the Babylonians, the Assyrians, the Armenians, the Persians, the descendant of Ham, the descendants of Japheth, the surrounding nations, not even to the great imperial powers of that time, the Egyptians, Greeks and Romans.

Those nations had many things to commend them. Not every one was evil and corrupt. Their immorality was no greater than that of the Jews, nor were the Jews perfect and without sin. God spoke to the Jews, because He wanted to. He appointed them to understand that God speaks and to receive and communicate His holy will and His intention to save the human race. The Almighty knew and still knows what they are like, just as He knows all other people. No one can escape His all-seeing eyes and perception. However that may be, He chooses and prepares a nation that had conquered large areas of land and that was not known to the world for its faith. It was only thanks to God's choice and God's words that that nation earned its favored position. We thank the Lord that He has pointed us to that people and enriched us by its values.

The Word received

The Jews were the first to receive God's word. The Bible is a gift which comes through the obedience of receiving. By predestination God did not take away freedom from the Jews as a people nor from individuals in the nation or outside the nation. On the contrary,

Reflections

freedom has been given to all men through the fact that man is made in God's image and form. The Lord is unimaginable without freedom.

The Israelites could have refused to receive God's words. But, just as God chose them, so they chose God. They did not choose Him in order to rule over Him, because no one can do that. They enthusiastically agreed to belong to the Lord in the conviction that there is no other god and that He is the best choice anyone can make.

Obedience is the touchstone for testing the accuracy, authority and power of God's word. The Savior Himself said, *If any man will do His will* (will of the Heavenly Father), *he shall know of the doctrine, whether it be of God, or whether I speak of Myself* (John 7:17). The Jews had at one time taken it upon themselves to test God's Word just as they tested other activities. They did what they were supposed to do. God can be experienced in the same way as we can experience the nearness and availability of our parents. He is close to those who will obey Him. The disobedient will not get to know Him, but He graciously reveals Himself to the obedient.

Throughout their history the Jews frequently exhibited disobedience. But they were more obedient than others. That is why they received the blessed revelation of God – they became the bearers of the revelation of the only true and undisputed Lord.

The Word passed on

God spoke and the children of Israel passed it on to others. This unnoticed people passed on a truth that was noticed. The Jews' language never became an international language such as English, Spanish, Chinese, French, Arabic or German. Few people can boast that they speak Hebrew, even less than know Dutch. But that little-known language gave us God's revelation. The Jews easily learnt foreign languages and forgot their own, and imperceptibly passed on their spiritual treasure to the people they lived amongst. They traveled from place to place, they were forcibly resettled and absorbed into other peoples, but the Scriptures traveled, firstly with them and then along its own paths. The descendants of the Israelites strictly preserved the word that had been entrusted to them. They faithfully communicated the holy word to the world even though they didn't preach much, and from time to time would betray God's plan by their behavior.

With the coming of the Lord Jesus to the earth the apostles emerged from within God's small nation and the Gospel began to be preached among the Greeks and the Romans. The gift of the Jews has reached very many people.

Our debt to the Jews

In rare moments of spiritual composure each one of us should ask himself: how much do we owe to this apparently unnoticed nation? Our debt does not form part of the international debt. We pay it off in the Spirit – for our debt to the Jews transcends the boundaries of indebtedness and super-indebtedness which nations repay – by expressing their gratitude to the greatest sons of the Jews. This debt arose in the shadow of Abraham and Moses. All the monotheistic religions emerged on the basis of the Scriptures: Judaism, Christianity and Islam. What have the Christians offered the Jews? With rare, very rare exceptions, the most deserving nation in the world receives what it least deserves: hatred to the extent of extermination, neglect, disrespect, contempt and persecution.

Reflections

The Jews don't need money, because the Bible is not for sale. Let us do what the Psalmist, King David recommends, *Bless ye God in the congregations, even the Lord,* (those who are) *from the fountain of Israel* (Ps. 68:26). Since we all in some way come from the fountain of Israel, we should all gather around God's Word and exalt the Lord in the congregations. Then we will repay our debt to the Jews and to all those who have contributed to the spreading of God's Word and the saving news of Christ the Savior.

Somewhere, far away

In the vast and populous land of China they call a church which normally does not have a paid pastor a meeting place. Once such meeting place is the church in a place called Ban-Shan (Half-Mountain). It is lead by Lu Guang Zen, a director of a building company which does business in an industrial zone.

The church/meeting place has its Biblical standards. Non-Christians are amazed at the high moral standards and admit that it can't be easy for them to live up to such principles. The authorities admit that the Christians are better citizens, show more respect for the laws, build good roads through their villages, and take care of the old, orphans and abandoned children. They are known for their kind deeds in the hospitals. They have a burning desire to help people and often intervene with the hospital authorities to get people into hospital who need treatment.

The Christians from Ban-Shan have become loyal friends of many of the local people. For example, the area is often hit by typhoons. They often need financial help, and the Christians are ready to help when disaster strikes. Everyone knows that they are

Aleksandar Birviš

like that because the Scriptures teach them not only to love God, but also their neighbors.

Brother Lu explains:

"One indication of how much the Christians are appreciated in our area is the helpfulness of the authorities: when we needed a plot of land for this church, we got it and the authorities approved our building plans.

Non-Christians are attracted by what they see: the Scriptures change people. And so they ask for their own copies."

"Every month," says brother Lu, "we distribute about fifty Bibles to non-Christians. Teachers, doctors, and nurses ask for Bibles even though they are not Christians. I ask them what they want a Bible for when they don't come to church and they aren't Christians. They say that the Scriptures contain many things which even those who are not Christians can use to reform their lives."

In 1980 there were five or six Christians in the Ban-Shan area. They began to meet in homes, to read the Bible and to pray. They did it in secret rather than publicly. During 1982 revival broke out. They had to change their meeting place three times. They built their fourth building in 1989. Many students come to the meeting to buy Bibles, mainly because they have seen that other students have Bibles and that the Bible has transformed them into examples to be followed. According to figures from 1990 this fellowship has 600 members and they meet on Sundays in three shifts.

It's interesting that they don't emphasize numbers in that church/ meeting place. They say they put the emphasis on quality. Each convert is warned of the seriousness of making a covenant with God: baptism is a serious step. They were expecting eighty-one people to be baptized in 1991. Before the baptism the past of everyone who wants to be baptized is investigated in detail. Their neighbors and

Reflections

friends must confirm their testimony of a changed life, and they have to regularly attend teaching sessions covering church doctrine. In this way the church is certain that they are clear about what is expected of them after baptism. There are no backsliders in Ban-Shan.*

* * *

This isn't China. We aren't even a part of it. We aren't ravaged by earthquakes, at least not today. But there is shooting. We are destroying our own homes and places of worship.

Where are our meeting-places? Where is our brother Lu? It's all here. Here, in our city and in other towns and villages, in existing meeting-places and in many places that will later become meeting-places – God wants to raise up a new Israel and to settle the debt to the old Israel. He desires brothers and sisters who will praise and worship Him as God's redeemed children.

We have the Scriptures too. We have been mandated as the new Israel, to receive what the Lord says to us, to obey and to apply it in our lives and pass it on to others. May God's Word multiply. May the one God be glorified: Father, Son and Holy Spirit.

Belgrade, 24th May 1992

---

* A Bulletin of the Bible Society of India (Bangalore), Vol. 5 (1990), No. 3 (Sept.-Dec.), pages 3-4.

THE SAVIOR GOES AWAY — WE REMAIN

Ascension Day

Subject: Christ ascends to heaven

Introductory reading: Ps. 24:7-10

Main reading: Acts 1:1-11

Almost imperceptibly, deafened by the daily news of war in neighboring countries and by political events in our own city and country, the days from Easter to this day have just flown by. Following the darkness it seems as if we have lost sight of the light. But God's light is here. Christ has not abandoned men, not even those who ignore Him. He wants to reveal Himself in these very days. So, just as we have bowed our heads in prayer, let us lift our eyes towards the saving words of the New Testament account of Christ's Ascension.

The former treatise have I made, O Theophilus, of all that Jesus began both to do and teach,

The writer of the Acts of the Apostles is the same man who wrote a Gospel (former treatise) for Theophilus. He is Luke the Evangelist.

The Evangelist wrote first about what Jesus did, and then about what Jesus taught. With the Lord, deeds come before words. For Christians it is important to act, for the Savior was a man of action. His works include the miracles. But His works primarily include salvation – the sacrifice that He made in order to save all that believe in Him.

Reflections

After works comes teaching. Christians cannot and shouldn't live without correct teaching, but they must not put that teaching before true deeds, right behavior, and helping others who are in trouble. Many people have lost their lives because official Christianity didn't consider them true believers, but there has never been a Church Council called to condemn missed opportunities and good deeds left undone. Christianity is obliged to establish a Gospel system of values, and in that system deeds come before orthodoxy.

Until the day in which He was taken up,

The Ascension is a turning point. Up to His ascension Christ lived on the earth; after the Ascension He reigns in heaven. By coming down to earth the Lord Jesus fulfilled the expectations of the ages. By His departure from the earth the Son of God fulfills the yearning of eternity.

... after that He through the Holy Ghost had given commandments unto the apostles whom He had chosen:

Christians were waiting for the Holy Spirit. The Savior didn't wait for Him, He already had Him. The Holy Spirit is the Spirit of Christ. Through this Spirit He gives His command to the apostles. Christ's commands are not written on stone or papyrus, or leather, or wood bark or paper. He writes them on the hearts of His apostles. And thus was fulfilled God's promise from the prophecy of Jeremiah (31:31-34) which states:

Behold, the days come, saith the LORD, that I will make a new covenant with the house of Israel, and with the house of Judah: Not according to the covenant that I made with their fathers in the day that I took them by the hand to bring them out of the land of Egypt; which My covenant they brake, although I was an husband unto them, saith the LORD: But this shall be the covenant that I will make with the house of Israel; After those days, saith the LORD, I will put My law in their inward parts, and write it in their hearts;

Aleksandar Birviš

and will be their God, and they shall be My people. And they shall teach no more every man his neighbour, and every man his brother, saying, Know the LORD: for they shall all know Me, from the least of them unto the greatest of them, saith the LORD: for I will forgive their iniquity, and I will remember their sin no more.

The first people to experience the establishment of a new covenant were the apostles. The Savior chose them to be in covenant with the living God and to receive, pass on and communicate the promised Good News. Later on, when the Holy Spirit came down, this task was broadened to include all Christians. God chooses each one that He will save and chooses those He will send. For each one He has purposed salvation and a mission. Circumstances differ and the tasks are not the same but there is only one salvation and the mission of the people of God is unique.

To whom also He shewed Himself alive after His passion by many infallible proofs,

To many people Christ's ascension is just a story. That is what the first enemies of our Lord wanted. During His life they tried to put Him down, and in particular to question His sonship. They had been taught that God cannot have a son. (As though what is possible for normal healthy people is impossible for God!). These objections were invalidated by the Savior rising from the dead.

Then they tried to argue that His resurrection hadn't happened and was just a trick. To rise from the dead is truly something extraordinary. Most people find it easier to assume that the Gospel account conceals some sort of deception, rather than to accept the holy words as true and authoritative for their life.

In the nature of things the apostles were at the mercy of the majority. They had first to have proof: the Lord appeared personally

Reflections

to them. Many times during the days from Easter to Ascension He came among them, to reassure them that He was alive. The power of death had fallen, faithlessness was dwindling, doubts were disappearing. Jesus is alive. That is definite.

... being seen of them forty days, and speaking of the things pertaining to the kingdom of God:

Why does Ascension fall this Thursday, ten days before Pentecost? Because Christ spent another forty days on the earth after His resurrection. He designated it as a time of demonstration and teaching.

His continuing appearances over those forty days were intended to convince His future witnesses of the truth of the victory over death. Those were the days when our victory over death was being formed – that is, the Christian hope. What we express when we celebrate Easter, along with all our words and thoughts as we say goodbye to someone who has died, is the product of Christ's concise and striking teaching which He gave in those forty days. We don't know what proofs He gave but they were certainly convincing. Not only the apostles, but many later Christians were ready to die rather than to deny the risen Lord.

His teachings concerned the Kingdom of God. A new world was being established, a true order, a new will and new relationships. In forty days Christ paved the way for a new political, legal system and social system. Day after day He set out before the apostles the order that would be established by the Holy Spirit, and not by this world. I assume that the apostles were eagerly awaiting the appearance of the Kingdom. They were not worried about the future because they knew that whatever their Lord was intending to do was safe.

Aleksandar Birviš

And, being assembled together with them, commanded them that they should not depart from Jerusalem, but wait for the Promise of the Father, which, saith He, ye have heard of Me.

The writer of the Acts of the Apostles points to a special command. From His many addresses the Lord had singled out one command: the apostles were not to leave Jerusalem until the Holy Spirit had been poured out on them. They could have been in a good or bad mood. Maybe some of them wanted to set out on their travels. They had heard, seen and learnt all they had wanted to hear, see and learn. Why not go off somewhere to broaden their horizons, and to refine their behavior and develop their tastes?

Christ looks at these things differently. Mission is not tourism. The Kingdom of God is not traveling to conferences, symposia and meetings. It is not discussions about tactics, strategy and vision. It is about receiving a mandate from the Holy Spirit. Until it comes we must not set out.

The Savior talks of the Holy Spirit as the promise of the Father. The Heavenly Father is concerned to provide power and uninterrupted existence for His children. Every age will have its unique aspects. The Gospel will overcome them all because the Holy Spirit reveals it and maintains it. The Spirit brings the Gospel to life and brings it back to life. That is the promise of the Father which does not depend on men. The only condition for us to become God's true children is to believe in the Father, Son and Holy Spirit, while the Father will keep His promise. The Holy Spirit is available to those who rely on the Father's promises and trust in God as the true Father.

For John truly baptized with water; but ye shall be baptized with the Holy Ghost not many days hence.

In this verse the Savior is talking about the impending outpouring of the Holy Spirit on the apostles. We talk about that event at Pentecost.

Reflections

God willing, we will look at it in more detail then. We must bear in mind that Pentecost is something that we know about today. At that moment the apostles had an inkling that something glorious was about to happen. But they didn't know anything definite.

I don't know what the apostles were thinking. I am sure they were impatient. The Kingdom was coming into existence. They were taught so by their (and our) Teacher. This time He said it would be *not many days hence.* So we shouldn't be surprised at their attitude.

When they therefore were come together, they asked of Him, saying, Lord, wilt Thou at this time restore again the kingdom to Israel?

Christ's disciples had the best teacher anyone could ever have. They didn't take advantage of it as they should have. They received His teaching but they were still engrossed in their own thoughts. They became better in words and deeds, but their desires were slow to change. Maybe they were secretly thinking about authority as giving orders and ruling over others. They expected they would get suitable positions in God's system and would be able to command not only evil spirits but also their fellow citizens.

Their other problem was the fact that their perspective was limited to their own nation. Today we call it nationalism. The Savior was teaching them about the Kingdom of God, while they kept asking about the Kingdom of Israel. He was instructing them how to overcome boundaries, while they were allowing boundaries to dominate them. Nobody asked them to turn their backs on their Jewish identity, or on their own people. But nationalism was beginning to limit their thinking.

The third thing that they couldn't stop thinking about was the timing of events. They thought that the Kingdom of Israel should come at once. They had had enough of Roman rule. They needed to liberate themselves from the occupying forces. Besides that they

Aleksandar Birviš

thought they needed to take this opportunity to seize power. They had given up so much for the blessings of Heaven. They ought now to get something during the time span of their earthly life.

And He said unto them, It is not for you to know the times or the seasons, which the Father hath put in His own power.

The Lord Jesus doesn't comment on the nationalism of His disciples. He first tries to calm their impatience. Times and seasons are certainly significant in the Christian life, but man cannot dictate when things will happen.

Christianity today is obsessed with investigating the times and seasons. Inadvertently the desire is revealed to hasten the Heavenly Father along, so as to alter the timetable of events relating to the end. Times are difficult and there is great suffering. Christ promised that the time will be kept short. Why can't things happen a bit quicker? For how long will the godless, violent and materialistic strut about, scorning God's people?

Men overlook that the Kingdom of God is fully under God's realm of authority. The Heavenly Father determines the events and those who will take part in them and how long they will last. There is no room for individual imagination.

But ye shall receive power, after that the Holy Ghost is come upon you:

The Savior is talking again about the promise of the Father. The Holy Spirit will give power. The power of the Holy Spirit will overcome internal enemies (amongst them impatience). It will also overcome external enemies: persecutors, seducers, false teachers and others.

The coming of the Holy Spirit will take place when the Father orders it. The Father cannot be forced to pour out His Holy Spirit. No one tells God what He can do, when He can do it and whom He can do it to. So let us not condemn Christians who are not at

Reflections

the same level of spirituality as us or whose spiritual perspectives are different from ours. The Father takes care of them.

… and ye shall be witnesses unto Me both in Jerusalem, and in all Judaea, and in Samaria, and unto the uttermost part of the earth.

What is the main purpose of the power of the Holy Spirit? To spread the good news about the Savior and salvation. We shouldn't think it is just about preaching. The Savior talks about witnesses. The Apostles – and all other Christians after them – witness: they pass on what they have heard, seen and touched. The Apostle John writes, *That which was from the beginning, which we have heard, which we have seen with our eyes, which we have looked upon, and our hands have handled, of the Word of life; (For the life was manifested, and we have seen it, and bear witness, and shew unto you that eternal life, which was with the Father, and was manifested unto us;)* (1 John 1:1-2).

Witnesses do not concern themselves with the past. They do not concern themselves with the future either. They describe events from the beginning, that is, what has happened in their experience and understanding. They have listened to the trustworthy Teacher. They have seen His deeds. They have touched with their hands. They have verified and considered. Not only do they not say anything false, they do not say anything superfluous. The content of their testimony is Christ, just Christ - the life, and not philosophy and history.

This testimony will cover the globe. Today we live in a world where more and more borders are springing up. "Sovereignty" and "independence" are in fashion – actually hidden obstacles to the all-embracing Word of God. But no divisions will stop the Christian witness and progress of the Gospel.

And when He had spoken these things, while they beheld, He was taken up; and a cloud received Him out of their sight.

Aleksandar Birviš

It is from this verse that the Ascension gets its name. The risen Christ ascends independently of the force of gravity. He changes His elevation effortlessly. The Apostles see it all. It is a miracle to them. It is a miracle to us too as it defies the laws of nature. When it encounters the Creator the creation cannot insist on its own rules.

I would like to quote here the words of Philaret of Moscow (1782-1867), a man who was at the head of the Russian Orthodox Church from 1821 and who in a special way left his mark on the intellectual life of nineteenth century Russia, "Just as Christ through His resurrection smashed the gates of hell and opened a way out of it, so by His ascension He opened the gates of heaven and opens the entrance into paradise for believers."

And while they looked stedfastly toward heaven as He went up, behold, two men stood by them in white apparel;

The miracle continues. Two angels appear, similar to those at the resurrection (Luke 24:4-7; John 20:12-13). They stand like men, standing beside the men and behaving like men, but they are not men. They are God's messengers – angels.

Which also said, Ye men of Galilee, why stand ye gazing up into heaven? this same Jesus, which is taken up from you into heaven, shall so come in like manner as ye have seen Him go into heaven.

The angelic message is the continuation of Christ's promise. The Lord said that He would come again. One further detail is added here: the Savior will come in the same way as He went away.

That means that His return will be visible and miraculous. Men will see Him even though many will not believe their own eyes. Who knows what they will think before that and if they will think at all? Will they have time to think?

Christ's second coming will be sudden although it will not be unexpected. The Apostles knew that the Lord Jesus would one day

Reflections

go away. Christianity today is also aware that He will come as ruler and judge. He will come in glory and of His rule there will be no end.

We must be on our guard. Some will give up. There are those who in spite of strict military regulations get slack while on guard and fall asleep. Let us not condemn but encourage. Our task is to live in accordance with God's will in order to welcome God's Son in a worthy manner.

★ ★ ★

We have considered Christ's sufferings in our spiritual exercises. By doing this we have strengthened our love for Christ and our love for one another. During the time of Easter our faith has been strengthened. We have realized that Christianity is the only system of beliefs where there already is an empty tomb. At Ascension time our hope is reinforced. That is what we are doing today. What does it matter if we are surrounded with difficulties? The one and only Almighty, the Lord Jesus Christ, holds all our circumstances and difficulties in His hand. He holds us and our lives — and the eternity of each one of us.

Final reading: Ps. 106:1-5

Blessing: Ps. 106:48

Belgrade, 3rd June 1992

THE ASCENSION

Introductory reading: Heb. 4:14-16
Main reading: Luke 24:50-53
Final Reading: Psalm 47

Meditation for the Lord's Supper

We praise the ascended Christ. He delighted His disciples by His presence. He met with them for forty days. The Immortal talked with mortals, the Eternal one with the temporal, the Almighty with the powerless.

In wonder and amazement the apostles listened to His teaching about the Kingdom of Heaven. They understood it was about them and about those who would come after them. God in Christ and with Christ has established a new reign. The Lord's new world has begun.

In the Ascension a small part of eternity is enacted before the eyes of mortal men. In one small space, before an insignificant number of people, in the presence of two angels, the work of salvation is brought to its completion for all inhabitants of the earth. Nothing is too small or limited for Christ. Death could not keep Him from life. Gravity could not keep Him from heaven.

Christ exists and lives. Whoever believes, believes for his own salvation. Whoever does not believe, does so to his own ruin.

Reflections

The Savior does not take account of men's condition or mood. He continues to live and work independently of human knowledge.

The risen and ascended Lord reigns. His rule can be disputed but not overturned. People can say what they like against Him because He does not take away our freedom of speech. But hatred and lies will not detract from or alter the reign of our Lord and Deliverer. He remains unshakeable and eternal on His throne.

Before His ascension the Savior told the followers of the Gospel to wait for the Holy Spirit. They could not hasten or delay the coming of the Father's promise. Maybe some of them were impatient, and some of them indifferent. Maybe some of them thought: "Why isn't the Holy Spirit poured out at once?" Others maybe said: "He can come when He likes, because I don't know anything about the Holy Spirit". All of them had to wait in prayer and fellowship, whatever they were thinking. God does not renege on His promises.

The Ascension of our Lord confirmed the apostles in their mission. They had been taught that their testimony would not be confined to one area alone, nor one nation or country. The news of the Savior had to penetrate everywhere that sin had penetrated. This realization took a long while to dawn upon them because of the many prejudices they had (material, tribal, political etc.) But in the end only those fellowships that moved out among the people survived.

As He was completing His work of salvation, the Lord Jesus left with them the message of His return. Salvation is not complete if it does not give the final solution for eternity. There is no true deliverance if we are saved from one misfortune only to fall straight into a new one.

The Lord Jesus will come again. His absence is only apparent and temporary. He is continually with His own by His Spirit and with all

Aleksandar Birviš

those who receive Him. This was seen and heard at Pentecost. When the time of the Savior's temporary absence is completed, eternity will erase what is temporary and Christians will be filled with joy at the glory of their Lord and will remain so.

The Ascension turns the gaze of the Christian to the hills whence our help comes (Ps. 121:1). Today all the powers seek to distract our eyes from Christ. Atrocities, inhuman acts, outpourings of hatred, bloodthirsty deeds, unbecoming behavior by members of the priesthood, the denial of truth and the human conscience, the inability to discern evil men and evil spirits, rejection of the Gospel, the encouragement of acts of savagery, malice and all sorts of other evils, deception, and threats — all this hinders us from seeing the real picture. We must add that today's television foments this, and narrows men's outlook even more and prevents them from considering Christ.

Still...

Christians have the prospect of seeing their Savior face to face. Until He comes again they seek His face in the four following forms. Or to express myself more specifically: these are my attempts not to lose sight of Christ as I use God's gifts in these four forms. Maybe God will reveal something different and something more to someone else. Let us be thankful and accept it.

First form: Scripture. On every page of Scripture we can see or sense the Lord Jesus Christ. He is most fully shown in the four Gospels. But our Savior acts, speaks, walks, looks, suffers, conquers, rejoices, blesses etc. in other books of the Bible, too. We know on the basis of the Scriptures that He is today in fellowship with the Heavenly Father and that He is praying for us. And everything else that we know about Him we have learned from the Scriptures. He instructs us as follows: *Search the Scriptures;* Jesus is thinking here primarily (maybe exclusively) about the Old Testament books – *for*

Reflections

in them ye think ye have eternal life: and they are they which testify of Me (John 5:39).

Second form: prayer. Christ fulfills our prayers. He is the essential power in this, and inspires, maintains and directs our prayer life. *And whatsoever ye shall ask in My name, that will I do, that the Father may be glorified in the Son. If ye shall ask any thing in My name, I will do it* (John 14:13-14). The prayers that Christ has answered are without number. With each one of our prayers the Father is revealed in the Son. God's glory appears. Many have never met Christ, nor God either, because they have never prayed in the name of Christ, i.e. they have never talked with the Father, trying out Christ as their representative, intermediary and participant in that conversation. If they do pray in this way, the Savior will reveal all things to them ever clearer, because the more gifts there are, the better we know the giver.

Third form: direct knowledge. This way of looking at Christ depends on the individual man or woman, who is sometimes insincere or is sincerely mislead. That is why it is a less reliable form than the others. Still, it has been applied since the beginning of Christianity. The Apostle Paul, writing in the Second Epistle to the Corinthians (3:18) says, *But we all, with open face beholding as in a glass the glory of the Lord, are changed into the same image from glory to glory, even as by the Spirit of the Lord.* God equips His faithful to look at Christ. He has given them the freedom (unveiled faces) to look on His glory. How can we differentiate between this and self-deception? Very simply. If someone says that they see Christ without being transformed from glory to glory, without becoming different and more like Christ, they are a fraud and a trickster of God's people. Seeing with unveiled face is a reality that transforms. Whoever is given this mercy cannot remain the same.

Aleksandar Birviš

Fourth form: examples. A Christian is transformed from glory to glory. The Lord's Spirit changes him. A man becomes an example to other Christians. By his life he draws their life into new glory. Later on, when he becomes spiritually independent, the man led by others becomes a guide himself. Being a spiritual example is a lifetime commitment. That is what being a Christian teacher means: an exemplary life right to the end. That is why it is written, *Remember them which have the rule over you, who have spoken unto you the word of God: whose faith follow, considering the end of their conversation* (Heb. 13:7). This is where Christianity has suffered its greatest losses: there are few born-again, transformed people who have remained as an example to others right to the end. Instead of others seeing Christ, they have seen those who would seduce them, and such men seduce them to their doom. But the Lord, on the other hand, always gives us an abundance of models, living and spiritual, who are sufficiently strong and clear and blessed. We see Christ in them.

A particular example is the Lord's Supper. It is not a human example, it is a form of God's distinct instruction. The Savior acquaints us with His sufferings. His body endured torment. His blood was poured out to the last drop. Through the example of the bread and wine Christians contemplate a life and a death, both of which were fully sacrificed for the resurrection of others. At the same time the Lord's Supper introduces us to Christ's indestructibility. We will share in communion until Christ comes again. Men took communion even in death camps. I know of a case where prisoners in a camp broke up the bread they were given into crumbs and they used a few drops of blood instead of wine. That was communion too. History is full of chilling stories, but Christ showed His indestructibility even in these anonymous examples.

Reflections

Now, when we remember the ascended Christ, we must think of those who have proved their spiritual calling in torture and blood. They went to be with the Lord ahead of us. Let us not be sad because of them. Let us not envy them. The ascended Christ has gone to the Father to prepare a place for us, too, in the courts of Heaven.

★   ★   ★

Christ's departure from the earth was not a loss. *Nevertheless I tell you the truth,* says the Lord, *It is expedient for you that I go away: for if I go not away, the Comforter will not come unto you; but if I depart, I will send Him unto you* (John 16:7). Ascension Day remains as the culmination of the Savior's works here on the earth, but with His ascension a whole new work opens up: the Holy Spirit comes to us, whom we worship and whom we praise together with the Father and the Son. Amen.

Belgrade, 7th June 1992

WHAT SHALL WE SAY ABOUT THE HOLY SPIRIT?

Sunday: Whitsun
Subject: Holy Spirit

Introductory reading. John 13:15-17

Main reading: Acts 2:1-41 (16-21)

Final reading: Ps. 104: 27-31

Today is Whitsun (Holy Trinity, or more rarely, Pentecost). It is a Christian festival parallel to the Jewish festival of Pentecost (Shavuot — Feast of Weeks), because it comes seven weeks after Easter (or rather, Passover for the Jews).

This festival is supposed to remind Christians of the day when the Holy Spirit was poured out on the apostles and disciples of Christ who were present. A sound like the roar of a storm was heard from the sky, and little flames of fire came down on the apostles and the others, looking like cloven tongues.

On that day the Christian Church was born. Up until that time Christians had been followers of a teacher, but at that point they were transformed into a spiritual organism whose head is Christ. Christians became both sowers and the actual seed of new life in the Spirit. At that moment the apostles spoke in various languages and began to speak forth the praise of God in those languages.

Reflections

The people were dumbfounded. Some were amazed and wondered what it could be. Others thought they knew and made fun of them. They said these men were drunk.

Less than two months before this the apostle Peter had cravenly denied Christ before two servant girls. In this moment he received special boldness. He got up and spoke before all the people. He explained what was going on, that this was the outpouring of the Holy Spirit that God had promised.

In his sermon the apostle Peter accused the people who had crucified Christ. His listeners repented in large numbers, the apostles baptized them and the Christian Church received its first three thousand members.

We don't have any more detailed explanation of the Holy Spirit in Scripture. We learn more about what He isn't than about what He is.

1

The Holy Spirit is definitely a Spirit. That means that He is not matter (substance). If we subscribe to the triune nature of man, as suggested by the words of the apostle Paul – spirit, soul and body (1 Thess. 5:23) – the Spirit is not soul. But our knowledge has not progressed much in this area – we cannot say anything more specific about the soul, and modern physics does not have a clear definition of matter.

When talking to the Samaritan woman, Christ says that God is Spirit (John 4:24). He says this to dispel certain prejudices, to caution that God is not bound to temples and that what is important to Him are not ceremonies but Spirit and truth (and even this cannot be determined and delineated intellectually and theologically). Later on, Church writers and teachers drew up a statement which says that

Aleksandar Birviš

God is in essence one, but has three persons (hypostases): Father, Son and Holy Spirit. That is where the name Holy Trinity comes from. (Both in the Roman Catholic and in the Protestant calendar the first week after Whitsun is dedicated to the Holy Trinity. God willing, we will talk about that in a week's time).

2

It goes without saying that the Holy Spirit is holy. Holiness has two meanings: a) separation from all that does not meet God's criteria (sublimity, purity, aloofness, righteousness etc.) and b) commitment to a clearly defined task.

The holiness of the Holy Spirit is transferable. Where He is at work holiness is evident: men, temples, specific times, places, actions. Where He withholds His action, holiness is lost, and there is apostasy, hardness of heart and cruelty.

3

Since they believe that the Holy Spirit is the third person of the Godhead, Christians generally also believe that He is Lord. The Biblical understanding of 'Lord' is of a God who exists of Himself. His existence is not dependent on anything else, nor limited by anything else, and least of all threatened by anything else. This is the Mosaic "I am that I am" and "I am" (Ex. 3:14; 6:3).

This is a question of faith, because man cannot imagine what it means to exist but not be created. Logic and science relate to the created world, but here we are talking about the Creator.

4

The Holy Spirit gives life. Through the Holy Spirit, life is made available first to man, but then also to all other living creatures.

Reflections

That is a source of faith and hope for Christians. We believe that the Holy Spirit witnesses to our spirits that we are children of God (Rom. 8:16). We hope that, no matter how much Christianity and the individual Christian may loose their cutting edge, the Holy Spirit will breathe in new life.

Because of this we believe in the indestructibility of Christianity. It endures even when its enemies are superior in strength and when it is infiltrated by degenerates and destroyers. The Holy Spirit is the only genuine internal strength of the Church.

Unspirituality is the same as death. All falling away from the source of spiritual life leads to stagnation and death. A large part of the Christian world today is involved in establishing and strengthening Christianity by means of the state, the nation, peoples, history, customs, etc. The Holy Spirit is absent from all these areas. There is no life in them, such freedom means nothing, and such rights as there are have no value. Darkness gives birth to darkness just as weeds give birth to weeds.

5

The key theological reason for the split[15] between the Eastern Orthodox and the Roman Catholic Church was the question of the source of the Holy Spirit. The Eastern Church adopted the statement that the Holy Spirit proceeds from the Father (John 15:26), whereas the Western Church maintained that He proceeds from the Father and the Son (*filioque*). For this reason countless numbers of books were written and burned, people were killed and other evils were perpetrated and are still being perpetrated to this day.

This question has never been so sharply defined among Protestants. For example the Lutherans have included in their basic documents of doctrine the Greek text of the Nicene-Constantinopolitan creed

Aleksandar Birviš

without appendices and the Latin text of the same creed with the addition of the word *filioque*.

6

The Holy Spirit is especially important as the bearer of prophetic and apostolic inspiration. It is the unanimous view of the Church that the Scriptures are the product of the Holy Spirit. The writers of the books of Scripture themselves hold to the view that holy people are the tools of God's Spirit and not the authors of the Bible. Later on Christians realized that the Holy Spirit also illumined their minds so that they could understand the Word of God.

This work of the Holy Spirit does not exclude the need for study, especially of the original languages: Hebrew, Aramaic and Greek. What we today call humanistic education arose out of this need to interpret the Bible. (It is in fact older than European humanism, and classical learning only appeared with the Renaissance).

7

The Holy Spirit is glorified together with the Father and Son, for there is one God and He must be glorified as a whole. This is how we should understand the very widespread phenomenon of spiritual renewal, new and old ways of reaching for spirituality, charismatic experiences, the desire to demonstrate the gifts of the Spirit again just as they were exercised at Pentecost and in the early church at Jerusalem and other places.

★ ★ ★

Today Whitsun means the same to us as it did at the beginning of Christianity. Unfortunately the Holy Spirit has been forgotten.

Reflections

Churches keep passing countless resolutions, memoranda, decrees, epistles and other documents. They usually contain no hint of the Holy Spirit, but it is all done in the name of some sort of spirituality. Spirituality is not in repetition but in renewal, in revival of true gospel values. This festival is intended to remind us of this.

Belgrade, 14th June 1992

I BELIEVE IN THE HOLY TRINITY

First Sunday after Whitsun
Subject: Holy Trinity

Introductory reading: Is. 6:1-4

Main reading: Matt. 28:19

Final reading: Rev. 4:6-8

During Whitsun we thought about the third person of the Godhead, i.e. the Holy Spirit. Many Christians feel the need to think more deeply about all the three persons of the Trinity: Father, Son and Holy Spirit. The Scriptures do not speak extensively or clearly about the persons of the Godhead. The term 'Holy Trinity' is not used in the Bible. But that does not give anyone the right to claim that the concept does not exist and that Christians should not think about it.

These things are not easy to grasp. We can't use any similes or illustrations to explain the meaning of these truths. Nor are words a reliable means to explain them because every word has its own connotations and ideas, whereas God who is not material cannot be categorized in this way. But I only have words at my disposal and I believe that they can be used to give a suitable explanation. As long as we approach the subject honestly and with love and do not contradict the Word of God and the truths and applications we find, our thoughts will be helpful, reliable and in accord with God's will.

Reflections

May God help us!

1

According to what we have just read from the Scriptures (and from other passages) there can be no doubt that there is one God, but He has three persons. These persons are the Father, the Son and the Holy Spirit. The Father is revealed as God and He is God. The Son is revealed as God and He is God. The Holy Spirit is revealed as God and He is God. Likewise God is revealed and He is the Father. God is revealed and He is the Son. God is revealed and He is the Spirit. Only three persons of the Godhead are revealed to us – no more and no less. That is what we believe, and if God wanted us to believe otherwise He would reveal it to us.

2

The three persons of the Godhead have different identities. The Father is not the Son. The Father is not the Holy Spirit. The Son is not the Father. The Son is not the Holy Spirit. The Holy Spirit is not the Father. The Holy Spirit is not the Son.

Each person of the Godhead is who He is. The Father begets the Son and gives the Spirit. The Son is begotten of the Father and accepted by the Spirit. The Holy Spirit proceeds from the Father and is glorified with the Son and acts with Him.

3

The persons of the Godhead are not a construction or something temporary. Neither are the Father, Son or Holy Spirit individually. God is triune not because it suits someone for Him to be like that, or because that is just a temporary arrangement that will change tomorrow. God is triune by His very nature. His individual

Aleksandar Birviš

persons are not like characters in a play, who cease to exist once the performance is over.

God is the Father by what He is. God is the Son by what He is. God is the Spirit by what He is. But He is all the time the same Lord. Within His nature each person is intrinsic to and inseparable from His being. The Father cannot be separated from God as such, nor can He be separated from the Son or the Holy Spirit. The Son cannot be separated from God as such, nor can He be separated from the Father, nor from the Holy Spirit. The Holy Spirit cannot be separated from God as such, nor can He be separated from the Father, nor from the Son. All this is the essence of God, and is unchanging.

4

The three persons of the Godhead are not three Gods; there is only one God. He is one by what He is, that is, in essence. This seems incomprehensible to men: three in the one and the one in three. Yes it is incomprehensible, but that is also how it is. That is why Christians believe even when something seems to make no sense.

The Father is eternal, the Son is eternal, and the Holy Spirit is eternal — they are not three eternal beings, but one eternal God. The Father is holy, the Son is holy, the Spirit is holy— they are not three holy beings, but one Holy God. The Father is self-existent, the Son is self-existent, and the Holy Spirit is self-existent— they are not three self-existent beings, but one self-existent God. The Father is almighty, the Son is almighty, and the Holy Spirit is almighty— they are not three almighty beings but one almighty God. The Father is love, the Son is love, and the Holy Spirit is love — they are not three loves, but one loving God. And everything else that the Christian says and thinks about God is said about the Father and the Son and

Reflections

the Holy Spirit — and that is always and everywhere the one and only God.

5

All three persons of the Godhead are equal, although they have differing characteristics. When the Lord Jesus says, *My Father is greater than I* (John 14:28), He is thinking of His going away and reigning once more in fellowship with the Father. This is a royal decree relating to a place of honor and not an expression of inequality between the persons of the Trinity. The relationships between the persons of the Godhead do not consist in positions of greater or lesser importance, but in the same powers and traits. That is why worship and the prayer life and daily Christian life are made up of a continual striving to please and give honor and glory to the one God: Father, Son and Holy Spirit.

Since God is Creator not creation, it would be pointless to look for the order and rules in Him which apply to and among created beings. I am convinced that many of our misunderstandings, and our arrogance too, are the result of some people not properly understanding the Creator, and assuming that He thinks like a created being. (Not to mention that this can lead to a lack of respect, because the creation is subject to decay).

Equality between the persons of the Trinity derives simply from the fact that they are not unequal, but are equal to one another. How we arrive at this realization is a different question. If anyone believes that the Father, Son and Holy Spirit exist, then they also believe that they are equal. The persons of the Godhead are not identical, because then there would be three Gods, or else there would be no reason for them to exist. The existence of three identical Gods excludes the possibility of God's existence as such. The existence of equal

Aleksandar Birviš

persons allows the statement, "In the name of the Father, Son and Holy Spirit" to remain correct, and does not disrupt the oneness of the essence of God.

* * *

God alone has immortality, dwelling in unapproachable light, whom no man has seen or can see (1 Tim. 6:16). The truth about the Trinity is an unfathomable mystery. Each of us can think about it and we should. Each of us should grasp the truth of the persons of the Trinity as far as his intellectual powers allow. Every Christian man and woman will enter into this mystery if they pray to God, study the scriptures and obey the Lord. Then each will become aware of the inadequacy of their own expression, but their thoughts and feelings and strivings will be focused on one very clear aim, that is to praise the Lord, that same triune God: Father, Son and Holy Spirit.

Belgrade, 21st June 1992

THE SPIRIT AND THE BRIDE SAY:

Introductory reading:

The King's daughter is all glorious within:
Her clothing is of wrought gold.
She shall be brought unto the King in raiment of needlework:
The virgins her companions that follow her shall be brought unto Thee.
With gladness and rejoicing shall they be brought:
They shall enter into the King's palace (Ps. 45:13-15).

Main reading:

And the Spirit and the bride say, Come. And let him
that heareth say, Come. And let him that is athirst come.
And whosoever will, let him take the water of life freely
(Rev. 22:17).

We have been talking about the Holy Spirit. God has helped us and we thank Him for that. I have tried — with God's help — to introduce you to the Holy Trinity, that is, to the irrefutably one God in three persons. Now it is time to look in more detail at the Church as the Bride of Christ. She is the companion and coworker of the Holy Spirit. Her voice becomes ever more important as Christ approaches us. She cries to her bridegroom, "Come!" Let us join her cry and the desire of her heart and say, "Yes, come, Lord Jesus!" (Rev. 22:20).

Aleksandar Birviš

Let me make clear straight away that I am not going to talk today about the Church as a local fellowship. Nor am I talking about the church as a building. I am not going to deal with the Church as an indisputable historical fact. I want to talk about the universal invisible Church made up of all the worthy and committed followers of the Lord Jesus Christ who bear the mark of His Holy Spirit.

Each one of us needs to decide whether he belongs to that Church or not. Let each one act as he sees right. The more seriously we take the Church, the more joyfully we will fulfill the will of God.

1

The Savior has only one Bride. The Church is one because there is perfect love between Christ and the Church, and it is not the love of a groom for more than one bride or a bride for more than one groom. Perfect love can only exist between one groom and one bride. Just one Bride – the Church – belongs to just one Groom – Christ.

The question arises, why are there so many denominations? The denominations (churches) are not Christ's Bride. They are types of association that have grown up over the years as a response to the believers' needs. Of course, there are many unnecessary deviations, concessions to human weaknesses, seduction of the naïve and self-deception of the blind, which is surely a form of disorder. But true, sincere, truth-loving, believing fellowships are trying to eliminate and root out internal evils and to contribute to the variety of the faith experience. They do not need to threaten the unity of the Church. The Church is one because God has blessed her as the Bride of Christ and that is what He wants her to be.

In one of His parables (Matt. 13:24-30) the Lord explains (Matt. 13:36-43) how the evil (the sons of the evil one — followers of the enemy) will insinuate themselves among His followers. They will

Reflections

look like Christians, but they will gnaw away at the Church from inside. This is not some impersonal force. From the beginning of creation to the moment when they are thrown into the fiery lake, evil spirits have names, and each of their followers has a name and surname. They are persons, but they are not the Church. They seek to destroy the spotless reputation of the Church — the innocence (virginity) of the Bride. In the end the Almighty will condemn them and cast them into the furnace of fire, where there will be weeping and gnashing of teeth.

On the other hand, men cannot unite all denominations into one united visible Church. They can try that from the most sincere and noble motives, but they won't succeed. The Lord Jesus in His High Priestly Prayer prayed to His and our heavenly Father that all His disciples might be one (John 17:21). Nowhere does He state that this prayer of His will be visibly fulfilled. The unity of the true Church is secret and not accessible to the human senses – just like the unity between the Father and the Son. It is achievable, but not by the power and will of men.

Christians should encourage one another in mutual understanding and tolerance. As a rule we don't preach against other churches in this fellowship. (I hope you have never heard me do so). Lack of understanding for others, demeaning others who think and believe differently from us, and showing intolerance towards them, is beneath the dignity of this pulpit and this church. In a time when men are struggling for human rights, for personal and general freedoms, such behavior does not contribute to the purity of the Gospel, nor to our efforts to bring spiritual revival. We should direct ourselves and our children toward unity, and the Lord will consummate that unity when He thinks the time is right.

Aleksandar Birviš

2

The Savior's Bride is the most perfect virgin. She has never belonged to anyone else. The Church is holy. Such an understanding of holiness seems outmoded to many. Today people laugh and take pity when a bride keeps herself pure for her future husband. But the Church knows of no other type of purity for itself and for its members.

The Bride of Christ is holy because nothing vulgar, dishonorable, or corrupt has happened in her past. The Church of Christ's chosen ones quickly rejected the temptation to cohabit with state, nation, tribe and class. She has never submitted to any man or group of men. On top of that, the true Church has never forced herself upon individuals or society.

The Church has developed among men. Today it is still in the world. But it does not belong to that world. In the past many dirty deeds were done in the name of the Church, in the name of Christ, in the name of God. They happen today too: much evil, violence, murder, extermination and bloodshed of all kinds is perpetrated in the name of religion.

Is it the Church doing it? No. Not the fellowship of Christ. Who is doing it then? It is Satan disguising himself as an angel (2 Cor. 11:14). The evil one tries with all his might to look like the light but he is and remains darkness. He would like to exhibit some kind of goodness, but there is only evil in him, not even a trace of good. The devil easily gathers unrenewed men around him and poisons them with enmity and wars. He was the one who devised holy crusades and holy empires. He leads men according to his will and leads them astray, unwitting into destruction. Christians need to be especially careful. "And what I say to you," says the Lord Jesus "I say to all: Watch!" (Mark 13:37).

Reflections

By belonging exclusively to Christ the Church demonstrates its singularity of purpose. That is the same as holiness. Christians have no other purpose: just Jesus! Everything else is marginal and temporary. Even the noblest deeds become dangerous when we take our eyes off Christ. Man is lulled into a sense that he is a good Christian and doesn't notice how near he is to destruction.

We exist and function because of Christ and for Christ. If we do good, we do it because we are following Him. If we build churches, hospitals, schools, houses, workshops and other things, or help others to build them, we do it for Christ. If we disapprove of something that is being built, because we can see where it is leading, we do that for Christ. If we sign up for the army or we refuse to wear uniform or bear arms, we don't do it for our own or someone else's benefit, but because of Christ's presence, because of His Gospel. If we want to be well-educated or, alternatively, we have an aversion to the conceit of academics and prefer simplicity — that too makes sense if we do it for Christ.

3

The Church of Christ is all-embracing. The Bride together with the Spirit calls the Bridegroom and all who want to listen to join in that call. Thanks to the Holy Spirit and the Good News of Christ the Church encompasses all generations and all time and space. The Spirit of God knows no boundaries, nor does it respect them. Those who once had some fleeting awareness of Christ and knew God through the prophets, join with the people of God and with the apostles and others who come after them. Each enters into the work of others and carries it on (John 4:37-38).

The Spirit carries the invitation on. The Bridegroom certainly hears it. Others hear Christ's invitation too. The upheaval in the

Aleksandar Birviš

world shows that the Lord is near. People are joining the fellowship of the redeemed. The number of members of the Church is increasing. New people are coming in. If men are not saved, they alone are guilty. God sends His servants in good time. The Almighty gives everyone an opportunity to hear the news of Christ.

The Church is united in inviting others. God expects people from all around to respond to the call. The Lord addresses each individual. The all-embracing fellowship of believers has a place for you and for me and for everyone else. No one is ordained for hell if he himself does not want to go there.

4

The fellowship of Christ knows where it is coming from. The Church is a heavenly institution. It began the moment the Holy Spirit descended on the apostles. He was poured out and is still being poured out today. Today the roar of the wind and the flaming tongues of fire will not be repeated, but that which began with the apostles has continued right up to this day and will continue until the Bride is united with her Groom, that is until the Savior's return.

No one has been able to destroy the continuity of existence and activity of the Church. Nothing has succeeded in negating the connection between the Church and Christ and the apostles. Why? Because the Holy Spirit is stronger than the destructive forces and spirits that hate Christ.

The fact that the Church has its origin in Christ and the apostles obliges Christians to live with their eyes on the Savior and His first disciples. No one has the right to state that he traces his origin to Christ and the apostles if he does not live a life that reflects this and demonstrates Christ-like integrity. Life without virtues, without blessing, without the mark (the seal) of the Holy Spirit may not claim

Reflections

to be the life of Christ and the apostles. Neither structure (*hierarchia*), nor gifts (*charisma*) are worth anything where there is no life (fruit or harvest) according to the will of God. The Savior specifically said, *Beware of false prophets, which come to you in sheep's clothing, but inwardly they are ravening wolves. Ye shall know them by their fruits. Do men gather grapes of thorns, or figs of thistles? Even so every good tree bringeth forth good fruit; but a corrupt tree bringeth forth evil fruit. A good tree cannot bring forth evil fruit, neither can a corrupt tree bring forth good fruit. Every tree that bringeth not forth good fruit is hewn down, and cast into the fire. Wherefore by their fruits ye shall know them. Not every one that saith unto Me, Lord, Lord, shall enter into the kingdom of heaven; but he that doeth the will of My Father which is in heaven* (Matt. 7:15-21). There is enough material here not just for one sermon but for a whole series. I shall concentrate this time on what relates to the Church as the Bride of Christ. The Lord will remove from her all that does not conform to God's will as envisaged by Christ and the apostles, for the Almighty promised, *Therefore the ungodly shall not stand in the judgment, nor sinners in the congregation of the righteous* (Ps. 1:5).

$$\star \quad \star \quad \star$$

The Lord wants each one of us to belong to such a Church as we have described. That is what this teaching is for. That is the reason we invite the unsaved and the unrepentant to repent and be saved at every service. That is how they join the one, holy, universal, Christian, apostolic Church in her waiting, as a Bride, for Christ to come. The Bride and the Spirit issue the invitation and ask who will join them. By our own personal, free and earnest desire to follow Christ, each one of us has been presented with an open door into the

Aleksandar Birviš

wonderful secret world of the Spirit and into spiritual unity with the Christ whom we desire and await.

We are the Bride. Who wants to join her? Come! And say the same to everyone, "Come!" And whoever hears let him say, "Come! Yes, come, Lord Jesus!"

Final reading:

Husbands, love your wives, even as Christ also loved the church, and gave Himself for it; That He might sanctify and cleanse it with the washing of water by the word, That He might present it to Himself a glorious church, not having spot, or wrinkle, or any such thing; but that it should be holy and without blemish (Eph. 5:25-27).

Belgrade, 28th June 1992

First Baptist Church, Belgrade Congregation
(credit Vicencio Žaknić)

THE WILL OF THE FATHER

Third Sunday after Whitsun
Subject: The Church trusts in Christ

Introductory reading:

O Zion, that bringest good tidings, get thee up into the high mountain; O Jerusalem, that bringest good tidings, lift up thy voice with strength; lift it up, be not afraid; say unto the cities of Judah, Behold your God! Behold, the Lord GOD will come with strong hand, and His arm shall rule for Him: behold, His reward is with Him, and His work before Him. He shall feed His flock like a shepherd: He shall gather the lambs with His arm, and carry them in His bosom, and shall gently lead those that are with young

(Isaiah 40:9-11).

Main reading:

Fear not, little flock; for it is your Father's good pleasure to give you the kingdom (Lk. 12:32).

What sort of church do we see? We see a gathering of people who meet more or less regularly at a fixed time to worship God. The church is an organized fellowship. It is called together by the Holy Spirit. The people in it are all different, but they share one aim: the Lord has invited them to meet with Him. That is a local visible church.

Reflections

The Church is not an organization. It is an organism. Its head is Christ. Every follower of Christ is a member, an organ in the Savior's body. The life of God is present in the Church because the Spirit of God is in it. Many would like the life of the Church to be very prominent and full of activity. The Church doesn't blow trumpets, doesn't fire from cannons and doesn't shake to the sound of earthquakes. The Savior teaches us, *But when thou doest alms, let not thy left hand know what thy right hand doeth* (Matt. 6:3). This is the characteristic of the individual and the fellowship: meek, or gentle, quiet, unobtrusive. The local church lives in virtue, not in a marriage celebration or a coronation.

The local church is focused on the needs of its locality. People in Belgrade or Niš, Kragujevac, Smederevo, Užice, or in Zagreb, Sarajevo, Sofia, Skopje, Tirana, Athens, Istanbul, Budapest, or in Hong Kong, Ubangi, Peking, San Paolo, New York, Sidney, Wellington, Lima and elsewhere need to be set free from sin. This is something that worries country people too. Our local churches in the towns have to deal with something which is not so obvious out in the country: a lack of common sense. Country people have been deprived of the truth like townspeople, but they have retained more common sense than urban men. The rhythm of life in the country keeps mainly in step with nature, whereas we townspeople have completely lost any sense of rhythm.

But the Church, however, lives by its own timetable. It has weekly, monthly, annual and longer cycles of events. Services, festivals, jubilees — come and go on their own schedule as much as possible, independently of other events.

Aleksandar Birviš

Fear not, little flock

When I spoke about the Good Shepherd on 10th May 1992, I said amongst other things that Christ liberates from fear. Christians should not fear for their Church. It is small, but it is in God's will.

At this time we need a word of encouragement. The people are being frightened by everyone. Everything around us is horrifying: war, death, poverty, inflation, hunger, refugees, victims of war, the disturbed, the robbed, the slaughtered, fire victims, displacement, violence, arson and who knows what else — it all causes fear, even more than people can bear. But it is clear to Christians: behind all these disturbances there is a peace which is intended for those who trust in Christ.

Besides this peace God has given us courage. Christians are by nature fearful: they fear God, they fear hell, they fear the authorities. But, for the very reason that they fear God, they have been given the courage to stand against hell, or even — when the Lord decides it is time — to also say to those in power "No!" or "Enough!"

I'll say it again: this is not personal bravery. It comes from God who in His enabling mercy gives us the strength. The Almighty has made the redeemed bold. But we need to be very careful. A Christian acts in God's name, and would be in great danger if he were to promote his own ideas and intentions as well as or instead of God's. It is a sin to lie. To lie in one's own name is a personal sin. To lie in God's name is the way to destruction.

In order for the Gospel to break through much more is necessary than just ordinary bravery and saying "God told me". Before we go on to what the Lord says to us as individuals, we need to receive what He has already said in the Scriptures. Then we must respect all that

Reflections

God has given, *For God is not the author of confusion, but of peace, as in all churches of the saints* (1. Cor. 14:33).

I should like to make something clear here. We are all living in the aftermath of revolution and coercion. It will take years for people to get free of the idea that anything can be improved by force, either by arms, or vocal protest, or by street demonstrations, public disturbances etc. Violence in the cause of justice, the imposition of truth, the enforcement of good, present evil for the sake of some future good — will bring neither justice, nor truth, nor anything good. Force only brings new fears; coup d'é·tat is the way of evil. The little flock must think differently: where people impose their own way, the voice of the Holy Spirit will not be heard; where men impose themselves, Christ will not be glorified — it will cause fear or at the very least apprehension.

Freedom from fear is the need of every human being. In environments where fear reigns, illnesses caused by fear are also rife, and children and the growth of young people is stunted. (I know from my own experience. When the Second World War broke out I stopped growing). Christ gives men the courage to do good and to progress. The little flock will grow if it can reduce its fear. If fear increases, the flock will not multiply.

What sort of things do the followers of Christ fear? They are afraid of their own smallness. To little people everything seems big. The fearful find everything frightening. In the dark even the rustle of leaves seems like the footsteps of a bear.

Fear can be caused by the power of the enemy. Christianity has to deal with a serious enemy, who has the whole world at his disposal. Lies are his natural characteristic and weapon of attack. Speaking of the devil, Christ says, *When he speaketh a lie, he speaketh of his own: for he is a liar, and the father of it* (John 8:44b). Unfortunately, lies

Aleksandar Birviš

creep in amongst the children of God too. If we don't stamp on them straightaway, they will spread like a cancer — thereby causing new fear. So let us boldly stamp out lies, firstly in ourselves, then in our immediate environment, and then further abroad, in the local fellowship, and in the region and areas we live in. If he loses lies as a means of attack, Satan will lose all his other weapons. *Submit yourselves therefore to God. Resist the devil, and he will flee from you*, writes the apostle James (4:7).

Corrosion from within is a cause of fear, but also its consequence. In order to preserve so-called peace in the home, many people — including Christians — pretend that they don't hear or see what is happening. Others add their own view of things and their own interpretation of events in order to avoid facing up to bitter and unpleasant facts. Within the local fellowship (sometimes further afield as well) something begins to eat away at the flock of God. This disease destroys from within. It is not "something" or "someone", it is the very antichrist himself. People who dream of unity feel division, those who love justice see injustice, those who yearn for peace become disturbed, those who long for joy are saddened, those who are open to God's Spirit become aware of unspirituality. They are all right. But their fearfulness is unfounded. It vanishes as soon as people grasp the role and function of evil spirits. If the body is sick it needs to be treated. Fear will not go on its own — it needs to be driven out.

Let us nurture our union with God. That will help us to drive out fear. Whoever has the Lord as his ally has nothing to fear. In the words of the song of King David, *Some trust in chariots, and some in horses: but we will remember the name of the LORD our God. They are brought down and fallen: but we are risen, and stand upright* (Ps. 20:7-8).

Reflections

Little Flock

All Christians should pray, "Increase our number, Lord!" But that shouldn't lead us to worship numbers for their own sake. Everyone, especially speakers, have a rush of pride when they have a large audience. Look at those who address mass meetings: they arouse the crowds and the crowds arouse them.

That is surely the temptation of mass evangelization too. Everyone would like to address huge crowds of people, but they find it difficult to go from door to door, talking to one man at a time. We imagine Christ and the apostles preaching in the mountains, the fields, in town squares and synagogues, but we overlook the conversation with the Samaritan woman, with Nicodemus, Lydia, the jailer and many other individuals.

There are two ways of avoiding this temptation: a) by encouraging individual salvation and spirituality and b) by encouraging the founding of small fellowships.

a) The salvation and spirituality of the individual has been neglected. With the appearance of national and state churches, church states and land divided on religious lines, individual salvation has been forgotten. So through the ages we have acquired Byzantine Christianity, the Latin church, Slavic Orthodoxy, Roman spirituality, Germanic mysticism, the Anglican Communion and so on. The individual has been left to social services and humanitarian (philanthropic) aid organizations. But salvation is intended for the individual: for you personally, me personally, your friend personally, but also for your enemy personally.

Aleksandar Birviš

The same applies to spirituality. Spirituality is not the task of the clergy or the monastic orders. It is the gift of God and a response to the personal faith of each Christian man and woman. Each person is spiritual in as far as he belongs to the Lord as the giver of mercy. *For whatsoever is born of God overcometh the world: and this is the victory that overcometh the world, even our faith. Who is he that overcometh the world, but he that believeth that Jesus is the Son of God?* (1 John 5:4-5).

b) A small fellowship should not always stay small. There are several numbers that appear in the gospels with special significance: three, seven, twelve, seventy-two. Let us try and think in terms of these numbers. *For where two or three are gathered together in My name, there am I in the midst of them* (Matt. 18:20). Where three members come together, we should find somewhere to hold regular meetings. (This should be done through the official channels and the authorities should be informed). When the group grows to seven, an elder should be appointed — and assistant if he needs one — with authority to teach the believers systematically and in a structured way, to preach the gospel and conduct funerals. When it reaches twelve members, the fellowship should look for a qualified pastor and teacher, someone who is spiritual and has the ability to do the job.

I believe that God will bless such an approach. A fellowship like this will quickly increase its membership six fold and reach seventy two members. As it continues to grow, the possibility of starting a new fellowship should be investigated. Half the fellowship should separate off, ideally according to where the people live, and form a new fellowship. And let them continue to praise God and grow.

Needles to say, but in these times of distorted values and deranged men I must say it: multiplication is a Gospel principle, but it must not be the cause of disputes and schisms. The Church will grow only if it grows in the fruit of the Spirit, of which the first is love.

The Will of the Father

The Heavenly Father is Father of the little flock. He is our Father, that is to say Father of all who call on His name and acknowledge Him as Father. His will is that the local fellowship should be small but should belong to the King.

God is no one's private Father. No one has the right to the Kingdom as his personal property. God's Church belongs to God. Although it starts with just a small group of people, usually just one or two families, it will not survive unless it transcends those limits. God is looking for people who will belong to Him because they have found in Him a Heavenly Father, and not because dad or mom, grandma or granddad, uncle or aunt or some other relative has taken the decision for them.

This has another human side to it. Christians must behave as befits the Father's dignity. How many people there are who are totally obsessed with their ancestors and family, but care little for the dignity of the Heavenly Father!

Clearly the Father expects courage. He gives His Kingdom to the little flock (the local church). These little folk are faced with a big task. The challenge to serve and to accept responsibility must be taken up. This is taught in every service, Bible study, sermon, prayer meeting. The business meetings of the church serve this purpose as do the structure of the fellowship, obedience, and the necessary sanctions and disciplinary measures. Christian literature,

Aleksandar Birviš

church music and other forms of worship also serve in realization of the Kingdom.

The Will of the Father is omnipotent. If He has given us the Kingdom, He will bring it to life. There are no grounds for doubting that the little flock will fulfill its great task. It will certainly fulfill it because that is the will of the Father. How will it fulfill it? More easily and completely if it trusts more fully in the Father. Difficulties arise when we lose our trust in God. The less trust there is in the Church, the weaker its faith is. Lack of faith stifles life. When the apostle Peter saw Christ walking on the stormy waters of the Sea of Galilee, he wanted to walk like that too. As long as he had faith, he was not afraid and kept on walking. Then he suddenly grew fearful, his confidence left him, his faith shrunk and he began to sink. He cried out for help, and the Lord Jesus pulled him out while at the same time rebuking him, *O thou of little faith, wherefore didst thou doubt?* (Matt. 14:31).

No one can oppose or go against the will of the Father. As He has ordained, so will His Kingdom be given. Thinkers and theologians may agree and disagree. Some men — especially those who have willingly submitted to the evil one — can speak evil of the King of Kings. But Christ will still be Lord. So the Father has decreed. He has decreed who will be King and what His Kingdom will be like.

The Kingdom is given

What will the Kingdom really be like? What can we say about God's Kingdom? We usually refer to the words of the Apostle Paul, ...*For the kingdom of God is not meat and drink; but righteousness, and peace, and joy in the Holy Ghost* (Rom. 14:17). These words contain a whole list of truths which we cannot ignore and which we need

Reflections

to consider. Since we are talking about the hope of the small flock I will draw your attention to several of the Savior's parables.

The first one is the Parable of the Sower (Matt. 13:3-9, 18-23). The Kingdom is given as an expression of the Father's trust. Christians have just the word this world needs. The Word of the Gospel is being spread among men. Some receive it, others don't, and it depends on the individual. Those who truly receive multiply the word by contributing to the salvation of others. The little flock holds a multifaceted word in its hands: proclamation, prayer, worship. Through the work of the Holy Spirit more and more people are coming to faith, repentance, forgiveness, justification, sanctification and glorification.

The second parable (Matt. 13:24-30, 37-43) is the one about the field sown with good seed, wheat and tares. The Church is sent into all the world. Each local church is responsible for its part of the human race. Among its number it comprises those who take salvation and the good things to others. But those who bring evil and unclean powers also appear. Men — and by this we mean adherents of God's Kingdom — would like to wipe out these others. But the Son of Man opposes that idea. He retains the right to separate out and condemn. Christians do not have that right. They must keep themselves from men of evil, but no one is allowed to kill and commit acts of violence in the name of the Kingdom of God.

I must mention something that is happening right now. The "White Eagles Society" announced on the eve of Vidovdan[16] 1992 through its leader that it will shortly be forming its own special "religious police". The task of this group would be to "drive out of Belgrade the religious sects that are corrupting Serbian youth." They are thinking specifically of Jehovah's Witnesses, Adventists and the Hare Krishna movement[17]. It seems very likely that this will happen

Aleksandar Birviš

and may even be approved by law. The "White Eagles" will use force. If they think it is necessary they will kill. Various human rights movements will protest, and demonstrate in front of our embassy in London or Copenhagen — and no one will take any notice. But there is no need to fear the "White Eagles". Eagles are vultures and birds of prey. That is what they are, whether they are black, white, brown or grey. The Lord Jesus says, *For wherever the carcass is, there the eagles will be gathered together* (Matt. 24:28; Luke 17:37). Society is in decay and it needs the eagles. We are the living Church and there is nothing for the eagles here. They will fly overhead, then fly off and land where they belong.

Let me remind you of a third parable which fits this situation. The Lord Jesus compared the Kingdom of God with a grain of mustard (Matt. 13:31-32). I shan't describe the plant. That's a job for the botanists. Instead I will apply our thinking to the little flock. The local church is small and not much to look at. But if it is constantly upheld by the Holy Spirit in righteousness, peace and joy, it will grow in two directions: firstly — it will spread its branches, and secondly — it will be of benefit to non-Christians too. The branches are new individuals and new local fellowships. We are surprised at the minute life and blessed growth of this same plant. But we should be concerned about something else: where are our new branches and why are there so few of them?

The next thing we need to think about is our service to those around us. The work done in caring for refugees is a good work. It started before these latest upheavals (1991/92). We were pleased that our eastern neighbor had taken a step towards freedom, and people no longer needed to escape from their country[18]. But even more depressing and disturbing human problems have appeared. Thank God, we have been able to make a difference in this too, and we will

Reflections

not stop doing even more. We will be blessed if we show the same concern for all, without considering race or faith, and without asking whether they will be converted or reject the good news of Christ. It is a big job for a small flock. It demands much sacrifice, additional prayer and a more ready faith.

We direct our faith towards receiving Christ's truths in a deeper way. In our specific situation it means we must once again take to heart the words of the Savior when He said, *That ye may be the children of your Father which is in heaven: for He maketh His sun to rise on the evil and on the good, and sendeth rain on the just and on the unjust* (Matt. 5:45). The little flock believes here and now that every refugee is my own companion in suffering, my brother and my friend.

★   ★   ★

Do not boast of the fact that you are chosen. God has set us apart for humble service, and not to be conceited and to lead people astray. The little flock does not dream about power, about ministerial positions, about revolution, about better living standards – although it is not indifferent to what is happening in society. New men in Christ know what awaits them and who it is who wants them to experience it. The Heavenly Father opens up a life of confidence and stability to every local church. It quickly becomes a reality, our reality.

Don't imagine you are the only ones who have been given boldness. There are others. The Lord didn't limit Himself to just one fellowship. Whoever thinks in a limited way, limits his faith. Whoever limits his faith is not able to accept the infinite and indomitable will of God. God is foreign to the haughty. The Almighty is repulsed by pride. Pride is evil because someone is trying to present themselves as being other than what they really are. It is also a sin against

Aleksandar Birviš

humility. Let us recognize that others too have worth in the eyes of the Almighty. Let us trust in their commitment to Christ.

Our trust in Christ will show that we are not alone. Every local church is a sister church to this one. Praise God, the little flock is not so little. Fear not, little flock, the Heavenly Father has made you great. He has given you great tasks, great victories and a vision of a great and living God. So look forward to the days that are coming with great confidence. Yours is an eternal Kingdom.

And I would ask those who do not belong to the little flock to think a while. There is room for you too in the little flock, in this Church. Fear not, there is no better place. It is the Father's will that you come into the Kingdom too.

Let us bow down to our mutual King, the one God: Father and Son and Holy Spirit. Amen.

Final reading: Ps. 78:52–54

Belgrade, 5th July 1992

GOOD NEWS FOR EVERY CREATURE

Fifth Sunday after Whitsun
Subject: The Church focused on people

Introductory reading: Ps. 96:1-10
Main reading: Mark 16:14-18

Afterward He appeared unto the eleven as they sat at meat, and upbraided them with their unbelief and hardness of heart, because they believed not them which had seen Him after He was risen. And He said unto them, Go ye into all the world, and preach the gospel to every creature. He that believeth and is baptized shall be saved; but he that believeth not shall be damned. And these signs shall follow them that believe; In My name shall they cast out devils; they shall speak with new tongues; They shall take up serpents; and if they drink any deadly thing, it shall not hurt them; they shall lay hands on the sick, and they shall recover.

All creation needs to encounter God. There is no creature that will hide before knowledge about the Lord. In vain will men forbid and proscribe that knowledge. The Savior is the personal Savior of all people: men, women and children. But He saves all other creatures too, because human sin has brought corruption to nature.

The Church must not be indifferent to this task. It is the Church that brings the news of the Savior, and brings Christ Himself to people. That is why the Church has the apostolate and why it is called apostolic.

265

Aleksandar Birviš

1

The Gospel is the Word about the redeeming Lord. Whom does He redeem? The sinner. Man is lost in sin. He cannot set himself free. Christ delivers from sin. He liberates the sinner.

The sinner has been pardoned and has received justification. God no longer sees him as unrighteous and does not punish him for his sin. Christ has redeemed fallen and ruined man. He who once cursed, now begins to praise the Lord.

In forty years or so it will be exactly 2000 years since Christ gave Himself as a sacrifice. From that time until the present, evil has been present in and amongst men. Sin has not changed, only the techniques have changed. For that reason the same Gospel is in force today. The same simple message leads us into eternal life and into glory.

2

The good news of Christ is addressed to all men. The Church is oriented towards all those who live on the earth.

The Church sends messengers and helpers to the places where God needs them. For us that certainly means our brothers in the Second Belgrade Baptist Church. For us, it means our brothers and sisters in Kovin, where we have a fellowship and where people regularly meet in the church to pray. We also help the Christians in Loznica – there are not many of them but they must know that we love them and take responsibility for them until they become independent.

But we should be praying that one day — as soon as possible — we can send someone to Erzerum. That is a place in the depth of Anatolia, the first Byzantine town captured by the Muslims and where the Gospel is no longer known. Maybe God has entrusted to

Reflections

this very fellowship the task of taking the Good News of Christ, of God who became man, to that place.

We probably need to be praying even more. We need to pray, for example, that God would show us whether He is expecting someone from this fellowship to help the brethren in Alma Ata? There is a beautiful new church building there. The members are Russians and Germans from the Trans-Volga region. The Germans have largely moved from the area, and there aren't many Russians. Very few people have tried to win the indigenous people, the Cossacks, to Christ. The Word of God has been translated into the Cossack language, and they are literate and have a culture of their own. Where are those who are prepared to learn their language and to adapt themselves to their way of life in order to witness to them about the Lord Jesus?

We should also be praying for a breakthrough of the gospel in North Korea – in Pyongyang – and in many other parts of the world. The Almighty is waiting for us in those parts of the world, maybe just for someone from this fellowship.

3

The task of the Christian is to proclaim Christ. It is an encounter with God. True joy is found in it. In spite of the new forms of entertainment that are constantly appearing, the world is becoming ever sadder. There are now teachers of good behavior who realize that people should be taught to smile, and man is the only creature who knows how to smile. I must admit that there is no evidence anywhere that the Lord Jesus ever laughed, but we see from His teaching that He had a sense of humor. However, today, so-called responsible people do very frivolous things, but they don't seem to

Aleksandar Birviš

be able to smile. The world needs joy, but there is no joy without the Kingdom of God and without Christ.

The Gospel proclaims the power of God's name. Evil spirits flee before the name of God. The Lord's name does miracles and brings holiness. The omission of the name of God causes the loss of power. That miraculous name breaks down the walls of ignorance, opposition, enmity and disbelief.

The Savior and salvation are inseparably joined. Wherever Christ is, there is salvation; where there is salvation, there is Christ. Faith in the Lord Jesus is proclaimed here too in this church. In fact we should be proclaiming nothing else but saving faith. Baptism only comes as the result of bold faith in which we share. Baptism is for those who are obedient and are ready for it. No one who believes should be prevented from being baptized.

God's signs are intended for those who believe. Those signs are intended for the internal life of the Church and not for those who do not believe. Believers will cast out evil spirits. Evil spirits are to be found all around and in many places. They flee from the name of the Lord.

Speaking in new languages is one of those signs. The Apostles didn't learn foreign languages. But, when it was necessary — for example on the day of Pentecost — they addressed the assembled people and they were understood. For the people this was a miracle, for them it was a sign: their Teacher was continuing to lead them through the activity of the Holy Spirit.

Immunity to poison was also a sign. Neither snakes nor men could poison them. God showed by this that He protects the life of His servants. He does not recommend them to deliberately step on snakes and to drink poison. But they should not fear the evil of snakes and men.

Reflections

Healing is for believers too. Prayers for the sick and the laying on of hands is not an act that should be performed like a theatrical performance. It is a modest fight against sickness.

This does not mean that if Christians pray for the sick they should not make use of doctors and their skill. On the contrary, where faith in Christ is firmer, healthcare is better and more comprehensive. General healthcare is a Protestant concept inherited from a Jewish principle: no settlement should lack a physician. So we pray for the sick but we also give them medical care and study medicine.

We don't announce signs and wonders in advance. They happen as a consequence.

The Church announces salvation. It calls men to repentance, to seek forgiveness and to accept God's justice, including justification before God on the basis of Christ's righteousness.

All people must hear that holiness is possible. Consecration is the natural Christian way of life. It is also natural that Christ's followers expect to come before God as a new people intended to praise the Lord. That is the content of Christian eternity.

4

Before eternity comes this everyday life of ours. In this life the Church, besides preaching, also offers teaching to all men. Christian teaching is part of a wider function in life that we call education. The content of our teaching is first and foremost correct teaching about God. It contains a number of points that we must not omit.

First: God is not an idol. Sinful man continually tries to make gods according to his own taste. He is apt to worship men and objects and phenomena and living beings and ideas of his own. Christianity strenuously opposes all idolatry.

Aleksandar Birviš

Second: There is one God. There is not more than one God, and no one can approach God merely as some distinct god or some special deity.

Third: God is Creator. Everything that exists exists because the Lord wanted it that way and made it so. Only He can create from nothing. That is what to create means: nothing becomes something. Men can convert things, work them, rework them, or shape them, but they cannot create. Only God can do that.

Fourth: God can do anything. He does everything and controls everything. Nothing is impossible for Him. Nothing can oppose His will and His power.

Fifth: God saves. The Almighty does not want man to perish. The good news, the Gospel, would not be good news if it were not news about salvation. What would Christ's beautiful words, and His all-wise thoughts and His exceptional and inexplicable miracles, be worth if we were not saved? Salvation is what is needed by every creature, because sin has spoiled all that God has created.

5

The Church motivates people. At services and in other types of church activity, each person should receive motivation. Meetings held in the church building encourage people to pray. Those who come should be encouraged and instructed. Those who don't attend but just walk past are affected by the sign outside and the cross on the building. Let them pause to think, at least.

Christians are encouraged to true worship of God. Each Christian encounter is a step closer to God's glory. Some walk faster, some slower. Some are willing to get to know God patiently, and Sunday by Sunday they listen to the interpretation of Scripture, and every Wednesday they enrich their prayer life. Some are not so patient,

Reflections

not so ready to learn, and not motivated to turn to God's Word every day. Nevertheless, each in his own way, some more, some less, contribute to the glory of the Lord. It shines forth from this place in all directions to the farthest point.

The sons and daughters of God are motivated to true generosity. There are those who are more prepared and those who are less prepared to make sacrifices. The Almighty is Lord of all good things. He has no need of anything, but He expects much. Why? Because by our gifts we express our love. The human race is by nature ungrateful. No matter what their customs are and their linguistic ability, men are generally ungrateful. Look how people forget their parents, don't remember their teachers, and pretend not to remember those who have done good to them. The Church shows the whole world a different attitude towards past and future generations: giving. We give to past generations out of gratitude, and to future generations through apostleship. Each prayer, each minute of time given to others, and every act of unselfishness, every sum of money, are investments in gratitude towards those who brought the Gospel to us and our neighbors, but also an investment in the future spread of the Gospel.

There is another encouragement that I think is important: the Church teaches people true respect for God. The Gospel needs to reach every creature, the Church needs to be present in all nations, tribes, tongues and states, related or unrelated, friendly or unfriendly. Why? Because the Lord is ruler above all rulers. He rules over those who acknowledge His rule and over those who do not acknowledge it. The Almighty is the only one who rules without any danger that His rule will be threatened tomorrow or that He will be deposed from His throne.

Aleksandar Birviš

Human relations are at their best when God's rule is kept in mind. The fellowship of God's children should be a role model of a social order. It doesn't need to learn from politicians, politicians need to learn from it. Disorder, disagreement and misunderstanding in the Church are doubly harmful: firstly — they bring disquiet and bitterness to men's hearts, and secondly — they destroy the example of good order among men. God does not love those who cause disputes amongst the brethren (Proverbs 6:19), but He has given the Church, which is to teach all men decency and order (1 Cor. 14:40).

6

The Gospel is the good and blessed news about Christ, but it also includes something unpleasant, the fact that the Lord is the supreme and most righteous judge. God's judgment is something that Christians must talk about. God willing, this will be the subject of a separate sermon. When the time comes I will not hesitate to preach on that subject. If the Lord gives us health and strength that will be on 25th October.

There is no other court of judgment above God's. Whatever He decrees must be enacted and cannot be changed, because all God's decisions are unchangeable and so are the decisions of His court. Don't grumble if God has appointed you for something unpleasant or something that seems unjust. Rather think about your sins, the cause of God's judgment. If you discover the causes and deal with them, God will suspend His judgment and your sentence will be quashed. He Who Knows All will not leave you in ignorance.

Neither despair that a human court will not understand you and that they do not pass just judgments. You always have someone you can appeal to. The Lord is above all judges. Christianity plants that knowledge into every follower of Christ. The Church tells all men:

Reflections

human justice is necessary but not perfect. The only way to perfect it and change it is by seeking God's will.

The Lord is the only true righteousness. No one can administer perfect justice simply because every judge is limited and restricted. Man cannot know everything and get to the bottom of everything. A judge can be most sincere in his desire to be just, and still miss something or lose sight of something. That never happens to the Lord.

★   ★   ★

The Son of God in His good will and humility came among men. All nations, tribes, tongues and all creation and matter must ascertain it. This is the shared task of the Church. This task was set even before the creation of the world, but is not finished. Each of us should get involved in God's work: both you and I in the same way as the prophets, apostles and all the other servants of God played their part.

If there is work to be done anywhere in the world, then it is those mighty works to which God appoints us. The Church is marching on, witnessing to the glory of Christ our God and our Savior: how He died for us on the cross of Calvary and rose mightily from the dark grave. We glorify Him, we worship Him, with united hearts and with one voice.

Final reading: Rev. 14:6-7

Belgrade, 19th July 1992

GOD CREATES A NEW MAN

Sixth Sunday after Whitsun
Subject: A new man

Introductory reading: Ps. 92:12-15
Main reading: Rev. 21:5-7

And He that sat upon the throne said, Behold, I make all things new. And He said unto me, Write: for these words are true and faithful.

And He said unto me, It is done. I am Alpha and Omega, the Beginning and the End. I will give unto him that is athirst of the fountain of the water of life freely. He that overcometh shall inherit all things; and I will be his God, and he shall be My son.

The man I want to tell you about is no longer alive on the earth today. He has gone to his Lord. Sometime before the First World War, he began to work as a craftsman, a simple tailor somewhere in Kosovo. As a young man he somehow came by a Bible. It was a large-format Bible (24 x 18 cm.). He read it and thought about it, slowly at first, to himself, and then out loud, then to himself again, and so on, never ceasing to do so.

Through his reading he was convicted of the truth of the Gospel. He mixed up many of the accounts and much was unclear to him. He tried to talk to people whose job it ought to have been to explain things to him – priests and school teachers. But they wouldn't talk to him.

Reflections

He wanted to become a monk. Then he heard a voice, "Don't let yourself be taken into captivity. I am preparing something else for you." He heeded the voice.

As a young tailor he wanted to get married. Friends and local matchmakers found various so-called "good prospects" for him, girls from prominent families with considerable dowries. Again he heard the voice, "Marry a poor girl. I have prepared other riches for you." He found a gentle and poor girl who bore him, as far as I remember, some nine children.

When the Second World War ended in Serbia (1944), his eldest daughter married a man in the Vojvodina[19]. He went to visit her new in-laws, as was the custom. In the little town where they lived he saw various different churches. He wanted to visit them.

"Not that one," they said to him, "that's a German church. We didn't go into that one even before the war. Now that the fascists have been driven out, it wouldn't do for you to go there."

On another occasion he wanted to go to a service in another church. It looked rather interesting as on the church tower there was a cockerel instead of a cross. This time they said to him:

"Not there. That's a Hungarian church. We don't go there."

Then they told him that one church was Slovak and another was Rusyn, and kept telling him not to go into them, but they never went to their own church even though it was close by and very beautiful.

He sought God's word. He wanted salvation. But his relatives kept telling him that this one and that one were not for Serbs.

At the time we are talking about, public transport was worse than it is now. So he often used to spend whole days in Belgrade, because his train was late or he'd missed one, or because they had changed the timetable. One day he was walking along Revolution Boulevard, and, passing the Djeram market he came to the well-known restaurant

Aleksandar Birviš

Lipov Lad. Then he saw our church at number 264. The signs were written in Cyrillic. He plucked up courage and went in.

He was met by the pastor who was not a Serb, but the man was not looking for people of his own nationality. He was looking for Christ and he found Him. He talked at length and in great depth. In a short space of time he and his wife were baptized and their sons and daughters were ready for baptism. Later on other members of the family, relatives and friends joined the church.

They all became new creations in Christ. The changes that took place in them, their work and behavior demonstrated that God does not abandon those who sincerely search for Him. Two thousand five hundred years ago the prophet Jeremiah recorded God's promise, *And ye shall seek Me, and find Me, when ye shall search for Me with all your heart* (Jer. 29:13). That promise is still as valid today as it was when the prophet was alive on the earth.

But our friends in Kosovo didn't manage to avoid all the troubles that that region has suffered from. The young people were forced to leave Kosovo and Metohija, the older ones died, but traces of what God had done remained. We believe that one day, by God's grace, we will once more see His children in those places. The remnant of the believers will come together again and multiply.

God gives birth to new men. He creates a people with specific knowledge, experiences and purpose out of men who were just wandering and searching. Change takes place in every such person. It needn't be something tangible and conscious. The Holy Spirit does this work independently of man's own ability to understand. He changes the sinful nature of every man even before that man believes in Him. And a faith that is able to respond to God's call is born.

What is God calling us to? He calls men to live in accordance with His will. In that way the Lord changes those who believe. *We*

Reflections

know, writes the apostle John, *that whosoever is born of God sinneth not; but he that is begotten of God keepeth himself, and that wicked one toucheth him not* (1 John 5:18).

New life is something that we can know. A new man knows that he is new by dint of the fact that he has new life. He knows that he has been born of God and sensitized to sin by Him. Only spiritually renewed people can oppose the evil one. That is why they are needed by every nation and every society.

The gift of new life encompasses the whole man. Man is pulled in so many different directions. The Apostle Paul describes this state of the unrenewed man in the well known passage in the Epistle to the Romans (7:19-25), *For the good that I would I do not: but the evil which I would not, that I do. Now if I do that I would not, it is no more I that do it, but sin that dwelleth in me. I find then a law, that, when I would do good, evil is present with me. For I delight in the law of God after the inward man: But I see another law in my members, warring against the law of my mind, and bringing me into captivity to the law of sin which is in my members. O wretched man that I am! who shall deliver me from the body of this death? I thank God through Jesus Christ our Lord. So then with the mind I myself serve the law of God; but with the flesh the law of sin.*

I don't want to spend time interpreting this passage now. (If God willing we are still here and able to meet together, I aim to interpret this passage on 21st February 1993). In this sermon I want to look at the action we are recommended to take: the new man must not stop struggling, but he knows which side has the victory. We need to thank God for that. Thanksgiving prevents us from eating ourselves away on the inside. God takes the distracted man and transforms him into a coherent person.

The Holy Spirit redirects man's main strivings, enlightens man's mind and constantly renews the nature of the spiritual man. The

Aleksandar Birviš

spiritual man does not grow old. He matures and bears fruit. In these fruits and in the virtues that are displayed is the victory of the Christian. The new man is a changed man — we can clearly see that. The essence of the change is that his shortcomings disappear and his virtues increase. Everything is transformed into gain. For the victor, God is everything, and the victor is a son of God.

In the victorious life of the new man a significant part is played by true faith in the Lord Jesus, *For whatsoever is born of God overcometh the world: and this is the victory that overcometh the world, even our faith. Who is he that overcometh the world, but he that believeth that Jesus is the Son of God?* (1 John 5:4-5).

These true and faithful words point to: a) Christ, who can and will do anything, and b) to the existence of those who are thirsty, the people whose greatest need is the Gospel.

a) Christ can and will do anything. He can make men new. He wants to do it and He does it in practice, *For God, who commanded the light to shine out of darkness, hath shined in our hearts, to give the light of the knowledge of the glory of God in the face of Jesus Christ* (2 Cor. 4:6).

b) There are people whose greatest need is the Gospel. They may not be aware of it, but they are thirsty for the life-giving water. They need to be told that the new life has come. All they have to do is to receive Christ: "I believe that Christ is the Son of God and that He saves me personally. All the rest has already been done." *And this is the record, that God hath given to us eternal life, and this life is in His Son. He that hath the Son hath life; and he that hath not the Son of God hath not life* (1 John 5:11-12).

Reflections

The new life is no political promise. Neither is it the invention of cunning priests. A Christian is a real, authentic human being. God has created the new man just like every other member of the human race. It is the Lord's desire that all men come to Him and be saved.

The old man hampers the new. He is like a scaly skin, like a dungeon that has been forced upon him. We need to reject the old man. Not because the old man is worn out, and is of no more use. In fact he would very much like to carry on living and enjoy life. We need to reject the old man because he belongs to the world of evil even if he himself does not do any evil. His desires are unworthy. The unconverted man has such strong, distorted desires that they simply consume him. He is being destroyed by them.

That is why it is necessary for every man to become a new man. Men mature as long as the truth matures in them. Where there is no truth, God's new man cannot be there either. Truth is by nature just and holy. It comes from the Holy Sovereign Lord.

Have you put the truth into practice in every area of your life? You haven't. Have you allowed it into every part? No. It's not surprising. It would be a miracle if you had. You have no power in yourself even though you are full of good desires. That is why the Gospel is preached to you. That is why Christ is given to you as a gift. That is why the power of the Savior's blood is made available to you. If you accept Him, you have chosen the right side. Trust in the Savior, for He is your Savior.

Come let us bow down to Christ! Come let us bow down to our Savior and Lord! Come let us bow down and fall on our faces with contrite hearts before Jesus Christ, Son of God, our King, Lord, Savior and Shepherd! To Him and the Heavenly Father and the Holy

Aleksandar Birviš

Spirit, the only God, be glory, honor and praise from now and for ever more. Amen.

Final reading: Ps. 84:5-8

Belgrade, 26th July 1992

I BELIEVE IN LOVE

Seventh Sunday after Whitsun
Subject: Love — the most excellent way

Introductory reading: 1 Cor. 13:1-13

Main reading: Rev. 3:9

Behold, I will make them of the synagogue of Satan, which say they are Jews, and are not, but do lie; behold, I will make them to come and worship before thy feet, and to know that I have loved thee.

I believe in love. *God is love; and he that dwelleth in love dwelleth in God, and God in him* (1 John 4:16). There is no one who could turn me from my faith in love, because they would be separating me from God — and I don't want that, nor will the irresistible love of God allow it. For this reason I place myself under the Lord's protection, even now. He guards and leads all those who serve Him. May He drive away every evil and all hatred, all intolerance and all lovelessness. There is no place for Satan, the devils and his evil spirits where men believe in love. Christ's love was victorious on the cross. It conquers today too.

I believe in the existence of love. That may seem silly and imprudent. Should one believe in love today? So much hatred, bloodthirstiness, fear, blindness, slander and murder have risen to the surface, that a man who believes in love doesn't seem in his right mind even to those closest to him. They will say that he has taken

Aleksandar Birviš

leave of his senses. Let them think I am deranged, I still believe that love exists and I believe in it. It is precisely because the world is without love that I am sure that it is not as it should be and must be destroyed soon. Love exists precisely because it is not of this world.

I believe in love as a fitting and consistent component of human life. Love gives worth. It motivates men and nations to do good things. A man without love cannot be a scientist, or an artist, a craftsman, a sportsman, a manual worker or a businessman. A man who has love can become all of these and more besides. Whatever he is, he is close to God and God is close to him.

I believe in love, because love uncovers secrets. One secret that it is worth delving into is the secret of love. To love, whom and what? To love, how and why? To love, when and where? With what, how much and when? I want to love as God loved: the Father gave His Son without asking who I was and how great my sins were. The Almighty knew all my wrongdoings. I do not doubt that God is all-knowing – nothing can be hidden from Him. But in spite of that, the Son of God washed and wiped everything clean with His blood. He does not allow any barriers to come between me and God. They all fell when His love was poured out.

I believe in love as the mother of prophecy. God so loved the human race that He sent messengers and His word. The Almighty spoke to men in their own language. He spoke to all men through chosen individuals. He still loves them today. He sends them His messages today too. When one group of prophets falls silent, God raises up other prophets. When the prophets disappear, apostles appear. If the apostles disappear, pastors and teachers appear. If the pastors and teachers are no longer able to function then prophets will emerge. Why? Because the Lord establishes different ministries

Reflections

and gives many abilities, all because of His love for men. He has no intention of leaving men without His holy life-giving words.

I believe in the love from which have come all blessed knowledge, revelations and discoveries. It was love that caused the Scriptures to be compiled and enabled me to know who God is and what He wants. The Holy Spirit prompted men to remember and record God's messages. Some of the Lord's words seemed unimportant and unintelligible at the time. The world made fun of God's chosen servants because of His word. They rejected and hindered them. But the Heavenly Father chose and trained new people to write down, compile, bind into books and publish His eternal revelations. Those people are very often unknown to us, but we still benefit from the fruit of their love today. They never saw us but they loved us because they loved the work God had given them. Through that work other knowledge, learning and instructions for everyday life have come down to us. From that love of God has also come resourcefulness: coherent thoughts, deepened spirituality and healed body.

I believe in love — the master artist. She has taken up her place between revelation and knowledge. Through her we become noble and approachable. Through love we draw near to God, even though it seems that God is lofty and far removed from everything that He has made. Art overcomes great distances. Love connects us with others, even with those who turn their backs on the Almighty. At a time when the distances between people are increasing at a frantic rate, the only true bridges are the bonds of God's love. That is why I trust them and am certain that every true art helps men to come closer to God and to one another. I do not shun music, painting, literature or the theatre — if they serve the Lord in a worthy manner. *Let every thing that hath breath praise the* LORD (Ps. 150:6).

Aleksandar Birviš

I believe in the love through which I believe. If it were not for God's love, I would not be much different from a clever animal, or I would be like a beautiful flowering weed, or a tree bearing refreshing fruit. But the Creator wanted me to be a man and so He gave me faith. He loves me and so I believe. I believe in God, righteousness, justice and judgment, but also in the Savior, salvation and deliverance. Love restores my faith. When my confidence grows weak, God's beloved Son speaks. He doesn't ask me, "Do you believe?", but "Do you love me more than the others?" The Almighty will not leave me without love. He is with me. He does not allow anyone or anything to separate me from the love of God which is in Christ Jesus our Lord (Rom. 8:39).

I believe in love as a force for good in society. It teaches me and enables me to understand the people about me and to be of assistance to them. I love my neighbor as myself. So I wish him freedom, health and prosperity. I am not content with bondage, disease and poverty. In fellowship with others we assist in the creation of a more just order, the healing of society and the individual, as well as in the fair distribution of goods and a fair and informed attitude towards nature. Love for God and ones neighbor demands that I work better, that I study more, that I give more generously and serve more humbly. Let the uneducated teach me, the incompetent rule over me, the dishonest condemn me, those dearest to me abuse me and those closest to me insult me — should I cease to believe in love because I am belittled and aggrieved? I love those I cannot see, and serve those who do not know me. People whom I have never spoken to listen to me. My writings are read in the main by men who have never heard of me. It is not I who am important to them but the truth which I communicate. God loves the human race. That is why He has placed us among men.

Reflections

I believe in love — the one true commitment. All that can be improved on I am interested in, with the passion of an explorer and a conqueror. I appropriate the good things of Christ. I must not be blind, deaf and dumb towards those who are in trouble: the lost, the afflicted, the naked, the homeless, the starving, the misunderstood, the rejected and the exiled. I love them all whether I approach them directly or someone else reaches out to them in the name of our Lord Jesus Christ. I am surrounded by my own weaknesses and the weaknesses of other people, both those I know and those I don't. We all belong to God because He has chosen us and redeemed us through the blood of Christ.

I believe in love for the Lord's Supper. I take communion *for God so loved the world, that He gave His only begotten Son, that whosoever believeth in Him should not perish, but have everlasting life* (John 3:16). The Lord's Supper reminds me of this. I join in with others who are thanking and praising Him. I endeavor to uphold the dignity of Christ's sacrifice with a thankful heart. I shun sin, seek forgiveness, am reconciled with my rivals and seek to be pleasing to God, and to be a blessing to my neighbor and those further away. I do not believe in my sinlessness or correctness before God, but I believe in the power of Christ's blood. And so I ask the Lord Jesus, that perfect lover of men, to accept my participation in communion.

I believe in love that can enable me to endure trials. The time has come that we have been praying for. The Almighty is shaking up the self-satisfied, the self-deluded and the self-contented. God is rooting out indifference. But to witness at this time requires greater forbearance, because people are disturbed by all that is going on. They easily take offence and offend others even more easily. They resort to violence at the drop of a hat. If I love them I must put up with them. I fall silent when they interrupt me. I am not afraid if

Aleksandar Birviš

they want to strike me. I will turn the other cheek if they slap me. If I only have two cheeks — because evil is not so easily stopped — I will pray to God for those who do evil to me.

I believe in love, the teacher of goodness. The Lord has already eradicated the intolerable bitterness, vindictiveness, malice and spite. But there are still many good qualities I need to learn. My desire is to be more like Christ in all things. I look to Him as my example because He is the embodiment and fulfillment of perfect goodness. I am in awe at what He has done. I ask myself: how can I be so bold, not to say impudent, to compare myself with Him? No, I am not bold or impudent, but Christ's example is irresistible. I don't have the strength to oppose Him. The character of the God–Man breaks down all resistance.

I believe in the love from which comes unselfishness. Man by nature puts himself at the centre of the world from the moment he is born. It seems that everything has to belong to him and to be just as he wants it. A baby grabs everything that it sees. As soon as it gets its hand on something it sticks it in its mouth. But it isn't hungry, just greedy. It grabs and holds on to everything it can. As the child grows its greed increases. Adults are the same, but they do it consciously, more skillfully and more surreptitiously. Who can stop them? Only Christ's love can stop them. The Lord Jesus condemned selfishness. On the cross every sin, including the sin of selfishness, was cut down and rejected. Selflessness shone forth from Calvary.

I believe in love for baptism. Many people call themselves Christians just because they have been baptized. Most of them don't even remember it, because they were baptized by others, and they are not aware of it even today. But the time is now here when they must think and decide for themselves. There are more and more of those who love Christ and it is of the greatest importance for them

Reflections

that they approach Him freely and consciously. No one is forced to be baptized, and in a free society no one should be forced to do such a thing. I know that we should love baptism because it comes from Christ. So I love all that comes before baptism, baptism itself and the life that comes after baptism.

I believe in love and that is why I belong to the fellowship of Christ. I joined out of love. I was received into it with love. There was room for me too with Christ. At one time I had no time for God, but God found time for me — what can I do but commit my life to Him? I did not have the power or the courage to make a decision for the Lord, but the Lord powerfully and boldly sacrificed Himself for me — how can I not sacrifice myself? I have always been and still am poor, but the Almighty put His riches at my disposal — how can I not make myself available to serve Him? I had no intellect of my own, but He used His great wisdom to make me wise — how can I not be His disciple for ever? In order to return this love, I love His work, I belong to His Church and I serve Him with the gift He has given me.

I believe in love for the Gospel and the evangelists. God loves soul-winners. No one comes to this service for his own sake, no one preaches for his own sake, no one sings for his own sake, no one prays for his own sake. Likewise no one sits down just for the sake of sitting or stands just for the sake of standing, nor prays just for the sake of it, or sings for the sake of it, or preaches for the sake of it. We are in the Church for God's glory and for His love. Everything that is done and that happens in the fellowship of Christ has its purpose: to glorify the Lord and to win new souls for the Savior and for salvation.

Yes, dear brothers and sisters, I believed in love, and I believe in love, and I will never cease to believe in love. Our Deliverer is

Aleksandar Birviš

love, and Jesus Christ is the same yesterday today and for ever" (Heb. 13:8).

Final reading: Ps. 117

Belgrade, 1ˢᵗ August 1992

LIFE IN THE LIGHT OF THE SPIRIT

Eighth Sunday after Whitsun
Subject: Fruit of the Spirit

Main reading: Eph. 5:6-10

Let no man deceive you with vain words: for because of these things cometh the wrath of God upon the children of disobedience. Be not ye therefore partakers with them. For ye were sometimes darkness, but now are ye light in the Lord: walk as children of light: (For the fruit of the Spirit is in all goodness and righteousness and truth;) Proving what is acceptable unto the Lord.

Spiritual life is not a fairy tale. It is a reality. Each one of us can be spiritual, but we can also refuse to live with God. Man does this on his own responsibility.

I must talk to you about life in the light of the Spirit. It is not good for Christians to be unspiritual. They are not even Christians then. They have the name, but they have no life. Nevertheless, unlike someone who is dead physically, they can escape from spiritual death even before the resurrection of the dead and the Savior's second coming.

You can escape spiritual death now. So I beg you to listen. Your spirit will come to life too.

Let no man deceive you with vain words…

Aleksandar Birviš

The Scriptures teach us that false teachers and false prophets will appear. As the days of Christ's second coming approach the number of seducers increases.

False teachers will know the Scriptures. Their mouths will be full of Biblical sayings, but by their lives and by their spirit they will deviate from God's words. They will cleverly interpret the Old and New Testaments. But they will make a new one of the Old and an old one of the New. Christ says that it is impossible to repair an old garment with new cloth, and that old wineskins cannot hold new wine (Luke 5:36-39). False teachers will oppose these words and other sayings of our Savior.

False prophets will appear with prophecies of their own invention. They will say that God has told them something. They may even persuade themselves that God has spoken to them. Others will tell them that they are good prophets. Whether they deceive themselves, or deceive others, or others deceive them, false prophets will exist and be active, and will browbeat, scold and lead men into destruction.

How are we to defend ourselves from the seducers? How can we oppose them? How can we know that their words are not just empty phrases?

The Holy Spirit has already taken care of that.

Firstly, seducers do not bring light nor do they point to the light. They generally see what is dark. They prefer to talk against something rather than for something.

Secondly, deceivers shun righteousness and truth. Their teachings and prophetic utterances are not in keeping with the spirit and practice of Scripture. They cannot be harmonised with the life of the Church. They want reform, but they are not reformers. They talk about renewal, but they remain ensnared by the past.

Reflections

Thirdly, deceivers love strange, incomprehensible and bombastic words. The words of the Christian should be flavored with salt (Mark 9:50; Col. 4:6). Seductive words are flavored with pepper or sugar.

For because of these things cometh the wrath of God upon the children of disobedience.

The acts of deceit that we have mentioned will not go unpunished. The Lord does not allow false teachers and false prophets to avoid His wrath.

God is not biased. He is not blinded by love such He does not see sin. He is not so filled with wrath that He punishes both the innocent and the guilty. He clearly sees those who are innocent, appreciates the good that they do and their goodness, and seeks to keep them in righteousness and justice, and encourages them to persist in the truth. He sees and corrects men, He hears them and knows them and He is ready to praise them and reward them.

This same God judges and punishes. If anyone opposes the voice of God's Spirit, he cannot expect to get by as if nothing has happened. The Holy Spirit takes note of virtues, because those virtues arise from the enlightenment that He gives to men.

Disobedience arouses God's wrath. In vain may a man appeal to his own skills and knowledge. Lies and deceit are not fruit of the Spirit. Opposition does not come from the Spirit of God. God does not intend to include the deceivers and the deceived amongst the believers, unless they truly repent.

God has not left anyone without the ability to reason. Christ has given to His fellowships people who can distinguish spirits. So we should not fear God's wrath, but we should flee from disobedience.

Be not ye therefore partakers with them.

Aleksandar Birviš

There can be no accommodation with impostors. Deceivers live around us and try and get alongside us. It is dangerous if we agree to let them live among us.

Have nothing in common with false teachers! Don't be in awe of their learning and their degrees — we have authentic experts who on top of their degrees are endorsed by the Holy Spirit. False teachers do not bear the fruit of the Spirit. Genuine teachers radiate goodness, righteousness and truth.

Have nothing in common with false prophets! We do not need to look for private prophecies when we have the Scriptures and when the Scriptures give us answers. When we see that there is no answer or the answers are not clear, then we will seek out prophets. How? We will pray to God, spend time in fasting, search the Word of God, and look within the fellowship of Christ. The Lord Jesus promises, *Howbeit when He, the Spirit of truth, is come, He will guide you into all truth: for He shall not speak of Himself; but whatsoever He shall hear, that shall He speak: and He will shew you things to come. He shall glorify Me: for He shall receive of Mine, and shall shew it unto you* (John 16:13-14).

If anyone makes use of lies, the Spirit of truth is not in him. We have nothing in common with such a man. If anybody devises something that does not agree with the Heavenly Father, he has dreamed it up himself, and we will not share in his words and deeds. If the prophet prophesies to glorify himself, and places the glory of Christ alongside himself or compares himself with Christ — let us keep away from him, because he is full of destruction.

For ye were sometimes darkness, but now are ye light in the Lord:

A firm approach to deceivers does not give Christians the right to think highly of themselves and to despise others. Even the holiest people can have a sinful past. The more spiritual a man is the stronger his awareness of the great redemption he has received. Christ has

Reflections

brought every one of His followers out of the darkness, out of sin and destruction.

Darkness — what an unpleasant word. It signifies life without God, or a condition without salvation. What are the characteristics of such a life? Allow me to mention just three:

One: darkness is the *absence of light*. In the spiritual life it means that we had nothing of that which comes from the Holy Spirit: no goodness, righteousness or truth. None of the other factors that we consider fruits of the Spirit (Gal. 5:22-23) were present in us, either: no love, no joy, no peace, no longsuffering, no kindness, no goodness, no faith, no gentleness, no self-control.

Two: in the darkness, *obstacles and dangers* are not visible. It is difficult to walk where there is no light. You cannot help tripping up, bumping into things, falling into holes in the ground, and you have to keep feeling your way. Darkness is full of painful surprises. It is no use being brave when you cannot see your enemy.

Three: darkness is a *source of apparitions*. You can imagine all sorts of things in the dark but you cannot substantiate any of them. Everything seems credible. In spiritual darkness, men believe in horoscopes, palm reading, tea leaves, drinking special water, visions of a new world order and the historic struggle of classes, races and castes.

Satan loves the darkness. Christ was arrested in the darkness even thought they could have arrested Him in broad daylight. Revolutions and political diversions are carried out at night, and what we call "night-life" is really just a veiled invitation to sin.

Each of us once lived in this darkness. Then the Holy Spirit spoke. A new day dawned. We met Christ and came into the light. I would remind you that this light "is in the Lord". Human enlightenment cannot bring spiritual light. The Heavenly Father has given us that

Aleksandar Birviš

light as a result of salvation. The Christian has crossed over from darkness to light and from sin to salvation.

Walk as children of light:

We belong to Christ. We are under obligation to live according to the new life that is in us.

Light brings out all that is good and all that is not. Our life is hidden with Christ in God (Col. 3:3). But our behavior is not hidden. It is public. Christian works must not be the subject of boasting, but the Christian nature must be known to men. It communicates the glory of God. The spirituality of an individual or a fellowship can be seen by the behavior of believers.

All those who have come out of the darkness into the light of the living God have experienced authentic life. Christians live with a special sense of dignity. We don't invent a unique lifestyle in terms of dress, footwear and the way we walk. There is no such thing as Christian etiquette. However, we belong to a people that God has declared as His own and whom He has marked as His own special people (Titus 2:14).

The character of Christ is immediately visible. I know of one of our sisters who somewhere in the early nineteen-fifties didn't dare tell her parents that she had become a Christian. She came to our church, and her parents knew and did not object much. But the change in her became obvious, even though she had always been a good daughter and as far as could be seen there was no change in her behavior. But one day her mother said, "You must have become a member of that church."

… For the fruit of the Spirit is in all goodness and righteousness and truth;

Reflections

This is the main thought of the passage that we are studying. Life in the light is life in the Holy Spirit. That life gives birth to virtues. Without them there is no spiritual life. By acquiring these virtues we acquire the Holy Spirit, and the greatest work of the Spirit in us is the attainment of virtues. These two are inseperable from each other, and from Christ who is our role model and the source of the Holy Spirit.

The unsaved can appear better and more devout than Christians in many ways. Christians should be ashamed if this happens, but — that's the way it is. Every Christian man and woman should ask themselves: why is a heathen, an unbeliever, a godless man or an idolater nobler, better, more full of love and more ready to make sacrifices than I am? I say that such a man is in darkness, yet we see there is more light shining from his darkness than from me and my enlightenment.

This should not concern us too much, however. When troubles come, the old man rears his ugly head, and the apparent virtues fall away like every other mask does. A small-scale civil war is enough to transform those who yesterday were peaceful neighbors and God-fearing citizens into bloodthirsty murderers. That is when we see who belongs to Christ and who has not emerged from the darkness.

The first product of the Spirit that is mentioned here is goodness. The light of the Holy Spirit has completely changed man's character. A former sinner has now become good by nature. (Of course, evil did not disappear overnight, but it is no longer part of the nature of the regenerate man). A true Christian will not become evil again even in the worst possible conditions.

Righteousness too arises from the light of the Holy Spirit. A sinner never obeyed the will of God. He obeyed the law because he had to. He was capable of being an excellent judge in the courts of this world provided he had a good knowledge of the law and if he

Aleksandar Birviš

found upholding the law a worthwhile and agreeable occupation. But without the activity of God's Spirit the sinner does not grasp his unrighteousness, even less so his own inability to be righteous. It is necessary that the Lord brings him to reason. Only then can a man expect something to happen to him. And that something is a miracle: Christ gifts the man His righteousness. If he believes in this the sinner becomes a righteous man: the Savior has imputed His righteousness to him (Phil. 3:9). It is by that righteousness that we can come before the throne of God even though we personally had no righteousness.

A similar thing applies to truth. We receive it through the merits of Christ. God first awoke in us a love for truth. Then the Lord Jesus came as the embodiment of truth. After that the truth became our truth and we became adherents of that truth. The Holy Spirit continued to maintain each Christian in a deeper and deeper understanding of that truth. We live in the truth and the truth lives in us.

This is an understanding of truth as a product of the Spirit. This fruit is applied in everyday life. Christians are certainly interested in theological truth, but they live in the truth in their everyday work: as a householder and a shopkeeper, a teacher and a politician, a street cleaner and a coach driver. In all the circumstances of life a Christian has Christ and Christ has the Christian; a Christian possesses the truth and the truth possesses the Christian.

... *Proving what is acceptable unto the Lord.*

The explanation of this verse also serves as the natural conclusion of the truths set out here. God has shown us goodness, righteousness and truth. He has delivered us from evil, unrighteousness and falsehood. Christ has conquered and now He reigns. The Holy Spirit sets us free and protects us from returning to the darkness.

Reflections

We have been given light. We have been warned not to have any part in anything dark or concealed. Light and darkness have nothing in common.

Life in the light, or life in Christ and the Holy Spirit, is a life of searching. Christian men and women continue to search untiringly all their lives. They don't peer into their neighbors' cooking pots or look under their beds. Christian men and women search out how and with what they can please God.

I will make so bold as to suggest a well-tested way to please God.

First: constant living prayer. Let us pray at a time set aside for prayer. Let us talk to God when we have to wait for something or are held up in traffic or we chase paperwork around government offices. Let us direct our prayers to God as we walk through residential neighborhoods: there are many unsaved people in those houses, yards, streets and squares. We need to pray constantly for all of them, and for others too.

We also need to commit ourselves to prayer after hearing or seeing or reading of anything happening around us. Radio, television and the newspapers inform us of all sorts of horrors. Behind each horror story there are people. People need God.

Second: regular study of the message of the Bible. We don't read the Bible so that we can boast how many times we have read it. We read it regularly because it is the Word of the living God. We study the Word with prayer and meditation. In this way we will get to know the Lord – the One Who Is – more deeply and more sincerely.

Reading the Bible encourages a more diverse prayer life and a more comprehensive development of our spiritual life. It must not be allowed to become a competition. The fellowship of believers — through preaching and Bible study — ensures harmonious study of

Aleksandar Birviš

the Scriptures. In this way we get to know God and His people and also ourselves.

Third: regular and genuine participation in church services. We like to come to the house of prayer. We love to see each other. We are blessed to have an opportunity to hear the Word of God and praise the Lord. This is all good and pleasant and useful — we enjoy church services more than anything else.

It is especially important that we know the fruit of the Spirit in this and that we receive that fruit. Services are a wonderful opportunity to do that and provide us with unique opportunities.

The Lord has given us this place. God has also given other places where He shows His goodness and mercy, and where we proclaim His righteousness and truth. There is life in church buildings. A life which is not according to man's understanding. Spiritual life often does not suit everyone's tastes. But God is not present in the Church in order to please us, rather we are there to please Him.

This act of pleasing God is done at specific times. Services have a schedule: daily, weekly, annual, or series covering various festivals. It is sin to forgo those special times, and to miss those services or to only come as and when it suit us, or, even worse, to come without any sort of pattern or discipline. That is a great loss, because in every opportunity that God gives us to worship Him, in every sanctified place, every worker and co-worker of God gathers spiritual blessings and increases in the fruit of the Spirit of God.

★   ★   ★

We are called to please God. It is up to us whether we will respond to God's invitation in a worthy manner. It is time for that response to be seen, heard and made known. May the Spirit of truth

Reflections

come and direct us into all truth, and goodness and righteousness. May He do it for us and for all followers of Christ.

Final reading: Ps. 118:19-21

Belgrade, 9th August 1992 / 23rd August 1992

STRENGTH, PROTECTION AND VICTORY

Introductory reading: Ps. 18:1-6

Main reading: Is. 59:16-17

And He saw that there was no man, and wondered that there was no intercessor: therefore His arm brought salvation unto Him; and His righteousness, it sustained Him. For He put on righteousness as a breastplate, and an helmet of salvation upon His head; and He put on the garments of vengeance for clothing, and was clad with zeal as a cloak.

Christ is your strength. The Lord Jesus is your protection. The Son of God is our victory.

1

Strength of faith comes from God. The Savior stretches out His hand to the weak in faith to dispel their doubts. No-one is without weaknesses. There will always be failures and shortcomings.

Who will give you the strength to stand against temptations and troubles? Great tribulations are coming upon the whole earth. The world does not notice. It is hurtling into oblivion. We should not be surprised, for all that you see around you is leading up to the end of the world.

Christians will not be part of the universal destruction. The Savior has come that His followers may have life in all its fullness, a special life (John 10:10). The power of life has come and is coming amongst men. God's power performs miracles. The Lord does not

Reflections

do them to make you wonder at Him, but so that you should stand when all else is falling apart.

Justice is a true foundation. Men and nations suffer because they are wallowing in injustice. In vain they rely on their own resources. They rely on all their knowledge to no avail. Quotations from the Scripture won't help either if injustice prevails. The foundation on which Christ's follower rests is God's justice.

No one may rely on their own righteousness, because human righteousness does not bring justice. Personal righteousness is an adornment, not a weapon. Adornments, medals and jewelry don't win wars. The strength of justice is in the Savior's superiority.

Your understanding does not direct you towards salvation. Why should it? Surely man is free to think what he wants? That is what you are struggling for: that your thoughts may be free, that your words may be free, that you may be free to do or not do what you intend or say.

But the redemptive Word is here. God saves, and that means that your mind must experience redemptive changes in its thinking. When you bring your weaknesses before God, you will receive strength from Him. If you boast to Him of your good qualities, your ingrained weakness will come to the fore.

God has reserved the right of vengeance for Himself. Just as judges once used to wear special robes (togas), so God's vengeance is the determinant of His justice. His Kingdom stands firm because He recompenses men for their intentions and deeds. Christianity gives special courage. Even the weakest Christian may suffer torture, and even death, because he knows that every injustice will cost someone dear. Even when you are defeated, you win, because the Lord's enemy is like chaff. He will be blown away by the power of Christ's breath, that is by the action of the Holy Spirit.

Aleksandar Birviš

The Lord insists on carrying out His decisions and decrees. He neglects nothing. By meting out justice He purifies the fellowship. The Almighty zealously carries out one more great deed: He brings the world to reason. In every nation, even in those where nothing is known about Christ, there are still certain rights and the need for righteousness. By responding to that need, God obliges the world to behave sensibly and soberly, and to realize that it must seek justice, righteousness and the one who brings all righteousness — God.

Men usually talk of a sense of or feel for justice, because they seek meanings and feelings. The Lord shows His zeal more readily than He explains things. He talks of His zeal for justice. Zeal in the Scriptures is a feeling of jealousy. The Almighty jealously preserves His right to decide what is to be considered justice and what is not; whom He will condemn and whom He will forgive. Through His zeal God also strengthens the fellowship and brings down the evil one.

2

The Heavenly Father is watching. He knows and sees what sort of people we are. He knows that weaknesses and shortcomings predominate. Men need a protector. Who is that to be? There is no such one among men. God decides Himself how to protect those who believe.

He is able to do that because He is almighty. Whoever believes in Him believes that He can do all things. No one need be afraid when he is under the protection of God, who knows no barriers. You are protected by the Almighty Lord.

The Savior taught men that they cannot trust human righteousness. Whose justice can protect us then? Can civil laws protect us? No. Christ's perfect righteousness protects you.

Reflections

God demonstrates this type of protection metaphorically: *He will not suffer thy foot to be moved: He that keepeth thee will not slumber* (Ps. 121:3). You will not descend into injustice. That is the promise of the Almighty and it is good to trust in Him.

Righteousness protects like armor. It protects you from all sides. If you don't want the powers of darkness to overcome you, be honest. Old brother Jacob Zhidkov who has long since gone to be with the Lord was the president of all the Evangelical Baptist Christians in the old Soviet Union. That was during the worst period of persecution just before the Second World War. Brother Zhidkov was for a time imprisoned on Sakhalin Island which was worse than Siberia. The authorities were trying to achieve two aims: 1) to turn those men into secret police informers 2) and to cause hate between them and the other inmates. They did not succeed in either of these aims with our brother. He never said anything bad about his country and her people, but he was never prepared to speak flatteringly about the government. As a committed Christian he would never flatter anyone. Nor would he hurt anyone. The camp inmates loved him and respected him as far as their circumstances allowed. They risked their lives, but were not prepared to witness falsely against him.

What was it that made that man earn the respect of both politicians and criminals, and even the camp authorities? Integrity. If you talk about faith, they don't believe. If you love them, they hardly feel it. If you have hope, that is unimportant to them. Integrity — that was something they could see, it was a basic form of justice and righteousness. They might make fun of a man of integrity, but one day they will appreciate him and love him. They will understand that he is a man of God and that he is under Christ's protection.

God has armed you with salvation. It is depicted as a helmet. The eyes of the saved man are protected so that they do not see

Aleksandar Birviš

immorality, as are his ears so that he does not hear unclean words, as are his lips so that they do not speak foul things; but especially his mind, so that he does not think as men think, but as God thinks.

3

It seems there is no room for Christ in the world. You think you are defeated in everything you have undertaken. Others think the same: they have lost more than they have gained.

But only the Lord Jesus is victorious. All wars are in vain. Victories are worth nothing because in the end there is only misery, and that is still defeat. The only war in which there is a real winner is Christ's war. The Savior is the true and indisputable victor.

The Savior's victory is a victory of justice over injustice. You have experienced many injustices, untruths, slander and attacks, spiritual, mental and physical. But none of it will remain as it was when you experienced it. You will see injustice disappearing and righteousness being established, untruths disappearing, and truth appearing, slander being rejected, and praise taking its place, attacks ceasing and completely new areas of the spirit, soul and body being built up.

For that reason it is necessary for the Lord to bring order to the world. That is His rule. The Kingdom of God is not "out there somewhere". It is amongst men. If God has defeated sin in you and me and established truth, that is the Kingdom of God. And where His Kingdom is, there is His victory. It doesn't matter how many people are present.

When I say the number is not important, I don't mean that this fellowship should be small. On the contrary, our conquests and Christ's victory are concerned with souls. Each conversion is a challenge, a struggle, an effort and a conquest. If we are Christ's

Reflections

soldiers, let us not be losers. This we dare not be both because of the unique name that has been given us, and because of the victory that has already been won on the cross.

The Lord does not allow for defeat. He has conquered. Whoever believes in Him, believes in His victory. Christianity is not a subject taught in school. It is life. Everything we learn in church is learnt for victory. It is natural that we should feel weak. You are not mistaken. Every man is insignificant and small —but God is great. You feel defeated and frustrated. This all contributes to your discouragement. But God is generous. He wipes out our defeats. He changes every frustration into conquest.

Righteousness and God's consistency cannot know defeat and loss. You constantly receive news from the world: injustice here, suffering there. Worldly men make fun of you: "Where is your God?" they say as if their gods are real rulers and true deities. They ask mockingly: "Why has He allowed a civil war? Why are innocent children being killed?"

Such sneering is enough to discourage you. But those are the questions of practical polytheists. They sacrifice everything to their gods: adults and children, young and old, the movable and the immovable. God never stood in the way of other religions, but the polytheist, the heathen and the atheist have paid a high price for their waywardness, both in this world and the next.

Is this not — when you take a deep, hard look at it — Christ's victory?

★ ★ ★

Aleksandar Birviš

Christ is your strength. Join together with those who believe that. Your Lord will give you power. You will receive strength from Him. He is the source of progress for those who trust in Him.

The Lord Jesus is your protection. Join together with those who believe that. Your Lord will give you the armor of justice and the helmet of salvation, the robe of His legislature and the mantle of His consistency. He is the source of protection for all who trust in Him.

The Son of God is our victory. We belong to His celebrated army. He will teach us how to fight against the power of darkness. From our suffering, exertion and blood, the rule of brightness will shine forth, that cannot be hidden, nor clouded over, nor stopped. The Kingdom of God has come.

Glory to Christ — our strength. Glory to the Lord Jesus — our protection. Glory to the Son of God — our victory.

Final reading: Eph. 6:10-20

Belgrade, 16th August 1992

THE TRANSFIGURATION

Today is Transfiguration in the Eastern Calendar. The three Gospel writers Matthew, Mark and Luke have recorded this event. I will read Luke's version (9:28-36), as translated by Professor Čarnić:

And it came to pass about an eight days after these sayings, He took Peter and John and James, and went up into a mountain to pray. And as He prayed, the fashion of His countenance was altered, and His raiment was white and glistering. And, behold, there talked with Him two men, which were Moses and Elias: Who appeared in glory, and spake of His decease which He should accomplish at Jerusalem. But Peter and they that were with him were heavy with sleep: and when they were awake, they saw His glory, and the two men that stood with Him. And it came to pass, as they departed from Him, Peter said unto Jesus, Master, it is good for us to be here: and let us make three tabernacles; one for Thee, and one for Moses, and one for Elias: not knowing what he said.

While he thus spake, there came a cloud, and overshadowed them: and they feared as they entered into the cloud. And there came a voice out of the cloud, saying, This is My beloved Son: hear Him. And when the voice was past, Jesus was found alone. And they kept it close, and told no man in those days any of those things which they had seen.

I hope that one day I will have time to talk in more detail about the Transfiguration. In this service I am going to ask five questions connected with the passage we read and try to answer them.

Aleksandar Birviš

First question: Why was the Savior transfigured on the mountain, and not down in the valley?

Answer: The Lord's intention was to teach us about effort. Do we want to have some experience of the glorified Christ? We must make some effort of our own. We mustn't say God is love, God can do all things, and God will give us everything, why should we make any effort to get this or that? God doesn't care for laziness. He does all things alone, He doesn't need to rely on human achievements, but He does not permit disorder, inaction and the human dislike of effort. Prayer too must be work, hard work before the Lord.

The Savior also wants Christians to get used to sublimity. Our thoughts are often very down-to-earth. It is good to think about earthly need, especially if we are to struggle for the good of our neighbors. But whoever wants to approach the glory of Christ must heed the words of the apostle Paul: *If ye then be risen with Christ, seek those things which are above, where Christ sitteth on the right hand of God. Set your affection on things above, not on things on the earth* (Col. 3:1-2).

Second question: Why was the Lord Jesus transfigured while He was praying?

Answer: The Lord was showing us that prayer is the time for transfiguration. Every sincere prayer is a sign that something is changing. The man or woman who prays is changing. After you have prayed, your neighbors become different. If they pray too, they become different people. Kingdoms and whole continents are changed by prayer.

There can be no doubt that the most important change is the transfiguration of the individual. Christ showed how His glory appears. Whoever prays readily and persistently to the Heavenly Father, will experience the appearing of the glory of God's Son. Believing in Christ's transfiguration we ourselves are transfigured.

Reflections

The way to obtain this is not through folk customs, or rituals of some kind, but prayer. Whoever prays consistently and persistently, will be transfigured and will see the transfigured Christ.

Third question: Why did Moses and Elijah appear?

Answer: Because the Law and the prophets were fulfilled in the Lord Jesus Christ. Moses is the representative of the Law, because the five books he wrote stand at the beginning of the Scriptures and represent the oldest comprehensive legal system in the world. Elijah left no writings, but what is recorded about him shows him as a prophet who is an example to others. He openly and fearlessly pointed to the will of God.

Obedience to the Law and Prophets is the only proper route to enter Christianity. We cannot continue to stand before Christ without respecting the Old Testament Scriptures. In the parable of the rich man and Lazarus (Luke 16:19-31) our Savior says that men have Moses and the prophets, and they should listen to them, and if they won't then it will be to no avail even if someone rises from the dead to call them to repentance. Transfiguration and growth in Christlikeness are possible if we are sincerely obedient to the Scriptures of both Old and New Testament.

The Lord Jesus says: *The law and the prophets were until John: since that time the kingdom of God is preached, and every man presseth into it. And it is easier for heaven and earth to pass, than one tittle of the law to fail* (Luke 16:16-17).

Fourth question: Why did Moses and Elijah talk to Christ about the frightening events which were to happen to our Savior in Jerusalem?

Answer: They talked about Christ's crucifixion and resurrection. The cross and the empty tomb are the key elements of saving faith. Whoever does not believe this is not a Christian and cannot be born

Aleksandar Birviš

of God. There can be no transfiguration where there is no faith in the crucified and resurrected Christ.

Transfiguration is a day when we should think about the meaning of true faith. As followers of Christ we will not persecute anyone because of heresy, but we will not deviate from the true faith that the Lord has entrusted to us. No appeasement or concessions. We believe in the crucified and resurrected Jesus, the Son of God and Lord.

Fifth and last question, of a more general nature: Why was the Transfiguration necessary?

Answer: The Transfiguration was necessary so that Christ's followers would grasp that their Teacher was the promised Messiah, the Son of the living God and that they would obey Him even when it appears that enemy forces have conquered. That is the command of the heavenly Father. We know Him and receive commands and knowledge from Him.

Even the freest man is obedient to someone. Before he meets the Savior, a man is enslaved to this world. Many people live in the conviction that they are free. They demonstrate this by their ability to do whatever they like. But these people are enslaved to their bodies and to this supposition that we have already mentioned that they are free. They are limited by their addiction to fleshly pleasures. Over time these pleasures become bitter, burdensome and destructive, but they are not able to get free from them. They are enslaved.

Christians are not slaves, but they obey the voice of the heavenly Father. They can choose not to obey Him. They are free to reject every voice, not just the voice of God. They have resolved not to do that. Instead of rejecting God, Christians praise Him: the victory is His, the Kingdom is His.

The Lord Jesus Christ is the chosen Son of God. Obey Him!

Belgrade, 19th August 1992

HOW CHRIST WOULD THINK

Tenth Sunday after Whitsun
Subject: The mind of Christ

Introductory reading: Ps. 27:1
Main reading: 1 Cor. 2:15-16

But he that is spiritual judgeth all things, yet he himself is judged of no man. For who hath known the mind of the Lord, that he may instruct Him? but we have the mind of Christ.

We are instructed to look to Christ. Thank God that we are able to do that. That is why we study the Savior's life and work. The Gospels are not just reading material for us. They show us how the Lord Jesus lived and what He did.

We want to do what our Lord did, to work as He did and think as He did. There are many people around who do not know how to think. We talk about manipulating people. A man doesn't know how to think for himself, so others force him to think like they think and to do as other people like.

Nobody forces us; we are attracted by Christ's thoughts. We can think like Christ, and we want to do so. Let's try.

Let us look at some everyday things going on at the moment.

What would Christ think about the civil war? Whether we like it or not war is raging all around us. Evil has raised its ugly head. The Savior certainly would not agree to evil. He has a wonderful

Aleksandar Birviš

word which instructs us on how to think about such things. He says, *Therefore all things whatsoever ye would that men should do to you, do ye even so to them: for this is the law and the prophets* (Matt. 7:12).

Imagine what would happen if all those who have taken up arms began to think like this. They talk or force a man into taking up arms but he thinks to himself: What I want them to do to me, I will do to them. Nobody wants their arm cut off, or their eyes gouged out or to be tortured in any way. How many problems would disappear in everyday life if men kept just to this principle!

War is a fact. The Lord Jesus would not pretend not to notice. He requires careful attention: His followers must be conscious of all that is happening, because all that is happening is part of God's plan. That is why the Savior says, *Watch ye therefore: for ye know not when the master of the house cometh, at even, or at midnight, or at the cockcrowing, or in the morning: Lest coming suddenly he find you sleeping. And what I say unto you I say unto all, Watch* (Mark 13:35-37).

The ministry of the spiritual watchman is for each of us. Each one of us is obliged to be God's watchman, to watch over himself, over the fellowship, over the neighbor in his care. There is no one who is excused from the obligation to struggle for the Gospel, because we do not know when the Lord Jesus will come again. We must be ready at any time.

Christ would certainly think about war in a way that people often don't think, namely, that there are no winners in war. Remember the parades we used to have on Victory Day (9th May). Over time they became more and more wretched and unimportant. The supposedly victorious nations had lost a great deal. They were all ruined internally.

In our times we should once again consider the Savior's parable of the talents (Matt. 25:14-30). In that parable God is not talking

Reflections

about people at war. He does not give His talent to generals but to men who need to work, and carry on working and increasing what they have. In a similar story which talks about bags of money and a silver coin called a *mina* (Luke 19:11-27), the nobleman says: *Do business till I come.* Business can prevent war, and work can heal the consequences of war.

In both of these parables of Christ we see the excuses of those who won't work. Their excuses cut no ice. Work brings blessing.

What would Christ think about the Constitution, elections and questions of power? We sometimes forget that power, whatever it is like, only comes when God decides, even if every political party believes that it has taken power by its own merits.

Christ says very clearly, *But seek ye first the kingdom of God, and His righteousness; and all these things shall be added unto you* (Matt. 6:33).

Earth's kingdoms crumble, lawlessness breaks out precisely because no one seeks the Kingdom of God. Instead of seeking God's Kingdom first, worldly men state openly that they are involved in politics because they seek power.

But power is from God and man should see what he needs to do with God's help and with the powers that God has given him.

Men talk so much about democracy that it has become a word no longer taken seriously, just as happened with the word revolution. It is worn out through overuse. However Christians have a kind of order where value is not lost.

The Kingdom of God is the most valuable thing. Christians have it today. There is no need to pay much regard to the values of this world, even though we are in this world and we have to think of them.

The Kingdom of God gives confidence. As long as men have existed, the question has been asked, "What will happen tomorrow?"

Aleksandar Birviš

Our King of Kings tells us: *Take therefore no thought for the morrow: for the morrow shall take thought for the things of itself. Sufficient unto the day is the evil thereof* (Matt. 6:34). However much we worry about tomorrow, it is still in God's hands.

The people of God serve Christ and so they should not be worried about eternity. Men create all sorts of power structures, and they are conscious that there is much that is deceptive in them, yet they behave as if they have given us the last word in politics. But even the Constitution has to be changed, sometimes very quickly, and with every new constitution we are told that it is something the human race should marvel at.

The human race is imperfect. It needs to understand its imperfection. Christians have the task of pointing out that we must simply follow the Lord and not worry about eternity. The Lord Jesus says, *If any man serve Me, let him follow Me; and where I am, there shall also My servant be: if any man serve Me, him will My Father honour* (John 12:26). In simple terms, if I serve the Lord, I will be where Christ is and the Heavenly Father will give me honor. If you serve the Lord, you will be where Christ is and the Heavenly Father will give you honor. Everything else is of secondary importance: the end of the world, the antichrist, the number of the beast etc. The Lord rules over times and events, He is the Almighty.

What would Christ think about the students' demands, about the situation in education, about the autonomy of the University? There are people who think that Christians shouldn't have opinions about such questions. But the Savior thought about learning, teaching and teaching establishments in His own way. He defined the relationships. So we read His words (Matt. 23:8-12): *But be not ye called Rabbi: for one is your Master, even Christ; and all ye are brethren.* The problem today in education and the upbringing of

Reflections

children is that everyone wants titles, but pupils are not brethren. Children are rivals and enemies. Academic institutions look more like boxing rings: in order to get better grades you are allowed to use methods which are without love and are of dubious integrity. Then the Lord Jesus said, *And call no man your father upon the earth: for one is your Father, which is in heaven.* It has been the rule since time immemorial that the teacher is like another parent. I am tremendously grateful to my first teacher, Stanika Todorović, the long-departed Mrs. "Caja", as she was nicknamed, for teaching me things which even my own mother did not teach me. Not to mention my teachers in secondary school and university. (You can read my preface to my translation of the Psalms). But no one may take the place of the Heavenly Father.

Christ continues: *Neither be ye called masters: for One is your Master, even Christ.* Christians know fundamentally that their first exalted teacher is the Lord Jesus. In Him there is freedom of education. The structured Christian approach to education is the only one that has been able to balance professionalism, general education and humanity. That is why we follow Christ, the true, perfect educator, teacher, professor, academic and expert.

The standards of the Son of God are not like human standards. Education and expertise are not a route to an easy life. Even less are they a means to control people. Our Lord teaches us, *But he that is greatest among you shall be your servant. And whosoever shall exalt himself shall be abased; and he that shall humble himself shall be exalted.* Not power, but service.

I don't mean to read politicians a lecture. Let's look at ourselves. Has the craving for power disappeared? Is this church an role model for service? What do we need to develop in order to serve as our Deliverer served? Let us search for the answers ourselves. I want to

Aleksandar Birviš

express the hope that at least the words that people hear from this pulpit are of service to someone.

What would Christ think about nature conservation? We have to admit that the two monotheistic religions, Christianity and Islam, have been destroyers of nature. The Byzantine Empire and the Romans were not famous for their protection of vegetation and woodlands – far from it: the Velebit range was denuded in order to build Venice, and even before the Turks came, large areas of woodland were sacrificed for iron smelting. Later on that destruction gathered pace still further.

We remember that in olden times Carthage supplied Rome with food. Wars were fought over its wheat. With the arrival of the Arabs the wheat fields became wildernesses. The colonial powers were no better. Not until the middle of this century did a new understanding arise, and people started saying: the sand has reached the coast, is anyone going to be able to stop the desert advancing?

But long before Byzantium and Rome, even before Islam, Christ said, *...that ye may be the children of your Father which is in heaven: for He maketh His sun to rise on the evil and on the good, and sendeth rain on the just and on the unjust* (Matt. 5:45).

The sun and rain are not man's possession. They do not belong to this world, or this church or state or individual. All nature comes from sun and water and belongs to the heavenly Father. God has given it to us. Christ teaches us to accept the gift and not to insult the Giver.

We all need to learn how to receive a gift from God. A gift should not be despised, nor is it given to entertain us, or to be destroyed. What man has received he should improve and multiply. If he does this and looks after it to the best of his ability, he will be blessed.

Reflections

A careless attitude to creation is an insult to God. Carelessness allows the seed of destruction to grow. As soon as He created him, God Himself placed man, whom He had just created, in the Garden of Eden to cultivate it and take care of it (Gen. 2:15). Everything that is neglected decays. The Heavenly Giver of gifts will not rejoice when He sees His gifts in poor condition or completely destroyed.

What would Christ think about what men call military intervention? I think the answer is simple and does not require a detailed explanation. Our Savior does not permit the use of arms. The problem is that men don't take any notice of this answer. That is why they suffer and why they are afraid.

Such fear is justified. The powerful and strong are not interested in what is right. In place of the truth they offer "political reality". What is that? That is another name for violence, but not the violence of the rough shameless young men from my street, but the violence of politicians, states, religions, and military and economic alliances. That is nothing new. The Byzantine Emperor Cantacuzene[20] brought the Turks here during the life of the Emperor Dušan, and "Christians" from the north leapt at the opportunity to extend their borders.[21]

Later on those alliances failed, but new ones were made. We got involved in some of them, and fought against others. What did they all want? Subjugation, exploitation, captivity, murder and pillage. That's what they do today, too. Armies come and go, but fears remain.

But Christ says, *...but be of good cheer; I have overcome the world* (John 16:33). Let us think like Christians. Let us obey the Son of God. When they attacked Christ, the apostle Peter pulled out a weapon. Then the Lord said: *Put up again thy sword into his place: for all they that take the sword shall perish with the sword* (Matt. 26:52). The

Aleksandar Birviš

Savior didn't say, "To war, to war, our cause is just!" but, "Put your sword away!"

★ ★ ★

Finally let us ask each other: How can we cultivate the mind of Christ?

First. Be open to the working of the Holy Spirit. You do not know how the Spirit of God works, but He knows what He is doing. He knows you better than anybody else. He has already found a way of impressing upon you the thoughts of God.

Second. Study the Gospels. They show the life and work of the Lord Jesus Christ. From them you can learn what the Savior thought and did. Every time you read try to think like Him and do His works. His thoughts will live in you together with the Spirit of Christ. They will control you and you will do His works. You will do even more, because that is what Christ promised (John 14:12).

Third. Carefully set the limits of your thoughts and words. Do not present them as if they are Christ's. Do not tell that lie and deceive people around you. Why should you lead them astray? Christ warns His people: *Take heed that no man deceive you. For many shall come in My name, saying, I am Christ; and shall deceive many (*Matt 24:4-5).

Fourth. Give thanks. You have the mind of Christ. Thank the Lord. Do not exalt yourself, and do not be ungrateful. The more spiritual he is, the more a man is thankful. *But he that is spiritual judgeth all things, yet he himself is judged of no man* (1 Cor. 2:15).

This is the mind of Christ in us and among us.

Final reading: Ps. 51:10-12

Belgrade, 23rd August 1992

FIVE PRAYER MINIATURES

We are praying for the mission of the Church according to the needs of the people around us. I see those needs in the following: more of the Gospel, deeper faith, greater calmness, more abundant love and strengthened hope.

1. More of the Gospel

The Father sends the Son. The Father and the Son send the Holy Spirit. In a similar way God sends Christians. The Holy Spirit stirs up individuals in the local church. The Church appoints and authorizes individuals. Those individuals move at God's direction.

In the Acts of the Apostle (13:1-5) we see how the fellowship in Antioch sent the apostles Barnabas and Paul (at that time he was still Saul):

Now there were in the church that was at Antioch certain prophets and teachers; as Barnabas, and Simeon that was called Niger, and Lucius of Cyrene, and Manaen, which had been brought up with Herod the tetrarch, and Saul. As they ministered to the Lord, and fasted, the Holy Ghost said, Separate me Barnabas and Saul for the work whereunto I have called them. And when they had fasted and prayed, and laid their hands on them, they sent them away. So they, being sent forth by the Holy Ghost, departed unto Seleucia; and from thence they sailed to Cyprus. And when they were at

Aleksandar Birviš

Salamis, they preached the word of God in the synagogues of the Jews: and they had also John to their minister.

Barnabas and Paul were apostles, that is ambassadors of the Lord. Their task was not to bring some special wisdom. Just as the Son of God set out and was ready to sacrifice Himself, so they set out to sacrifice themselves. Just as Christ was stronger than death, so the two of them set out to encounter new life, the renewal of the spiritually dead, and their own resurrection. That is why the apostle Paul writes, *For I am now ready to be offered, and the time of my departure is at hand. I have fought a good fight, I have finished my course, I have kept the faith: Henceforth there is laid up for me a crown of righteousness, which the Lord, the righteous Judge, shall give me at that Day: and not to me only, but unto all them also that love His appearing* (2 Tim. 4:6-8).

The Gospel is a proclamation. Multiplication of the Gospel means proclamation and sacrifice. Are we ready to bring more of the Gospel to this world? Then we must sacrifice ourselves: our conceit must die, our intolerance, our pushiness, our impatience, our prejudice – but even our impartiality must die and only Christ remain as the sole fullness of God's revelation (Col. 2:9).

Let us sacrifice ourselves. The Gospel will be more complete.

Belgrade, 1ˢᵗ July 1992

2. Deeper faith

Mission is the work of God. Who is sent by God? The one who has truly experienced God. The Lord does not require that all Christian experience should be the same, or even very similar. But all experiences amongst Christians must be Christian.

Let us remind ourselves of the experience of the prophet Isaiah (Isa. 6). The Prophet had a vision of the glory of God. That included

Reflections

the Lord on His throne, seraphim with six wings, an awe-inspiring temple and frightening voices and smoke. An earthquake. The Prophet is terrified. He is not afraid of what he sees and hears. He is terrified at the thought that he is sinful because he has said unworthy things or at least things that were not in accordance with God's will. One of the seraphim picks up a piece of coal from the altar with his tongs and touches Isaiah's lips. The Prophet is purified. In future he will speak God's words. The Lord calls and Isaiah replies, "Here I am, send me."

Our experiences are not like this. Nevertheless each one of us is appointed for some work of God. Christ speaks to His Heavenly Father about each follower of His: *As Thou hast sent Me into the world, even so have I also sent them into the world.* (John 17:18). The question is not "Have we been sent?" but, "What have we been sent to do?".

Belief in mission is not some private revelation. It is fulfilled in a commitment and complete obedience to the will of God. A true prophet speaks in God's name but he does not act like God. He dare not do that because he is conscious of his insignificance.

We are praying for mission (apostleship) in accordance with Scripture, according to the will of the local fellowship and in a way acceptable to all, that is, in accordance with the will of the living God.

When a Christian witnesses to someone in the street, when he knocks on someone's door, when he gives someone a tract or a book, when he helps someone in trouble, he does it because he believes. The deeper his faith is the more ready he is to fulfill the tasks that he is sent to perform. Without this deeper faith, the man of God would be no different from the man of the world. The man of the world can do good works because the saving spark of Christ is smoldering in him (John 1:9). But, when a Christian does the same things, he

Aleksandar Birviš

has the awareness, the readiness and the enthusiasm to turn faith into action.

A deeper faith understands other people. It is not afraid of men and women who think differently and hold different beliefs. When the Lord Jesus told the apostles to throw their nets into the sea (Luke 5:4), they indicated to Him (at least that is what we see from the response and actions of the apostle Peter) that they were doing it out of obedience, and not because of the Savior's professional opinion, because they knew their trade well, and the lake that they were fishing. It turned out that God's Word was the key to them making a catch.

Depth indicates something else: we do not need to fear others' opinions. We need to fear our own sinfulness. In our situation that means this: if we grasp our own sin and sinfulness, then we will not find it a waste of time listening to other voices (Jews, Muslims, Orthodox, Roman Catholics, and other Protestant believers, even those who have no faith, but have something to say).

Belgrade, 8th September 1992

3. Greater calmness

God wants His children to be at peace. When the apostle Paul greets the fellowship in Thessalonica, he writes: *Now the Lord of peace Himself give you peace always by all means* (2 Thess. 3:16). In another place he expands this idea, ... *and the peace of God, which passeth all understanding, shall keep your hearts and minds through Christ Jesus. Finally, brethren, whatsoever things are true, whatsoever things are honest, whatsoever things are just, whatsoever things are pure, whatsoever things are lovely, whatsoever things are of good report; if there be any virtue, and if there be any praise, think on these things. Those things, which ye have both learned,*

Reflections

and received, and heard, and seen in me, do: and the God of peace shall be with you (Phil. 4:7-9).

Peace protects a man. A man thinks, wishes and feels both when he is at peace and when he is disturbed. Disturbed thoughts, a disturbed will and disturbed feelings may be interesting but they distance us from God. Calmness makes an individual self-controlled, and a fellowship strong, united and blessed.

Christians have received peace from Christ. He said, *Peace I leave with you, My peace I give unto you: not as the world giveth, give I unto you. Let not your heart be troubled, neither let it be afraid* (John 14:27). The calmness that has been given is calmness in Christ. He warned His followers in advance: *These things I have spoken unto you, that in Me ye might have peace. In the world ye shall have tribulation: but be of good cheer; I have overcome the world* (John 16:33).

The calmness of the children of God does not depend on our circumstances. Our circumstances are in the hands of Almighty God. Whoever trusts in Him has nothing to fear. The Lord promises, *Moreover I will make a covenant of peace with them; it shall be an everlasting covenant with them: and I will place them, and multiply them, and will set My sanctuary in the midst of them for evermore. My tabernacle also shall be with them: yea, I will be their God, and they shall be My people* (Ezek. 37:26-27).

Whoever puts any store by calmness and truly desires it must stop fretting. People here are beginning to use the phrase "holy unease". You won't find that in the Scriptures. So I do not intend to talk about it, but I will raise my voice against anxiety gladly and enthusiastically, because this should not be part of the Christian life. If we feel apprehension, let us examine our love, for, *There is no fear in love; but perfect love casteth out fear: because fear hath torment. He that feareth is not made perfect in love* (1 John 4:18).

Aleksandar Birviš

A well-tried route to maintaining and perfecting the peace that has been given us is described in the first half of the first Psalm (Ps. 1:1-3), *Blessed is the man that walketh not in the counsel of the ungodly, nor standeth in the way of sinners, nor sitteth in the seat of the scornful. But his delight is in the law of the* LORD; *and in His law doth he meditate day and night. And he shall be like a tree planted by the rivers of water, that bringeth forth his fruit in his season; his leaf also shall not wither; and whatsoever he doeth shall prosper.*

Let us take this path. Let us follow the example of those who live this way.

Belgrade, 15th July 1992

4. Richer love

According to the First Letter of John (4:16): *God is love; and he that dwelleth in love dwelleth in God, and God in him.* Love is the constant theme of evangelical Christianity. A lot of sentimental stuff is said about it. In order to avoid that I will refer to some events from the Middle Ages. About the time that Saint Sava[22] died in Bulgaria (1235), Peter Nolasco founded a sort of charitable society, the Mercedarian Order (Mercedarian meaning "those who pay the ransom"), in Spain. It was made up of nobles, priests and monks. It was founded somewhere between 1218 and 1234. The main activity of the order was the purchasing of slaves from Muslims. It is a well-known fact that in Muslim thinking, those who are not Muslims are *raya*, which means "herd". Every Muslim can keep them as slaves. Peter Nolasco and his colleagues collected money and jewels and used it to ransom Christians who were in slavery. Nolasco himself made two trips to Africa, probably to Algeria and Morocco. It is believed that he personally redeemed 890 slaves: men, women,

Reflections

girls, boys and children. It is calculated that over the centuries the Mercedarians redeemed more than 70,000 slaves.

Why did Peter Nolasco do this? Because that was the need of the time. Someone had to do it. Who? A man in whom God's love was at work, and who understood Christ's words, *Greater love hath no man than this, that a man lay down his life for his friends* (John 15:13). Such people don't work on their own. They join with others and help each other; they collect good things and multiply love.

Christians deepen their love. The apostle John writes, *Hereby perceive we the love of God, because He laid down His life for us: and we ought to lay down our lives for the brethren* (1 John 3:16). Love is perfected in action. Christ's love becomes visible on the cross of Calvary. How can our love be seen? The same apostle goes on to say, *But whoso hath this world's good, and seeth his brother have need, and shutteth up his bowels of compassion from him, how dwelleth the love of God in him? My little children, let us not love in word, neither in tongue; but in deed and in truth* (1 John 3:17-18). It is fairly simple: let us do something for the refugees and the exiles, let us do something for the deprived and impoverished, let us help those who are already doing something.

Love for our neighbor is eternal. We may have to redeem our neighbors today and lay down our lives for our faith and for men of faith. Who knows whether someone will once again class us as *raya*? Maybe someone will persecute us like slaves. That time is not far away and nor are the people. The people who today are waving human rights and freedoms in front of our eyes are those same people who will abolish them when they come to power.

That is not the number one priority for Christians. They do all they can to contribute to the liberation of their neighbors. People around us are in slavery to sin, Satan, evil spirits and evil in general. Christians will show their love if they commit to reducing the

Aleksandar Birviš

number of sinners in the world. The apostle James teaches us at the end of his epistle (5:19), *Brethren, if any of you do err from the truth, and one convert him; Let him know, that he which converteth the sinner from the error of his way shall save a soul from death, and shall hide a multitude of sins.*

Let us act like this in our prayers and in our lives as a whole.

Belgrade, 22nd July 1992

5. Strengthened hope

The average man in Belgrade today, and most people in Serbia, are just living to get by. Man struggles to live by making sacrifices. If he belongs to the privileged minority, he gives up various enjoyments. If he belongs to the majority, he gives up almost everything. Our fellow citizens are interested in what will happen after this but they haven't time for that. Besides that they avoid such questions because they are afraid to confront the truth: that they will meet God and their personal responsibilities, but they would rather believe that God does not exist.

This type of spiritual shallowness is the surest way to fall into complete hopelessness and despair. Christ offered hope. Do Christians offer hope? Not really. Christians have caused two world wars, devised camps for the extermination of the Jews, Poles, Serbs, Russians, Gypsies, and have discovered weapons of mass murder. They have accepted violence in politics and public administration as something quite normal. It is Christians who have caused the slaughter that is happening around us (1991/92.).

Do Christians have the right to offer anyone hope? No. But we are not talking about the right, but the duty: Christians are under an obligation to proclaim hope. The closer the Church is to man and the further it is from the politicians, the more it can recognise the

Reflections

present and the future times, the condemnation of the world and the hope in Christ.

The Word of God teaches us that ... *the creature itself also shall be delivered from the bondage of corruption into the glorious liberty of the children of God. For we know that the whole creation groaneth and travaileth in pain together until now. And not only they, but ourselves also, which have the firstfruits of the Spirit, even we ourselves groan within ourselves, waiting for the adoption, to wit, the redemption of our body. For we are saved by hope: but hope that is seen is not hope: for what a man seeth, why doth he yet hope for? But if we hope for that we see not, then do we with patience wait for it.*

Likewise the Spirit also helpeth our infirmities: for we know not what we should pray for as we ought: but the Spirit itself maketh intercession for us with groanings which cannot be uttered. And He that searcheth the hearts knoweth what is the mind of the Spirit, because He maketh intercession for the saints according to the will of God (Rom. 8:21-27).

The Christian hope is stronger in those believers who wait patiently. Many lose hope because they are impatient. They propose something pleasant, sensible, noble, useful and good and they would like to have it straightaway. They think that the seed bears fruit as soon as it is sowed. The Preacher says (Ecc. 8:5-6), *Whoso keepeth the commandment shall feel no evil thing: and a wise man's heart discerneth both time and judgment. Because to every purpose there is time and judgment, therefore the misery of man is great upon him.*

Obedience removes hidden dangers. Christians are not without help. The Holy Spirit helps each of them. The helpless only think that they have nothing to hope for. They should pray to the best of their abilities. The Spirit of God encourages them and teaches them to pray even when they do not speak any words but only utter sighs.

True hope is not linked only to the resurrection of the dead and Christ's second coming. God has made us His sons, and so we also

Aleksandar Birviš

have hope for everyday life. The righteous man has many trials, but the Lord delivers him from them all (Ps. 34:19). But we do not just believe that … *all things work together for good to them that love God, to them who are the called according to His purpose* (Rom. 8:28) – we know it.

This is what the sons and daughters of God believe. They know this and it strengthens their hope.

Belgrade, 29th July 1992/5th August 1992

The above teachings were given as closing words at prayer meetings held on Wednesday evenings in the (first) Baptist Church in Belgrade. Not many people were there to hear them: about thirty people on average. But those who listened were regular and patient.

The writer of these studies is their spiritual pastor. Their desire to listen is proof that they deserved more than they heard. Words that are written down like this can be read many times. Even if they are not of great value, their usefulness increases every time they are read and studied.

Glory be to God for all things.

Reflections

ADDRESSES ON SPECIAL OCCASSIONS

THE AUTHORITY OF THE SCRIPTURES IN RELATION TO THE CHURCH

In June 1968, major disturbances flared up at Belgrade University and at other Yugoslav Universities, as well as in other countries. The ruling circles in our country were very much taken aback. The President of the Republic[23] appeared on television after an unpleasant chain of events in which the police beat up not only some students but also a top political figure who had come to negotiate with the students. The President appeared on our screens with his tie undone, his shirt unbuttoned, his face unsmiling and eyes stern. This was not the man that the people were used to, the person before whom people had shouted and cheered.

Why? Because he too had realized, perhaps for the first time, that he must make concessions. He was not the only one. All the leading people had to retreat before a phenomenon that was difficult to understand entirely but which represented defiance of authority.

I will leave further consideration of this question of authority to the psychologists, educationalists, sociologists and political analysts. It will certainly be interesting to read what the experts have to say. My task is not to deviate from the information they provide and not to get involved in their controversies, because the questions that we have and the arguments that concern us are of a different nature.

I hope that it will not be boring if this question seems at first purely theoretical, and if people think that it has no impact on their lives.

Reflections

Authority

How can we say authority in our language[24]? I think the best word would be competence[25]. Authority defines the criteria, sets the rules which someone or something must be governed by if it respects that authority.

Authority is accepted either willingly or unwillingly. Authority is not based on force but on irresistibility or on necessity, where there is no other option.

The one who has the authority is able or should be able to do what needs to be done and what he wants. His actions are an expression of his care for and realization of that same authority, for the good of those over whom he has authority.

The word authority is often used for the person in authority themselves. So we talk about the authority for the question of wheat or ethnic minorities or hunting reservations or South America etc.

The person in authority carries out the task that falls within his area of responsibility. He carries out that task with the help of his position and/or his official activity in society. Compliance and cooperation are demanded on the basis of his competence.

Such an understanding of authority covers people, for example, the authority of fathers, mothers, elders, political powers-that-be, rulers, teachers and so on. It can also apply to institutions, for example the authority of government, the police, the army, school etc. The authority of the Church either as an organism, or as the local church or parish, also falls into this category.

The concept of authority can be broadened to cover the spoken or written word, or both of them together. The reliability of those words must be established and accepted. It is best when that acceptance is

331

Aleksandar Birviš

voluntary, but some words of command and demands made in special circumstances come with an element of compulsion.

In everyday life the authority of certain words means that one can trust the announcement of those words. They are based on truth – or apparent truth in the case of deception – and they are believed because of that validity.

Such an expanded concept of authority covers the authority of Scripture too.

The Scripture

The Scriptures are God's Word. Every word comes from the source of that communication to the one who receives it. God's Word stands between God and man. It is communicated by God who is His own authority. The Lord is the power and the authority in everything and for everything. If it were not so He would not be God.

Since God is the authority by His own supremacy, His Word is authoritative by the very fact that it is His. As far as its accuracy and acceptance are concerned the key question is not one of proving its claims but of proving its source. It is wrong to ask, "Is the Bible true?" because in asking this we do not know what we are trying to prove and how we can prove it. It is correct to ask, "Are the Scriptures God's Word?" because it is the answer to that question that makes the Bible truthful or not, and therefore acceptable or not.

We should approach proof in that way. In order to arrive at proof one should have some previously proven truths and well-tried methods. That is possible in mathematics and other sciences, at least it would appear so, because today any mathematician worth their

Reflections

salt would admit that there are cracks even in the edifices of these sciences.

As well as logical, deductive and inductive proof, some assumptions can be proved experimentally. First of all it is necessary to establish what an experiment is. It is a phenomenon that is deliberately caused and controlled. If I want to conduct an experiment with God and with the things of God, I must take into account two factors: my own will and God's manifestation. I expect God to behave according to my will and to act in accordance with my senses and my ability to observe phenomena. But if God were to submit to my expectations or anyone else's expectations, then He would not be independent, and would not be God. The same applies to His actions: if they were to be caused and controlled by man and limited to man's sense and abilities, then God would be a created being; yet God is not created precisely because He is God.

In other words: if God were to submit Himself to proof He would not be God but a concept, an object, and all those other things which fall within the domain of philosophy and the human mind.

Experience

How can we prove that the Scriptures are God's word? We are left with evidence based on experience. Whose experience? Certainly on authoritative experience, that being the experience of people who live according to Scripture and God's will. Such people have existed from the beginning of the human race. Their experiences are genuine, because it would be dishonest to suggest that all of them, widely separated in time and space, could have agreed to lie to us and our generation.

Aleksandar Birviš

I am deliberately not talking about the experience of the Church, because this experience arose in people who existed not only before organized Christianity, but even before the Bible took on its final form. God Himself spoke even before there were people who would receive His Word. To put God's Word in a time frame means to give an *a priori* negative answer to the question of the origin of God's Word, thereby excluding the impartiality and validity of the answers.

What does the experience of God's people tell us?

The Jews have been a literate people from earliest times. They steadfastly wrote down the words spoken through inspiration in the name of the Lord. Those words were authoritative for the life of the whole people and each individual. They were first and foremost words about the covenant with God (Ex. 20:23 to 23:33), and then the whole of the Law, that is the Pentateuch.

Therefore as early as 621 BC we have a reliable witness in the Bible itself that these texts were authoritative for the life of the whole Jewish nation. They are called the Book of the Law (2 Kings. 22:8 and 11), the Book (verses 8 and 10), the Book of the Covenant (chap. 23:2), and later the Book of the Law of the Lord given by Moses (2 Chr. 34:14).

Here we note that these books were used in worship. Did the authority of the temple give authority to the book? No, because at that time the temple was a hotbed of paganism and other wicked practices. We might rather say that the holy book brought holiness back to the temple: the ruler and the priests accepted the teachings from the book as God's call for direct and decisive action in eliminating firstly from the temple and then from among the people everything that did not conform to God's will as set out in the book they had found.

This action does not need much interpretation. It speaks for itself. In Jewish society, in the Jewish way of praying and thinking the Scriptures were authoritative because they were the Word of God and not because the authority of the Scriptures derived from the temple or the priesthood or some written agreement (consensus) of the whole nation.

The people of God, the believers, simply accept what God has already given as His Word. In the light of the Bible itself, this is not questioned. And the affirmative answer arises as the natural response to God.

A Book about God

We must keep in mind the other aspect of authority: the Bible is the only book, the only source of information, that gives authoritative statements about God. It is amazing how little attention people pay to this fact. Let me mention a few matters relating to this.

1. People pray most often by reading prayers from a prayer book. They do not know how to pray, and sometimes are afraid to pray in their own words. Many people cannot be expected to. But why do people not read the Psalms or other parts of the Bible that can serve as a conversation with God? Why don't they direct their thoughts to the Almighty when they read passages from His word?

2. The newspapers are full of horoscopes and other means of "peering into the future". The readers, of whom there are very many, are trying to discover what God wants, but they are going about it in the wrong way. If they use this method they will not discover the future, but they will fall into the clutches of evil powers. Astrology and its related activities are literate, but they are abominable to God. Men must not

Aleksandar Birviš

overlook the fact that the revelation of God is found only in the Bible.

3. Today a lot is talked about the introduction of religious education in schools. It is becoming quite an issue. But what does it mean? Children and school pupils will have one or two lessons each week, if they agree to it, when the teacher will present to them truths of a religion that as minors they do not have the right to embrace but must accept as their own. An imposed collection of truths must be accepted voluntarily. Why should we introduce minors, especially at the time when they are required by law to attend school, to an endless circle of freedoms and restrictions, when they are not really old enough to grasp it? Is it not better for the family, which no one can choose anyway, to read the Bible together and meditate together on what they have read, then pray together and thereby contribute to the renewal and ennoblement of each member of the family?

4. An authoritative knowledge of God cannot be given by any school of philosophy. Man tries to discover God and this is a constant source of torment.

I remember when Yuri Gagarin[26] first flew into space, just enough to escape from the earth's gravity. Around that time I overhead a conversation between two bus conductors in Belgrade. They were sitting outside a bar at the bus terminus on the route which then used to end somewhere around Karaburma[27]. They weren't particularly sober and were waxing philosophical.

"Have you seen what the Russians have done, mate?"

"Yeah, I've seen it. Er, what have they done?"

"They've flown into space."

Reflections

"Where's that?" asked the other.

"A long way away. A very long way. More'n you and me'll ever travel."

"And what did they find there?"

"Nothing. They said they didn't even find God there," said the first one in a mocking tone.

"Of course not, that's not where they lost him."

Isn't that right? Men have lost God here on Earth. They have denied the revelations, and trusted their own discoveries. They won't find God that way. The Bible teaches that only a man with a pure heart will see God (Matt. 5:8). The cleansing of the heart can be accomplished only by the power of Christ's blood (1 John 1:8). No one can discover that apart from the Bible.

5. Many books fall apart very quickly. Some are forgotten, no longer of any use. Some are enjoyed only by experts. But no book from ancient times has been so uniquely and so completely preserved as the Bible. Other old reading material can be interesting but cannot bring salvation. It can't change men. The world can seek after that kind of thing all it likes. Indeed the reading of ancient texts can become quite fashionable. But fashions come and go and men will grow out of this fad too. Only the Word that does not change and that does not need to change, the Bible, will remain. It speaks of God, it will continue to speak of God and it alone will change men and nations.

By the very fact that it makes authoritative statements about God, the Bible is the authority. It is validated by the personal revelation of the Almighty. The Bible is the authority in a negative sense as well,

Aleksandar Birviš

for there is no other authority: there is no other source that talks about the One who is, the Lord.

I don't mean to insult the Muslims by this remark. They believe that the Koran is the final and most complete revelation of God. But the Muslims believe and the Koran also acknowledges and accepts a number of books of God. That is the third religious article of the six articles of the faith, the so-called Iman šarti[28], or prerequisites for someone to be a Muslim. Islam recognizes the following as the books of God: Tevrat (Torah or the Pentateuch of Moses), Zebur (Psalms), Injil (the Gospel or New Testament) and the Koran. Whoever does not believe this is not a Muslim. The Koran mentions the Bible, but the Bible does not mention the Koran, so we as the people of the Scriptures cannot take it into consideration when we are studying the question of authority.

Man is not able to come to an authoritative knowledge of God himself. Human knowledge can reach great distances but not great depths. We do not have the answer to some questions such as, "What is quantity? What is number? What is electricity? What is politics? What is darkness? Where does the darkness come from? What is light? Where does it come from? How was water created?" and so on. But we are used to that. It is even more difficult to talk about God with such an approach. The above questions relate to the created world, but finding valid knowledge about the Creator is even less possible, if man does not rely on what he discovers about himself.

Certainty

In such a state of affairs we need to ask about certainty. Finite man needs to know the infinite, or to be specific, the infinite God. In other words: how can I know that what I know is true? On what

Reflections

basis is my knowledge reliable and undoubtable? Theoretically and democratically speaking everything is open to doubt and nothing is reliable by the very fact that it fell into human hands.

The certainty of the Bible rests on experience and the impossibility of disputing it.

Experiences of certainty can be personal and general. Personal experiences are not verifiable. They need not be false but it is impossible to show that they are true. The Bible is full of personal experiences. We believe that they are true and of inestimable worth. But we cannot rely on them when we talk about the certainty and the authority of God's word. That would be like a man grabbing himself by his ears or his hair, if he isn't bald, and trying to lift himself off the ground.

Things are different when it comes to general experiences. They can be false. Skilful and dishonest leaders can bring whole nations into a state of collective hallucination. But those circumstances pass, everyone inevitably sobers up and then accounts have to be settled. However the Bible is not subject to these changes. The Bible has come into existence over a considerable period amongst different nations, not exclusively the Jewish people. If we take into account that whole civilizations were born and died out, then it is unimaginable that all those generations were deluded. The men of God who took part in the writing of the Scriptures were men of different ages, of differing social standings, varying greatly in education, with no uniformity of language, or orthography, or ways of speaking or political viewpoints. This is a well-known fact and it can be proved historically, scientifically and logically, to a degree of reliability that is greater than some facts from modern history. The Bible is reliable and unquestionable, its certainty is without dispute, and its authority clear.

Aleksandar Birviš

We can talk about the impossibility of disputing the Bible first and foremost by studying the history of the Bible itself. During its history it has been the most frequently and most violently attacked book. All sorts of people have attacked it. The godless have questioned it because it talks about God. Modernists because it is "behind the times". Academics have claimed that it is made up of fairy tales and myths. The uneducated have rejected it as being the invention of priests. Some didn't like it because the ordinary people were reading it, so they banned it or revised it. Others, out of a desire to make it available to the masses, were careless in translation and its publication, and people were confused.

There were attempts to impose it on people, as well as the opposite approach: going to the greatest lengths to ensure that people did not even know that it existed. Our nation is a pretty good example of this ignorance.

None of these approaches, nor many others, have been able to disprove the Scriptures.

Nevertheless a series of attempts has successfully diverted people away from God's Word and from faith in God. Those people are false Christians. Godlessness and faithlessness spread quickest and are most difficult to eradicate where dishonesty, inconsistency, struggle for power and immorality are cultivated under the guise of piety. The people who act like this and call themselves Christians, believers, Biblical Christians, the converted, born-again etc., very quickly and effectively destroy faith in God and the authority of God's words. Such attacks on the Bible are most effective and most painful: truths are no longer truths, faith is no longer the basis for hope and it offers no proof or demonstration, it merely deceives the people.

Reflections

Enlightenment

The authority of the Scriptures is inconceivable without enlightenment. This entails the work of the Holy Spirit in those who receive: God making the message of His Word understandable and acceptable. The Holy Spirit is the source of the key stimuli for the emergence and formation of the Scriptures. As far as the authority and acceptance of the Bible are concerned, He is a key factor in this too.

The key level in enlightenment, that is the understanding of the intervention and function of the Holy Spirit, is the recognition of Christ as the fullness of revelation. God, in His good will and pleasure, has allowed His fullness to dwell permanently in the Lord Jesus Christ (Col. 1:19). Whoever wants to understand God in a worthy manner, needs to understand Christ. In Christ the fullness of the Godhead dwells bodily and permanently. The Savior was an ordinary but perfect man and perfect God.

Christ is the key content of the Scriptures. The true authority of God's Word is in Christ as the incarnate Word of the living God. The Lord Jesus is the undisputed and unquestioned authority. He rules over all principalities and powers (Col. 2:9-10). All authority is given to Him in heaven and on earth (Matt. 28:18).

The fullness of God is revealed to Christians and given to them if they believe in it in the same way that Christ is revealed in the Scriptures. God wants His children to know the boundless love which Christ has towards people and to be filled to all the fullness of God. No one can fully grasp this but God has demonstrated it and fulfilled it (Eph. 3:19).

Aleksandar Birviš

The Church

We seem to be coming to the subject of the Church and its authority almost without realizing it. According to the Scriptures (Eph. 1:23), the Church is the fullness of Christ who fills all in all. The Church is His mysterious body. As far as authority is concerned this definition says the following:

1. The authority of the Church proceeds from Christ's authority. The Church is authoritative if the Lord grants it that authority. But the founder of the Church established only the local church in Jerusalem. The image of the body and the head relates to the visible and the invisible Church. Christ is the invisible head of the visible local church or parish community.

2. The authority of the Church depends on how you define the Church. In Biblical terms, the Church is first and foremost a specific gathering of people, who are responsibly, consciously and enthusiastically gathered around Christ. This gathering is spiritual: the Savior is absent in the body, but present by His Holy Spirit. If we accept that this means the local church, then Christ is present in it, and He leads its leaders: priests, supervisors (bishops), elders (presbyters), servants (deacons) and so on. Men and women are not the authority in the Church, they are servants to whom Christ has entrusted duties and given them gifts relating to those duties, including the duty of leadership.

If we accept the principle that the Church comprises a large number of local churches, then it is difficult to see Christ in it.

Reflections

Instead of gathering around Christ we see a hierarchical system centered around authority. A specific visible head is appointed, who supposedly acquires power in Christ's name, and strives to increase that power. The different forms of power support worldly power: autocracy, autocephaly, autonomy, parliament or national assembly, administrative division, ethnic division and – an insatiable thirst for pomp and titles. When defined in this way the Church sets itself up over the Scriptures, and becomes its owner, the authorized distributor, interpreter and publisher.

We must bear in mind that the authority of Christ's apostles and other followers rests on Christ (2 Cor. 12:19; 10:11; 1 Thess. 2:13; 5:27; 2 Thess. 2:15; 3:14). Church ministries and subsequently established offices cannot take precedence over the Scriptures.

Man in his pride asserts boldly that the Church has defined what the Scripture is and what makes up the Scriptures. That doesn't hold water theologically or historically. Theologically that would mean that the Church, however we define it, can subordinate the Holy Spirit, who inspired the Scriptures, to itself. Historically this is even less tenable: the Church merely acknowledged the insuppressible authority of God's Word and formed its own opinion.

No one is denying the role of Christianity in preserving the Bible. But that was accomplished by God in His mercy and understanding of the needs of the human race. The Lord could have taken a different course of action. I believe firmly that God would even today give the human race the Bible if the heathen were to destroy it. For that task He would not need you, nor me, nor even the whole of Christianity. The Almighty could do it single-handed, independently and perfectly.

Aleksandar Birviš

Nevertheless...

Nevertheless, the Almighty has directed His attention toward humans. He works with them. And so men took part in the creation of the Bible, in maintaining it and preserving it, translating, compiling, delivering, reading, interpreting and applying it to life. Our interpretations may differ, and our understanding and deductions vary, but may God forbid that our life should be disunited and unworthy of the Lord's purposes. The Scripture remains, remains unique, and nothing can replace it. Thank God, those who believe in the name of the Father, Son and Holy Spirit need nothing else.

Address given in the Novi Sad Pentecostal Church 12th December 1991

ADDRESS AT THE OPENING OF
HOLY TRINITY CHURCH[29]

17th April 1992, at 12 o'clock

Ladies and gentlemen, respected friends[30] and dear brothers and sisters,

I would like to be able to tell you a story appropriate for this special occasion for which we are gathered. But my creative powers are insufficient, and I have no original inspiration.

Instead I ask you to recall one of Christ's parables (Matt. 20:1-16). I take the liberty of quoting it from the second edition of my own translation:

For the kingdom of heaven is like unto a man that is an householder, which went out early in the morning to hire labourers into his vineyard. And when he had agreed with the labourers for a penny a day, he sent them into his vineyard. And he went out about the third hour, and saw others standing idle in the marketplace, And said unto them; Go ye also into the vineyard, and whatsoever is right I will give you. And they went their way. Again he went out about the sixth and ninth hour, and did likewise. And about the eleventh hour he went out, and found others standing idle, and saith unto them, Why stand ye here all the day idle? They say unto him, Because no man hath hired us. He saith unto them, Go ye also into the vineyard; and whatsoever is right, that shall ye receive.

So when even was come, the lord of the vineyard saith unto his steward, Call the labourers, and give them their hire, beginning from the last unto

Aleksandar Birviš

the first. And when they came that were hired about the eleventh hour, they received every man a penny. But when the first came, they supposed that they should have received more; and they likewise received every man a penny. And when they had received it, they murmured against the goodman of the house, Saying, These last have wrought but one hour, and thou hast made them equal unto us, which have borne the burden and heat of the day. But he answered one of them, and said, Friend, I do thee no wrong: didst not thou agree with me for a penny? Take that thine is, and go thy way: I will give unto this last, even as unto thee. Is it not lawful for me to do what I will with mine own? Is thine eye evil, because I am good? So the last shall be first, and the first last: for many be called, but few chosen.

I assume that the majority of you are familiar with this parable. I do not propose to interpret it on this special occasion. I hope that I will have opportunities, God willing and with the agreement of the elders of this church, to go more deeply into Christ's parables in this place.

As a man from whom God has not withheld an understanding of the Scriptures, I make so bold as to apply the parable of the Savior that we read to this town in which we live.

Belgrade, saved by God, is God's vineyard. Over the centuries this vineyard has been given spiritual stewards. The first two citizens of the town whose names and surnames we know were Jews. We do not know how much they contributed to the spiritual life of the city, but I assume that in a place where everyone knew everyone else they must have talked about their faith amongst other things. During Roman and Byzantine times this town was peopled by Christians of various levels of spirituality. Other Slav peoples and the Magyars who received the Christian faith from Constantinople left their mark, as did a considerable number of emigrants from areas under Roman control.

Reflections

Through the town, maybe along this very street, passed the first Muslims, considerably before Suleyman the Magnificent. The city was constantly under attack, and thus in 1048 and 1049 the Pechenegs marched through it. A little more than a hundred years later (1151-1155) the Muslim army of the Hungarian King together with mercenaries from Maghreb (Kalisia) marched through on their way to fight against Byzantium.

It is not known whether the Bogumils came through Belgrade. This unfortunately exterminated movement was well-known during that same twelfth century and later. The Bogumils were cultivators too, and blessed are those who had understanding for what they were doing. Their significance is yet to be recognised.

Large movements of people took place in the Balkans from the fourteenth century onwards. Byzantium brought the Turks. The Turks by their amazing persistence, their strict administrative structure, and wise government changed the tribal, national, social and religious picture of all areas from Constantinople to Vienna.

Nevertheless, right up to the eighteenth century no trace of evangelical Christianity had reached Belgrade. Instead of that another group of hardworking religious ambassadors appeared: in 1613 a small number of Jesuits opened the first Grammar School[31] in Belgrade. Next year it will be 380 years since Stefan Szini (a Magyar) and Marin de Bonis (from Sibenik) founded the school. The Jesuits ran the school until 1632, when they had to leave. The Grammar School was founded again in 1724. It was forced to close down in 1739, when the Ottoman Turks conquered Belgrade for the second time. (It was not far from here, near the corner of Emperor Dusan Street and Dubrovnik Street).

We had to wait a while until new evangelical voices were heard. It was not until a century later that we heard something about the

Aleksandar Birviš

Protestant faith. A few emigrants who had converted came to the vineyard from Austria and Germany. Under Turkish rule there were many wars and revolts, and spiritual life died out.

After the First Uprising[32] against the Turks in Serbia the railway reached Belgrade. With it (from 1880 onwards, to be exact) came a new wave of Roman Catholics, but also Lutherans. Thanks to the European policy of Obrenovic[33], new workers came to this vineyard.

At that time the Nazarenes and Baptists were first heard of in Belgrade. At the beginning of this century the Adventists arrived, too. In the first half of this century our esteemed brothers who are gathered today in this wonderful building of the Holy Trinity Church appeared.

The vineyard is expanding. The workers are multiplying. Although it is not yet time for the silver coin that has been earned to be given, some of the older workers are annoyed. We know in advance what the Lord will say. Let us not be angry; instead let us give thanks.

I greet all the vineyard workers of all generations. Thank you for agreeing to work in the Lord's vineyard. Let the new workers live and work. We are looking forward to receiving the silver coin and joyfully awaiting the one who will surely come and of whose Kingdom there will be no end. We greet Him too, "Welcome, Christ, Perfect Light!"

Ave, Lux Serenissima[34]!

THE DESIRED TIME

(Address given at a meeting of the Association of Evangelical Ministers and Believers)

Dear brothers and sisters, fellow-workers and friends in the good and redemptive news of our Lord and Savior Jesus Christ.

Glory to the Lord who has granted us to see these days!

We are people of faith. We look on these days as a people who believe, as individuals with a confidence. The Savior says, *And when these things begin to come to pass, then look up, and lift up your heads; for your redemption draweth nigh* (Luke 21:28). The time of multiple blessings has come.

First. We have desired this time. We knew that these days would come. We are conscious of what they bring: trouble, at first glance, only trouble. Let us not be deceived: we believe that the world will be destroyed, we are convinced that it must disappear. It is of no worth. The world lies in the power of the evil one (1 John 5:19). What need have we of this world?

The world has turned its back on the Creator; it rejects the Savior, and will not receive the Comforter. Does God need the world? No. Do the people of God need the world? No.

We thank the Lord for giving us the mercy to live in these very days. They are challenging days. Believers are being called to stand up. (I personally feel as though I am short of time: why am I not,

Aleksandar Birviš

say, fifteen years younger, so that I could take up all the invitations that I have so eagerly been waiting for).

Second. Sin, especially the sin of dishonesty, is multiplying. These troubled times encourage it. There is more and more dishonesty on the large scale as well as the small. The boundaries of integrity are narrowing dramatically: everything that is not actually forcibly prevented is allowed, and there is no real force. This is insinuating itself amongst Christians too. Instead of being enthusiastic about good they are advised to show calculated self-interest. That is the very reason why the Gospel way of life is constantly faced with two challenges: how to remain uncorrupted and how to win others when integrity not only is not appealing but is actually laughable to many people.

Evangelical Christianity can and must maintain a high level of honor and integrity. If not, it will alienate itself from God and be lost. On the one hand it is and must be above worldliness. This can be achieved through integrity and spirituality. On the other hands we have the demands of our environment. They have grown tremendously. Christianity must respond to them. At one time they were mostly needs for help in education and the health service. Today they are the demands of political culture, parliamentarianism, economics and especially of ecology (where Christians must urgently have their say).

Third. The current violent events are diverting attention away from the Gospel. We mustn't let that happen. With each day we are nearer the resurrection of the dead, the transfiguration of the living and the all-embracing rule of God.

What should we do in these circumstances? We must immediately reject the following: a) a lack of understanding for the eschatological moment in which we live, b) wrestling with

Reflections

non-existent problems, c) our reliance on good contacts and d) indifference to professionalism.

Please don't feel I am trying your patience if I explain what I mean in more detail.

a) A lack of understanding for the time in which we live. It is rightfully said among evangelical Christians that we must oppose the spirit of the times. Preachers and ordinary believers allow themselves to criticize certain modes of dress, hairstyles, education, behavior etc. By straining such gnats Christians miss the camels: mediocrity, self-satisfaction, entanglement in wordly (and even underwordly) politics, contempt for those who have different beliefs etc.

b) Wrestling with non-existent problems. For example a bootleg edition of the Bible has appeared in our parts (in Latin script, translation by Kršćanska Sadašnjost[35], without the deuterocanonical texts, but with textual additions in the protocanonical books). The book names the publishers as being Kršćanska Sadašnjost of Zagreb and a non-existent Bible society.

The press that is mentioned is a British press that has never printed any such thing. It is obvious that the publication is a fraud, an infringement of copyright, a misrepresentation and an unauthorized publication. Some biblical Christians are mixed up in this "business". But no one mentions this problem; everyone pretends that they don't know – yet somebody must know something – and many preachers in their sermons are talking about the clumsy way some deuterocanonical additions have been left in the Book of the Prophet Daniel and so on. There can be no doubt that the true problem is a

Aleksandar Birviš

question of translation and publishing fraud, and believers have not even raised the question of the canon.

The same applies to the confrontation of theological modernism and liberalism from our pulpits. That problem does not exist in the majority of churches. The problem is the clear and positive representation of biblical truths, and not academic viewpoints.

c) Reliance on good contacts. The Gospel says that the saved are those who are born not of blood, nor of the will of the flesh, nor of the will of man, but of God (John 1:13). Within Christianity family, tribal, national, social and other similar ties must not be decisive. However, in this country the evangelical faith is linked to a small number of people. Most fellowships have grown out of house groups or families. The temptation is ever present to replace the body of Christ with a family business, where the Savior becomes a sort of tribal leader. In the same way there is the centuries-old custom of making Christianity the mark of a nation. Such churches are a picture of oppression and imposition, where clan links are expanded and elevated above the Gospel. We will only be successful in opposing this if we honor the old Jewish custom that the apostle Paul mentions when he says that the heir, as long as he is a child, is no different from a slave, though he is master of all; but he is under guardians and stewards until the time appointed by his father (Gal. 4:1). Until God says His word, let us not interfere with our own unfulfilled desires and plans.

d) Indifference to professionalism. Evangelical Christianity must not allow itself to be dragged down by the general decline in educational values. The basic intention of preaching and

Reflections

teaching is to win others for the Savior and salvation. No one should take part in this without first checking his facts. It is inexcusable to give inaccurate and misleading information, to mix up ideas, and not to discriminate. For example, the Reformation and Protestantism are not the same, nor are divorce and separation, trinity and trinity, a man of prayer and a book of prayer.[36] What is more, in parts of the country where people speak correctly and where they think about what they say, a crucifix is not the same as a cross. Our service is the service of the public word. Each word should be as specific and as unambiguous as possible, with due respect shown to the rules of speech and expression. We are all learners before Christ. We are all learners for ever.

★　★　★

I say this in the belief that we can come to a joint decision. It would be advantageous and the honest thing to do for all those who preach the Word to agree on a Charter of Honor and Integrity, i.e. a Professional Code, and to establish a three-man committee to work on the Charter and to give authoritative interpretation and rulings on the basis of the Charter.

There is nothing stopping us from doing what is best and most acceptable to God. Let us strengthen our confidence in the Founder and Perfector of our faith. Without that confidence I would not be standing before you today. Thank you for hearing me out, and glory to God for all things.

Belgrade, Simina 8, 20th June 1992

FOR THE WOMEN'S CONFERENCE

BELGRADE '92.

Introductory reading: based on Psalm 133

> *Behold, how good and how pleasant it is*
> *When sisters are in agreement as one!*
> *It is like sanctified oil,*
> *Like God's holy anointing,*
> *That spreads with gentleness and glory,*
> *As the dew on the mount of Hermon,*
> *Which flows upon the mountains of Zion.*
> *The LORD allotted to those in agreement*
> *His blessing and life everlasting*[37].

Prayer:

Come, Heavenly Father. We pray that You will graciously look on this gathering of our sisters in Christ. Thank You for making them our sisters, and for giving us the privilege of being their brothers and all of us together Your children.

Come, Son of God. We pray that You will graciously protect this gathering of our sisters. Thank You that Your sacrifice has brought all of them into new life, so that we have the honor of sharing with them in all the gifts and redemptive ministries of Your Kingdom.

Reflections

Come, Holy Spirit. We pray that You will graciously lead this gathering of our sisters. Thank You for bringing joy and comfort in these troubled times, so that we can joyfully look together with our sisters to the time that is coming.

Come, You who alone are Lord. You are truly God and we pray that You will graciously fulfill all the sisterly aspirations of this gathering. Thank You that You have not forgotten us and for having time for us. Thank You that our sisters are still active in spite of their busy lives and jobs. Bless their efforts in the fellowships and ministries where they are. Bless them and keep them. Let the light of your countenance shine upon them and be gracious to them. Look on them and give them peace, both for this meeting and for all who hear their word and feel the results of their work.

Glory to God, Glory to the only God: Father, Son and Holy Spirit! Amen.

Main reading:

Ex. 38:8

And he made the laver of brass, and the foot of it of brass, of the lookingglasses of the women assembling, which assembled at the door of the tabernacle of the congregation.

Dear sisters,

You have surely noticed that the introductory reading is similar to the one hundred and thirty third Psalm, but the words sound a little different from that Psalm. Instead of the Psalm our reading is a greeting. The main reading is not in the usual translation, but it is still completely biblical. I translated it from the original Hebrew with the help of my humble translating ability.

Aleksandar Birviš

Why have I done that? Because this gathering deserves to be better informed than ordinary readers of the Scriptures, because you are sisters who serve, sisters who make sacrifices and who are near to the Holy place.

That is what I want to say to you as your unworthy brother.

A word about ministry

God has opened up, and continues to open up opportunities for all sorts of ministries. We don't know what the ministries were at the door of the tabernacle of meeting. Each of these jobs was connected with the holy place. The names of these women workers are not mentioned, nor are we told whether they belonged to any chosen tribe or social class. Neither are we told anywhere what their rights were.

But does anyone need a greater right or anything else in addition to the nearness of God? That is why we thank the Lord today that He has given our sisters a place near the holy place and that He has given us such sisters. Their commitment begins at the doors of the temple not made by human hands. All our thoughts, desires and feelings begin with our mothers, sisters, wives, and female co-workers because true Christian women are at the entrance into the holy place. We cannot imagine our way to consecration without our sisters.

The women served. They did not ask whether they were necessary and what their ministry would be. They simply made themselves available to the Lord and to Moses, His chosen one.

Reflections

A word about mirrors

In the time of Moses, and for a good time after that, mirrors were made of polished bronze. They were not as good as today's, but they were enough for beauty purposes.

The women servants in the temple were no exception: they too no doubt liked to look at their reflection and perhaps to ask themselves surreptitiously, "Mirror, mirror, on the wall. Who is the fairest of them all?"

When the time came for the portable temple to be built in the wilderness, these consecrated women brought their gift. They had no money. They possessed no lands. They had no cattle, fruit or vegetables. They no longer had any jewelry as Aaron had taken it all to make the golden calf (Ex. 32:2-4a). If they gave their dresses, they would sin against decency; if they gave food, they would condemn themselves to starve, and sin against life.

The consecrated women showed that it is important to be prepared to give, and a gift was found. They gave their mirrors: probably pretty small, maybe a little larger but not particularly large. That was enough for God as it came from committed and joyful hearts.

We have no information as to how Moses and the others looked on this sacrifice. Moses was both gentle and strict. Maybe he spoke words of rejection like some ancient Jewish teachers: "God does not need the tools of female vanity". In that case God's warning or human criticism would have been justified: "When you were in Egypt you had a privileged position. You did not taste the suffering of the Jews. You felt it even less when you lived in a foreign country. At that time these women were suffering and the only joy they had was to be beautiful for their husbands. Now they are offering their only joy".

It is possible that Moses did not look so arrogantly on the women. Why should we not suppose that, instructed by the learning of two continents and eighty years of experience he said: "There is no such thing as a little gift and a small giver before the Lord. Thank you, sisters and servants"?

For us today, our sisters are God's gift by the simple fact that we have them. Humanity is lost in the wilderness. All have gone astray and made a mess of things. The Almighty has entrusted to Christians the building of the temple not built with human hands. So our sisters are living stones being built by the Holy Spirit into a spiritual house and a holy priesthood. Together with us they bring holy sacrifices, spiritual, mental and physical sacrifices. Thanks to this cooperation we are acceptable to God by the intervention of the Lord Jesus Christ (see 1 Pet. 2:5).

A word about the laver

Men, especially preachers, consider themselves the guardians of the pure faith. Baptists have no dogmatists. There is no complete body of Baptist beliefs. From time to time leading brethren come together and go over old and modern heresies, and decide what should be believed. This serves as a signpost so that they do not go off into some false teaching.

This is a necessary task but it is not exclusively a man's task. However, I have shared in the work of our churches for more than forty years, but there has not been one case where one of the members of these theological committees was a sister. Maybe somewhere outside of the Balkans, but nothing like that has ever happened here.

Reflections

But nevertheless our sisters preserve the purity of the faith better than can ever be done through confessional principles. The Apostle James wrote: *Pure religion and undefiled before God and the Father is this, To visit the fatherless and widows in their affliction, and to keep himself unspotted from the world* (James 1:27). This is where our sisters "lave" our faith. This is how we know that our confession does not have the flavor of the world, rather we are washed in the blood of the heavenly Lamb.

By their work and their virtues our sisters are building our spiritual laver. Their efforts cleanse us of the zeal for inquisition. We are sometimes unaware that there is in each of us a little seed of judgmentalism towards those who have different beliefs, opinions and interpretations. God has given our sisters simplicity of heart, and they see things in a different way. Thank God for that different way: away from worldliness, closer to sacrifice.

★   ★   ★

The Belgrade church is glad to host this gathering of our sisters. I would like our contribution to be greater, in order to match the merits of our sisters. But our greatness is in our poverty. So I ask you: accept our poverty; it is our gift of grace. Share it freely with us and the Lord will bless this meeting and your efforts to glorify God, to enrich His Bride and save more souls.

Glory to the crucified and risen Lord Jesus Christ. May He bless you. Begin in His name. Amen.

Belgrade, 20th Sept 1992

EDUCATION: CONDITIONS, DEVELOPMENT AND PURPOSE (I)

Beginning of the academic year

Introductory reading: Ps. 16:1–11

Main reading: 2 Chr. 17:1–13

And Jehoshaphat his son reigned in his stead, and strengthened himself against Israel. And he placed forces in all the fenced cities of Judah, and set garrisons in the land of Judah, and in the cities of Ephraim, which Asa his father had taken. And the LORD was with Jehoshaphat, because he walked in the first ways of his father David, and sought not unto Baalim; But sought to the Lord God of his father, and walked in His commandments, and not after the doings of Israel. Therefore the LORD stablished the kingdom in his hand; and all Judah brought to Jehoshaphat presents; and he had riches and honour in abundance. And his heart was lifted up in the ways of the LORD: moreover he took away the high places and groves out of Judah.

Also in the third year of his reign he sent to his princes, even to Benhail, and to Obadiah, and to Zechariah, and to Nethaneel, and to Michaiah, to teach in the cities of Judah. And with them he sent Levites, even Shemaiah, and Nethaniah, and Zebadiah, and Asahel, and Shemiramoth, and Jehonathan, and Adonijah, and Tobijah, and Tobadonijah, Levites; and with them Elishama and Jehoram, priests. And they taught in Judah, and had the book of the law of the LORD with them, and went about throughout all the cities of Judah, and taught the people.

Reflections

And the fear of the LORD fell upon all the kingdoms of the lands that were round about Judah, so that they made no war against Jehoshaphat. Also some of the Philistines brought Jehoshaphat presents, and tribute silver; and the Arabians brought him flocks, seven thousand and seven hundred rams, and seven thousand and seven hundred he goats.

And Jehoshaphat waxed great exceedingly; and he built in Judah castles, and cities of store. And he had much business in the cities of Judah: and the men of war, mighty men of valour, were in Jerusalem.

Today we are talking about the beginning of the academic year. And so God's Word about Jehoshaphat's attempts to stir up the leading minds amongst his people to teach the people is of interest and worth studying. He knew what the people needed, and how to give it to them and the Lord played His part.

What were the steps he took first?

The first was defense against the enemy. The King appointed watchmen on all sides. One could not yield to the enemy, because where there are enemies there is no education. The same is true for our education system and our children: the family and the Church need to deploy watchmen. Nothing that is opposed to Christ and that hates God must get past.

Watchmen throughout the country

One unit of guards must protect from paganism. There is no genuine education without the knowledge that there is a God and that His will is alone and unique. How can this be done? Through the simple ethos of obedience. In the family all must know who the father is. Both the mother and the children must submit to the father's will in the home, and the father submit to God. The father seeks to rule reasonably and gently, with a combination of love and

Aleksandar Birviš

wisdom. The life and work of the Church is similar. The Church is by nature a free gathering of free people; but it is not an association, it is a living body. Its elections and committees serve to discover God's will, which is essential for all.

Christians must establish a similar watch against idolatry. Men listen to God's Word and watch God's people. Whom does the family worship? Who rules the Church? If the mother is constantly complaining that the father's earnings are very small, will not then the children believe that money is the main household god? If the father continually grumbles about his bosses, everyone in the house will think that their lives are ruled by office gods of some kind. There can also be idolatry in schools. Children and young people become attached to certain objects, scientific and unscientific movements, artistic and non–artistic trends and the vagaries of fashion. Schools should oppose the creation and worship of stars in sport, entertainment, politics and other areas. The younger generations will not grow up properly if they are obsessed with idols. Idolatry is common and, sadly, a voluntary immaturity. It doesn't stop as people get older, it only disappears before the awareness of one unique and exclusive God.

A guard should be established against unnecessary words. It is a sin to talk about all and everything. It is an even greater sin to mention God when the time is not right. The Lord is angry with all those who take His name in vain and speak evil of Him. Every curse and every harsh word is a sin. The habit of swearing almost every other word is a dangerous ploy of Satan. There is no justification for such behavior. Where people swear there is no education. It is a misconception to think that we will be valued as a nation or a country when we have so many curses and swear words which are

Reflections

so proudly encouraged by young and old alike, by those in the lowest and those in the highest positions.

Our common enemy is laziness and lack of concern for our church services. So we need to mount a guard there too. Christians must consider these things before their own consciences and before God: Why do I miss services? The value of a church is measured by the number of people attending, on Sunday morning, on Sunday evening, and during the week. The spiritual growth of an individual can be clearly measured by attendance at services and participation in the activities of the church. Let us beware of the attitude that it is enough to honor God in our hearts, and that services are a restriction of freedom if we are obliged to attend regularly. We must bear in mind this simple commercial and social fact: where freedom is used as an excuse for laziness and indifference, that freedom is very quickly lost. The guards must be especially careful, because if we lose our commitment we lose the fellowship, the body of Christ, and that means we lose the Savior.

We need to mount a guard over the doors of the family. Marriage and the family are God's institution. They are the basis of a healthy society and a viable state. The Scripture sees the Church, too, as an extended family: we are brothers and sister to each other. We want our education system to have the correct foundations. We want education to make a difference. We pray that God will preserve and protect marriage and the family. There is no need for me to emphasize how important this is. The Savior Himself grew up in a family and He took care of His mother to the end of His life on earth. Of course, the family must not become an idol. Christ does not allow the family or the nation or country or anything else to be more important than the Kingdom of God. This is the watch we must mount over our parents, their parents, our children, grandchildren,

Aleksandar Birviš

our relatives and those close to us. Through this watch the upbringing of children is established and is given direction. The school is only one of the participants in the upbringing of children. The Church and the family also have their part to play.

A guard also protects the sanctity of the individual. There is no country in the world where there are no adults who know who and what they are, what they are not, where they fit in and who they belong to. In man himself Christ resolves that question in its entirety. The fellowship of the children of God also behaves like a person. It is the body of Christ. When it is linked to its head (the Lord Jesus) in the proper way, it knows who and what it is, or is not, where it fits in and whom it belongs to. It is alive just like the personality of an individual is alive. An individual can be killed, just like a fellowship. Satan is a murderer from the beginning (John 8:44). For education not to be distorted it is essential that neither the body nor the soul nor the spirit, both of the individual and the fellowship, should be killed.

This guard and the previous one remind us of the special need to protect our bodies. The apostle Paul warns us, *And be not drunk with wine, wherein is excess; but be filled with the Spirit* (Eph. 5:18). *Flee fornication. Every sin that a man doeth is without the body; but he that committeth fornication sinneth against his own body* (1 Cor. 6:18). The same apostle also gives us the justification for such behavior. He writes, *For no man ever yet hated his own flesh; but nourisheth and cherisheth it, even as the Lord the church* (Eph. 5:29). We take care of the body as the Savior takes care of the fellowship of God's children. We do not allow anything to trouble the human body, no matter whether it is my body or the body of some other human being. Such cleanliness and purity must firstly become the habit of those who belong to the Son of God, but also of all others who come into

Reflections

contact with Christians. Without this we cannot expect a successful education system.

The spiritual guards are the Scriptures, our conscience and our Church. They do not protect our own property, but they do protect us from other people's property. Christians learn integrity at the very first step. I hope that a converted man will not become a robber, a hijacker, a criminal, a thief, counterfeiter or trickster. But is this entirely true? If I should be at the service on Sunday at 9 o'clock, and I arrive at a 9.15, have I not short-changed God by a quarter of an hour? Have I not stolen a quarter of an hour from those who arrived on time? Not counting God, I have robbed people of more than five hours if there were only twenty of them. The Lord's gift must not be wasted, and time is a gift from the Lord. We all steal a little here and there. *See then that ye walk circumspectly, not as fools, but as wise, Redeeming the time, because the days are evil* (Eph. 5:15-16). Not using our time is to waste the Lord's property. In the same way, goods used incorrectly (money, food, clothing, books, etc.) are stolen goods. Let us mount a guard in good time; otherwise we will all become thieves.

Dishonesty does not begin with a theft but with a lie. That is Satan's product above all other products for, *When he speaketh a lie, he speaketh of his own: for he is a liar, and the father of it* (John 8:44). We therefore need to mount a guard against lies. Men lie using words. Read today's newspapers. Just take one page and underline the sentences where the statements given have no proof. Then just reread the bits that are not underlined. That should be the truth. Compare that with the Bible and the life of the Church. You will have to reject a lot, maybe two thirds. The rest is something that is supposedly truth, but it could be supposed that it is not true. Now it is clear how little truth there is in daily life. Let us try, for example

Aleksandar Birviš

in the evening, to read ourselves as we have read the newspaper. Let us examine our words and actions just in one day. Let us reject all that we know has no proof or reason. Then let us examine what we have not rejected. Let us compare that with the Bible and the life of Christ's Church. Look at what is left. Let us think upon it. Let us nurture that. That is where truth is springing up.

There is one more guard that we should mount: let us pray and fight against excessive personal desires. It is good to strive towards something. It is even better to achieve it. However, those who want to get rich ... *fall into temptation and a snare, and into many foolish and hurtful lusts* (1 Tim. 6:9). So it is with material wealth. It is the same with mental and spiritual wealth. Whoever wants to be more skilful, cleverer, better educated, a better artist, a more spiritual Christian or a more generous philanthropist, he will also fall into a trap. There is a great danger of losing one's humility, condemning others, deposing more capable people, grabbing for honors. To want what is not ours, to envy others their achievements and to acquire something in a dishonest way, those are all sins of desire or envy. This was precisely the kind of evil deed that the evil one got enmeshed in: he wanted what was not his and was not becoming of him.

An ordered life

These and other guards are the first precondition. Whoever wants a good education system must prevent that which is not good. But even the best guards cannot make fertile land out of a desert. Cursing the darkness will not bring light, and education is the bringing of light.

The second precondition can be reduced to the following: to walk in God's will.

Reflections

We hear descriptions and explanations of Christ's way at every service. Calls are made from this pulpit: to change one's life, to live according to God's will and to strengthen one's life in accordance with God's will. So I will limit myself. I will talk about what we should believe and do on the basis of today's scripture reading.

King Jehoshaphat placed guards all over the land of Judah and in the cities of Ephraim, which his father Asa had won. God has entrusted us with certain values. He wants us to maintain and promote them. Revolutionaries claim that it is possible to create a better life by destroying the past. Some even acquire riches in this way: they enslave and carry off the inheritance of many generations, and then indulge in lasciviousness and dissipation. The people of God do not do such things, because they are a thrifty people. Christians respect the achievements of their forebears and seek to preserve them, to improve them, to develop them and to multiply them. Education is based on tried-and-tested values. Where values are destroyed, society loses out. In a matter of days the problems, unrest and hunger will start.

The people gave gifts to their ruler. A good education system demands a good foundation. Poverty can be cured by education, but education cannot be cured by poverty. On the contrary, all upbringing demands investment. Wiser and better investments lead to a more enlightened people. A more enlightened people work more cleverly, live more honestly and acquire true riches. Poverty will not cease, because Christians will always have the poor (John 12:8). But even the poor are better off where they are understood. Whoever wants a healthy education system needs a healthy economy, healthy money and proper investments.

Education can be acquired even in times of anarchy, but true enlightenment relies on a worthy authority. It says of King

Aleksandar Birviš

Jehoshaphat, *And his heart took delight in the ways of the LORD; moreover he removed the high places and wooden images from Judah.* We have the ridiculous situation today that a policeman can be punished if he is too rough in arresting a criminal, but no one is held responsible if methods are used against demonstrators that endanger their health and their lives.[38] The Bible looks on authority as protection. Good education is possible where people know what authority is, what its duties are, what powers it has and where and how it can act. Every authority has its weapon (Rom. 13:4). If it uses it in accordance with God's will, then there is no fear for those who are being educated: they will be successfully educated.

$$\star \quad \star \quad \star$$

These are the preconditions we must talk about at the beginning of the academic year. Each parent, each teacher, but also each pupil must know where to start. Before sowing his seed every year a good farmer makes the effort to prepare the land. Upbringing, education and enlightenment have their time of sowing: that is the beginning of the academic year.

Christians should grasp before others how important it is to create the conditions which I am talking about. Let us strengthen our guard, and sort out our lives. Don't let us allow our children and young people to experience disappointment in the family or Church. We can't expect anything better from the world, for the whole world is in the sway of the evil one (1 John 5:19). It seems to me that people today with even a little power of reasoning can see that the world has nothing to offer. This is the time for all to hear and understand that the solutions are elsewhere. Christ is the only Savior.

We say this today, too, in the name of the Lord Jesus.

Reflections

Don't look at your circumstances. Don't be put off by people and events. Believe in the Son of God. Turn to Him and worship Him. He alone is worthy of all glory and honor. We praise Him and His Heavenly Father and the Holy Spirit, the only God, and we thank Him now and always and forever.

Amen.

Closing reading: Is. 48:16–17

Belgrade, 27th September 1992

EDUCATION: CONDITIONS, DEVELOPMENT AND PURPOSE (II)

The academic year

Introductory reading: Ps. 16:1-11

Main reading: 2 Chr. 17:1-13

And Jehoshaphat his son reigned in his stead, and strengthened himself against Israel. And he placed forces in all the fenced cities of Judah, and set garrisons in the land of Judah, and in the cities of Ephraim, which Asa his father had taken. And the LORD was with Jehoshaphat, because he walked in the first ways of his father David, and sought not unto Baalim; But sought to the Lord God of his father, and walked in His commandments, and not after the doings of Israel. Therefore the LORD stablished the kingdom in his hand; and all Judah brought to Jehoshaphat presents; and he had riches and honour in abundance. And his heart was lifted up in the ways of the LORD: moreover he took away the high places and groves out of Judah.

Also in the third year of his reign he sent to his princes, even to Benhail, and to Obadiah, and to Zechariah, and to Nethaneel, and to Michaiah, to teach in the cities of Judah. And with them he sent Levites, even Shemaiah, and Nethaniah, and Zebadiah, and Asahel, and Shemiramoth, and Jehonathan, and Adonijah, and Tobijah, and Tobadonijah, Levites; and with them Elishama and Jehoram, priests. And they taught in Judah, and had the book of the law of the LORD with them, and went about throughout all the cities of Judah, and taught the people.

And the fear of the LORD fell upon all the kingdoms of the lands that were round about Judah, so that they made no war against Jehoshaphat. Also some of the Philistines brought Jehoshaphat presents, and tribute silver; and the Arabians brought him flocks, seven thousand and seven hundred rams, and seven thousand and seven hundred he goats.

And Jehoshaphat waxed great exceedingly; and he built in Judah castles, and cities of store. And he had much business in the cities of Judah: and the men of war, mighty men of valour, were in Jerusalem.

Last Sunday, 27ᵗʰ September, we spoke and prayed about the beginning of the academic year. I listed a number of things relating to conditions (preconditions) for a good education system. I described ten spiritual guards in accordance with the Ten Commandments. I set out other steps to be taken too. Social order and the economy play their part, they have a good and beneficial effect.

We immediately observe that Jehoshaphat had a vision for an education system that was intended for the whole nation. Leaders, Levites and priests were sent around all the cities of the country. I do not believe that education was withheld from the peasant population. The cities were the places where people gathered. Teaching and discussions took place in meeting places that were accessible to all. The listeners were probably mainly men. But the king's plan did not relate only to them; he was thinking of the whole nation. I assume that whole families would come to the teaching sessions.

Education should be comprehensive and accessible to all. Literacy and knowledge are not privileges but duties. These first few days of the school years are accompanied by the cries of parents "Where are we going to find books, pens and pencils, where are we going to get the money for it all?" It is a heavy burden and literacy rates can hardly improve in times when people do not even know how they will survive the winter. Hunger and nakedness are not far from us.

Aleksandar Birviš

But this burden too will be born by the one who says, *Come unto Me, all ye that labour and are heavy laden, and I will give you rest. Take My yoke upon you, and learn of Me; for I am meek and lowly in heart: and ye shall find rest unto your souls* (Matt. 11:28-29). We must bear in mind that the beginning of every academic year is a call to parents not only to spend money but to study. People usually think that parents need to study again in order to help their children. We understand that need, but the first need is that parents should know God as deeply as possible, and then, armed with that knowledge of God, study their children. Every child is a book. No, our little girl or boy is not a book, they are a whole series of books.

King Jehoshaphat took the Book of the Law of the Lord as the basis of his education system. There can be no healthy education without knowledge of God's will. It is not important for a school whether Religious Education is on the curriculum or not. The whole nation should set out to discover God's will. Instead of waiting for the government to take decisions, the Lord's people should turn to themselves. Let those who have the knowledge and who can teach go from house to house, let them gather the people around the Church, and let them speak to them about the will of God. Let the Church focus its efforts on training teachers. Teachers are people. Investment in them is not the same as investment in buildings and things. And it is a good thing that they are not the same: human values are restored if they are based on God's will, which is reliable and clear and indestructible because it is written in the Bible. The Law of the Lord is a part of God's Word, and it remains forever (Is. 40:8).

Every fall when we think about the school system, we realize that our concepts of education and its content and organization need to change. Men of this world say the same. They have reached these conclusions by observing the education system. They have carried

Reflections

out very serious study, in order to find out the causes of the condition that it is in.

We don't need to interfere in their work. They are professionals and I assume they do their work conscientiously. I would rather spend time on some symbolic and secret meanings of God's word.

Primary education

King Josiah sent out leaders, Levites and priests. Let us imagine they represent three levels of education: primary, secondary and higher. Basic spiritual education covers knowledge of society and the social system in accordance with God's will as applied to life in justification and righteousness. Secondary education covers service to God and our behavior before Him: readiness for consecration. Higher education is a sacrifice, the discovery of truth, entrance into the holy place and the appearance of God's glory.

The leaders were called: *Ben-Hail, Obadiah, Zechariah, Nethanel, and Michaiah.* Their five names mean as follows: Son of Strength, the Lord's Servant, the Lord has Remembered, God has Given, and Who is Like the Lord. The aim of primary education is the realization that everything that exists around us exists because it was made through the action of one force. That force is creative and it has its consequences. It is the Lord. Whoever wants to belong to Him must serve Him. The Almighty will not forget it. He remembers His servants. He gives them different gifts, not because people curried favor with Him, but because He is the Lord (The One Who Is). No one is like the Lord. Men must have these truths before them in their relationships one with another. To neglect truth is to weaken authority, lead people astray and corrupt society.

Aleksandar Birviš

Secondary education

Secondary education in the spiritual life is important in the Almighty's eyes. That is why the number of Levites is much greater. God declares and demands that those who belong to Him be regular at services and that they behave as He has commanded. The names of the nine Levites were: *Shemaiah, Nethaniah, Zebadiah, Asahel, Shemiramoth, Jehonathan, Adonijah, Tobijah, and Tobadonijah.* Translated from Hebrew the names mean: the Lord has Heard, the Lord has Given, the Lord has Rewarded, God has Made, My Name is the Heights, the Lord has Given, (my) Master is Lord, the Lord is Good, and My Master the Lord is Good. The aim of secondary spiritual education is to know the Lord more deeply and to become better grounded in salvation. The repentant sinner and suffering man cries out. Often he does not even know who to cry out to. Whoever has set out to serve the Savior, knows two things: 1) that he is unworthy and sinful, and 2) whom to turn to. Repentance and conversion are closely linked. God hears and answers. He gives salvation to all who turn to Him. He sets no preconditions. God has granted salvation because He wanted to. God also rewards according to His undisputed will. All our efforts and tears and suffering are not fruitless: those who are saved gain even when it looks as though all is lost. God always does something.

The Almighty is especially at work at the middle level of spiritual education and is teaching us spiritual growth. He is molding the Christian man and woman: He saves them from falling, develops their awareness and conscience, strengthens them in their responsibilities and establishes them as individuals. The spiritual heights become accessible to them. Of course those heights conceal temptations. The man who stands on the heights can easily become proud. I

Reflections

remember when the first mountaineer stood on the highest summit on the globe, and the British Queen interrupted preparations for her coronation to congratulate him. What a boost that was to his pride! The next temptation is to despise those who are below us. In the spiritual realm that is a sin just like pride. Pride asks, "Who is like me?" and contempt says, "No one is like me!"

The spiritual school sees this danger, and heals man of pride and scorn. The Lord implants the awareness that He is the only giver of all achievements. Sometimes He gives an extra thorn in the flesh, some sort of painful restriction. This keeps His followers meek; they don't show off and don't seek honor, privileges and esteem. At the same time, Christians go deeper into truth and life thus making the Lord ever more fully their Master. The Word of Christ is applicable to all creatures and every situation: *I am Alpha and Omega, the Beginning and the Ending, saith the Lord, which is, and which was, and which is to come, the Almighty* (Rev. 1:8). The Word is also intended for individuals; whoever truly regards the Lord as the Almighty, is under the best possible protection from temptation.

On the spiritual heights men and women discover God's goodness. In the book of Exodus (24:9-11) we read, *Then went up Moses, and Aaron, Nadab, and Abihu, and seventy of the elders of Israel: And they saw the God of Israel: and there was under His feet as it were a paved work of a sapphire stone, and as it were the body of heaven in his clearness. And upon the nobles of the children of Israel He laid not His hand: also they saw God, and did eat and drink.* God is good toward those who approach Him in a worthy manner. He is obviously good to all things, both men and other creatures. We learn from the book of Job (1:6-12) that God has patience even with Satan. But God's special goodness is shown to those who are close to Him. They are deemed worthy of good cheer and spared the Lord's wrath.

Aleksandar Birviš

By giving thanks and having fellowship in food and drink – which is a wholehearted participation in the Lord's Supper – we graduate from the secondary spiritual school and enter higher education.

Higher education

We could represent higher education by the two priests who are mentioned. They were called Elisama and Joram. Their task as priests was to bring sacrifices, to preserve and pass on revelation, to bear the truth, to look towards the Holy Place and receive the glory of the Lord. The name Elisama means 'God has heard', and Joram 'the Lord is exalted'. The highest spirituality is simple spirituality. The believer commits himself to God and follows God's example in the Lord Jesus Christ. A spiritual man and a spiritual woman pray with the conviction that God will hear them individually and that they can talk to Him. This is the same attitude that the believer has when he studies the Bible. In the Bible he discovers the will of God, God's voice, but at this level Christians learn to speak the language of God. That is not some special power. On the contrary, the Almighty works through weak people. As it says in the Scripture: *Likewise the Spirit also helpeth our infirmities: for we know not what we should pray for as we ought: but the Spirit itself maketh intercession for us with groanings which cannot be uttered* (Rom. 8:26).

Life in the Spirit constantly unfolds in the presence of God's glory. That life is not always cheerful, but it is full of joy and radiates undisturbed serenity. All lies and masks, facades and hindrances have been stripped off and the spiritual man glorifies the Lord with every word, action and thought. He lives on the heights, and as well as the heights he understands God's depths too. The Lord is infinitely exalted because He infinitely humbled Himself. He came down

Reflections

among men, not to rule, but to serve. The spiritual man adopts the exalted way of thinking and the exalted way of acting from Christ. *Let this mind be in you,* says the Apostle Paul, *which was also in Christ Jesus: Who, being in the form of God, thought it not robbery to be equal with God: But made Himself of no reputation, and took upon Him the form of a servant, and was made in the likeness of men: And being found in fashion as a man, He humbled Himself, and became obedient unto death, even the death of the cross* (Phil. 2:5-8).

At this level believers encounter the truth and so are free. God's preeminence obliges them to live by the truth and to make careful use of their freedom. In accordance with the advice given by the Apostle Peter, they behave as free, and not using their liberty... *for a cloke of maliciousness, but as the servants of God* (1 Pet. 2:16). Their freedom goes a long way. They judge all things, but are judged by no one (1 Cor. 2:15). On the other hand, their service keeps them in the realm of everyday reality, and they don't imagine that they are something more than they are, but they humbly accept what they are.

Consequences

It now remains for us to consider what the results of such a concept of education are when it is adopted and implemented. I am not going to make any special conclusion. I will just read the closing words from our main reading for today and make some short comments on them.

And the fear of the LORD fell upon all the kingdoms of the lands that were round about Judah,

Every country has neighbors. There isn't one country that doesn't have problems with them. Island states such as Cuba, Ireland, Japan, the Philippines, Great Britain and others have "foreign policy

Aleksandar Birviš

problems". The problems that countries have with their neighbors are not small ones: disputes are constantly arising and the fear of war is ever present. When there are extensive and far-reaching changes in the spiritual life of a country, God pacifies its neighbors.

... so that they made no war against Jehoshaphat.

King Jehoshaphat didn't need to defend himself. His enemies did not rise up against him. Nobody tried to kill him, even though he had destroyed many pagan temples of various tribes and nations. His country did not yield to its surroundings, either spiritually nor culturally. Why? Because the whole nation promoted true education, the Law of the Lord. Let us take the example of the Scandinavian countries: they had problems one with another right up until spiritual renewal came and then they sorted everything out peacefully and live to this day without bad feelings.

Also some of the Philistines brought Jehoshaphat presents, and tribute silver ...

The Philistines were both militarily and politically like Austria is towards our country today in their relations with Jehoshaphat's country. The Jews had a weaker economy, limited trade, different values, a different system of encouraging values and a completely different religion. But Jehoshaphat took no notice of that. He strengthened integrity and honesty in the nation, increased true knowledge and focused his people on seeking God's will and glory. The Lord's response was real and it could be measured and counted.

... and the Arabians brought him flocks, seven thousand and seven hundred rams, and seven thousand and seven hundred he goats.

The consequences of Divine education are ever more obvious and tangible. The Arabs are the descendants of Ishmael, a people who troubled the Jews, because through the Arabs the Jews suffered as a result of Abraham' impatience. We see how the Arabs work for

Jehoshaphat and the Jews and bring them food. At that time, between 870 and 850 BC, those were huge quantities. The Arabs of the time didn't have the technical capability, or literacy, or a country, or agriculture. They kept cattle, gathered fruit, did a little weaving and a lot of warring. But the Lord, indirectly, changed them too. They now respected the Jews as brothers and neighbors, and concentrated on working better, and showed their respect in an appropriate way.

And Jehoshaphat waxed great exceedingly...

Do we want a forward-looking society? Do we seek a successful country? Let us turn to the Lord. Let's stop talking and pray. Let us fill the existing churches. Let us build new ones. Let us work and do business and especially study honestly, with love and with a solid understanding of our profession. The Lord will do the rest.

... and he built in Judah castles, and cities of store.

An advanced society is not a wasteful society. On the contrary, honest people are thrifty, because carelessness and waste are forms of dishonesty. Careless and wasteful people steal albeit not from specific people, but theft is still theft. Jehoshaphat carefully guarded the food. God could have asked him at any time, "King, where are my gifts?" Jehoshaphat could show anyone that he was not destroying what God had given. Among the people of God people know where things are and what to use them for.

And he had much business in the cities of Judah...

It wasn't only money, cattle and food that came as a result of spiritual education. God gives other benefits too. He doesn't ration them out, He always gives a little more than is necessary.

... and the men of war, mighty men of valor, were in Jerusalem.

The army is mentioned after the other property. A sanctified people do not consider an army the most important pillar of power. God's will does not exclude the need for defense, but where the

Aleksandar Birviš

people look to the Lord and believe that He is Almighty, conspiracies and internal enemies are no longer hiding behind every bush. The Lord is the fortress and defense of His faithful followers. He can do it with an army, but He can do it without as well. People and kingdoms rise and fall at His will. In His will freedom appears.

★ ★ ★

A question arises here not related to school: Is this possible today, in this country, in this city? Of course it is. And what's more, it is necessary today, it is essential.

Don't expect the country to change. You change. Look at your idols and your sins and reject them. Repent. Look to Christ: He delivers you and saves you. Turn to Him. Accept God's Word. Begin to study today. We are here to help one another. If you want to study, teachers can be found. The Scriptures are intended for you too. The Church exists so that you can join it. It isn't only the academic year that has begun. Your new life in God: Father, Son and Holy Spirit, is also beginning.

Final reading: Is. 48:16–17

Belgrade, 4th October 1992

Dr. Aleksandar Birviš with his wife Vera Hill Birviš
(credit Vicencio Žaknić)

Appendix

WHY I WRITE OUT MY SERMONS

More often than not preachers don't write down what they are going to say. Listeners like a man who speaks without any notes. They feel that they are witnessing the direct working of the Holy Spirit.

I used to do that too, for a long while. Then one day God revealed two things to me:

One: By preaching without notes I am not pleasing my Lord but indulging my laziness and human tastes. Writing and preparing a well-polished sermon requires hard work, and no one should become a preacher if he is afraid of hard work.

Two: My colleagues and listeners began to write down, copy, duplicate, quote and retell my sermons. And it would often differ from what I had actually said. In order to preserve the original text I began to write everything down. The written word remains. It doesn't depend on how much of it is remembered and understood. It is there. The reader can read it at any time, verify it and interpret it. Readers who have never heard me preach, and even those who will live after me, can do the same.

I have made use of and quoted various Serbian translations of the Bible (Daničić-Karadžić, Čarnić and others), and I have used my own translations of the Gospels, the Psalms, etc.

Once a man begins to write, he cannot do without it. One of the first journalists of Politika and the editor of Politika's Entertainment magazine, the late Bogdan Popović, Uncle Boca, used to say, "Writing is the scabies of the soul. The more you scratch it, the more it itches."

Notes

[1] **Stevan Nemanja**. Grand Prince of the Medieval Serb state of Raška 1168-1196

[2] **Bogumils**. Gnostic dualistic sect in Bulgaria and Bosnia 950-1396

[3] **Quirinus Kuhlmann**. Kuhlmann (1651-89) is one of the most eccentric authors of seventeenth-century Germany. Before being burned at the stake in Russia as a heretic, he had been expelled from the University of Leyden, traveled to England, and gone to Constantinople to try to convert the Sultan.

[4] This relates to the political maneuverings by the presidents of the various republics of the former Yugoslavia immediately prior to the outbreak of war.

[5] **Dedinje, Topčider**. Elite districts of Belgrade.

[6] **Osijek**. Osijek, Croatia is the location of the Evangelical Theological Seminary where many of the current generation of pastors in the republics of the former Yugoslavia were trained. Dr Birviš was himself Dean of the Seminary for a time.

[7] A **Youth With A Mission (YWAM)** team.

[8] **White Eagles** (Beli Orlovi). Serbian paramilitary group active in the civil wars in the former Yugoslavia.

[9] **Iskušenje**. The word used here can mean both temptation and trial or ordeal in Serbian.

[10] **Demolished Baptist Church**. The old building of the First Baptist Church in Belgrade was forcibly demolished in 1973 by the communist authorities to make way for housing development. The believers were without a building for some time.

[11] **The Kalevala** is an epic poem which Elias Lönnrot compiled from Finnish folk lore in the 19th century. It is commonly called the Finnish-Karelian national epic and is traditionally thought of as one of the most significant works of Finnish language literature.

[12] **Dositej Obradović** (1742-1811). Serbian writer and translator. First Serbian minister of education.

[13] **Vuk (Stefanović) Karadžić** (1787-1864). Serbian linguist and reformer of the Serbian Language and orthography. Translated the New Testament into Serbian (1847) with the support of the British and Foreign Bible Society.

[14] **Karić family**. Controlled a number of large Serbian companies – a mobile telephone network, a television station, a private business school. Were later investigated for corruption.

[15] **Schism**. The Great Schism (1054) when Rome and Constantinople split into 2 churches.

[16] **Vidovdan** (St Vitus' day). June 28th. A significant date in Serbian history and mythology. Date of the Battle of Kosovo and the assassination of Archduke Franz Ferdinand in Sarajevo in 1914.

[17] Source: newspaper articles *Najavljuju obračun s podzemljem* ["War to be declared on underworld"] (Politika, 27/06/1992, p.11) and *Uhapšeni Bokan i Vučinić* ["Bokan and Vučinić arrested"] (Politika, 28.06. 1992., str. 20).

[18] In the period immediately before the fall of Communism in Romania large numbers of Romania refugees had escaped into Serbia.

[19] **Vojvodina**. The northern, flatland area of Serbia bordering on Hungary. An ethnically mixed region with significant Hungarian, Slovak, Romanian and Rusyn communities, under Austro-Hungarian rule until the end of World War I.

[20] **Cantacuzene**. John VI Kantakouzenos (1292-1383), Byzantine emperor 1347-1354.

[21] **Christians of the north**. Probably a reference to the Crusades of the 14th and 15th centuries, launched ostensibly to counter the expansion of the Ottoman Empire, which included the recapture of Belgrade in 1444.

[22] **Saint Sava**. Prince Rastko Nemanjić (1175-1236) son of Serbian ruler Stefan Nemanja. First Serbian Archbishop and founder of the independent Serbian Orthodox Church, revered in Serbia as the Illuminator for his work in enlightening the Serbian people.

[23] **President of the Republic** – referring to Josip Broz Tito, the illustrious Yugoslav head of state from the Second World War until his death in 1980.

[24] **authority**. The Serbian word *autoritet* is a loan-word from other European languages – Birviš was very insistent on using an authentic Serbian vocabulary wherever possible.

[25] **competence.** An approximation of the word Birviš uses – *merodavnost* – which could loosely be translated as 'authority' or 'competence'.

[26] **Yuri Gagarin** (1934-1968). First Russian cosmonaut. Flew in space in the Russian spacecraft Vostok 1 12th April 1961.

[27] **Karaburma**. An urban neighborhood of Belgrade.

[28] **Iman šarti**. A term derived from Turkish and used in Bosnia, as with other Islamic terms used here.

[29] **Holy Trinity Church**. The main Belgrade Evangelical (Pentecostal) Church, its new building then completed in the centre of Belgrade.

[30] **respected friends**. A greeting directed towards a number of public figures that attended the opening.

[31] **Grammar school**. *Gimnazija* – non-vocational secondary schools usually seen as preparation for university.

[32] **First Serbian Uprising**. 1804

[33] **Obrenović**. Miloš Obrenović (1780-1860). Prince of Serbia 1815-39 and 1858-60.

[34] **Ave, Lux Serenissima**. Latin – Hail most serene Light.

[35] **Kršćanska Sadašnjost**. Croatian Christian publishing house, Zagreb.

[36] Birviš here uses two archaic words for "book of prayer" and "man of prayer" that sound very similar in Serbian.

[37] **Psalm 133**. The Serbian is Birviš's own translation from the Hebrew, here rendered in English as closely as possible to his translation.

[38] **methods... used...** A reference to numerous occurrences of police brutality used against pro-democracy demonstrations in the 1990s in Serbia.

Printed in the United States
By Bookmasters